D0632182

To Maria & Nan,
It was great meeting
you! Enjoy!

— Marsha Low

10/14/12

The Orange Robe

My Eighteen Years as a Yogic Nun

Marsha Goluboff Low

iUniverse, Inc.
Bloomington

The Orange Robe

My Eighteen Years as a Yogic Nun

Copyright © 2010 by Marsha Goluboff Low

All rights reserved. No part of this book may be used or reproduced by any means, graphic, electronic, or mechanical, including photocopying, recording, taping or by any information storage retrieval system without the written permission of the publisher except in the case of brief quotations embodied in critical articles and reviews.

iUniverse books may be ordered through booksellers or by contacting:

iUniverse
1663 Liberty Drive
Bloomington, IN 47403
www.iuniverse.com
1-800-Authors (1-800-288-4677)

Because of the dynamic nature of the Internet, any web addresses or links contained in this book may have changed since publication and may no longer be valid. The views expressed in this work are solely those of the author and do not necessarily reflect the views of the publisher, and the publisher hereby disclaims any responsibility for them.

ISBN: 978-1-4502-3013-1 (sc)
ISBN: 978-1-4502-3012-4 (e)

Printed in the United States of America
iUniverse rev. date: 06/06/11

For Max and Mina

There is a road, no simple highway
Between the dawn and the dark of night
And if you go, no one may follow
That path is for your steps alone

The Grateful Dead

Table of Contents

Preface

This book is an account of the eighteen years I spent abroad with Ananda Marga, an Indian-based yoga organization whose name means "The Path of Bliss." I was in my early twenties when I first got involved with the group and went overseas to work full time for it when I was twenty-four.

After leaving the organization and returning to this country, my early attempts to write about my experiences were like a series of snapshots—just brief descriptions of mostly humorous events. Some delved deeper, into attitudes and prejudices I had unconsciously brought along. A few of my accounts mentioned that I had belonged to a yoga group, but none offered details or referred to Ananda Marga by name. I didn't want potential readers to know I had been in what they might consider a cult. By editing Ananda Marga out of my story, it was as if I were removing it from my life as well. As time went on, however, I began to realize that any account without an exploration of Ananda Marga and my relationship to it would not be worth writing, as the story would lack the whole structure and context in which it had taken place.

I must admit that fear also had something to do with my initial reluctance. I was wary of putting down anything that current members of the group might construe as negative *pracar* or publicity. Stories had been floating around Ananda Marga for years, tales of monks who had run afoul of the organization and ended up dead. Although the truth of these stories to my knowledge has never been substantiated, I didn't want to take any chances of winding up dead or of living under a kind of Ananda Marga *fatwa* à la Salman Rushdie. As it is, even though I don't consider myself to have portrayed anyone unfairly or inaccurately, I did change the names of all Ananda Marga members mentioned in the book except for the Guru's, as well as all other names except for those of family members and a few close friends.

I wish to emphasize that the book is the account of my personal experience of Ananda Marga; others in the organization may have experienced things differently depending on their own psychological and spiritual makeup. To help create the world of Ananda Marga for the reader, I have retained the group's terminology and numerous Sanskrit and Hindi terms. Unfamiliar terms (those not listed in an English dictionary) used repeatedly throughout the text are italicized only when they first occur.

Here, then, are some basic facts about Ananda Marga.[1] It was founded in 1955 in the small town of Jamalpur in the state of Bihar, India, by Prabhat Rainjan Sarkar, later known to his followers as Shrii Shrii Anandamurti, or "he who attracts others as the embodiment of bliss." Soon drawing disciples through what many described as a magnetic and spiritual presence, Sarkar left his job as a railway official and began to train missionaries to spread his teaching of self-realization and service to humanity through Tantra Yoga,[2] which he sometimes described as an "intuitional science." In 1962, Anandamurti initiated his first monk. In 1966, he created an order of nuns. In 1970, shortly before Anandamurti was arrested and charged with arranging the

---

[1] The full name of Ananda Marga is *Ananda Marga Pracaraka Samgha*, which means, "The Society for the Propagation of the Path of Bliss."

[2] Tantra: Ananda Marga defines tantra as "that which liberates from crudeness." Its essence is to awaken the spiritual force within the individual and unify it with Cosmic Consciousness. Ananda Marga does not teach the sexual methods that many Westerners associate with tantra. Some descriptions of Ananda Marga practices appear later in the book.

kidnapping and murder of six former disciples,[3] Ananda Marga arrived in the United States.

In the fall of 1970, an Ananda Marga teacher came to the campus of the University of Pennsylvania, where I was a twenty-one-year-old student. Four years later, in the summer of 1974, I left the United States for the Ananda Marga training center in India to become a "didi," a yogic nun in orange robes.

---

[3] More on the imprisonment of Anandamurti will appear later in the book.

Chapter 1

Early Days

Out of breath, still clutching the student newspaper I'd just been reading, I ran into Hill Hall and quickly found the room where the yoga teacher was supposed to be. According to the paper, he was on campus to give a talk and teach meditation. I knew I was too late for the talk but was hoping to get a chance to learn how to meditate. I had recently been reading about Zen and was taken with the idea that anyone could achieve a deep state of peace through meditation. Just a month or two earlier, a bad experience with LSD had sent me to the psych ward of the university's hospital. Like a lot of people my age, I'd been searching for something. Drugs hadn't been it—nor had college: Penn had proved too big and impersonal for my taste, and I was looking forward to graduating in a few months, one semester early, having managed to put together just enough credits to do so. Not that I had any idea what I'd be doing after graduation. The last thing I wanted was to move back in with my parents. My father was old enough to be my grandfather, and neither he nor my mother, it seemed to me, had a clue as to who I really was.

The small room was crowded with students—mostly hippie types with long hair and bell-bottoms who were sitting on the carpet, drinking tea or meditating with their backs against the walls. My eyes gravitated to a dreamy-looking young woman with long blond hair and blue eyes. Dressed all in white, she was sitting on the floor in the middle of the room and was talking to some students. What struck me was the look of utter contentment on her face. Finding myself drawn to her, I went over and sat down, introducing myself when there was a pause in the conversation. Instead of saying hello, she drew her hands together and brought them to the middle of her forehead and down to her chest and said, "My name's Mangala."

"Are you the yoga teacher?"

"Oh, no. That's Dada[4] Viirananda," she said, smiling. "He's teaching students in the room next door. I met him in India, where I've been studying meditation, and now I'm traveling with him around the United States, helping to arrange classes."

"Can I go to India, too?" I found myself asking. I felt immediately embarrassed by my question—asking for permission like a small child!—but she answered as if it were the most ordinary in the world. "If you want to," she said.

I was offered some sassafras tea and sipped it while awaiting my turn to meet the yogi. When it came, I found myself sitting cross-legged opposite an Indian man with a beard and shoulder-length hair, wearing flowing orange robes. The lesson was brief. He gave me a two-syllable mantra[5] and told me to meditate twice a day, in the morning and evening.

A few weeks later, I went to a retreat organized by the yoga group (called Ananda Marga) in a nineteenth-century mansion in Fairmount Park. It was my favorite time of year and the weather was perfect. Both mornings, I awoke to skies of deep blue and a touch of chill in the air. Autumn colors were nearly at their peak, and the vibrant reds and yellows of maples made a striking contrast with the dark, rambling house. The mansion's shabby air

---

[4] Dada: The male teachers were called Dada (brother); the female teachers, Didi (sister).

[5] mantra: "That which can liberate the mind." A mantra often consists of two syllables and is repeated with the breath.

of lost grandeur blended in perfectly with the melancholy beauty of a season soon to succumb to cold and darkness. A perfect setting for a yoga retreat, I thought.

But something inside wouldn't let me enjoy it: a painful, all-too-familiar sense of inadequacy and self-consciousness that would not let me be. On Saturday afternoon, while everyone else was outside enjoying the sun, I spent the time lying on my bunk, hiding. Later, when I went to see Dada Viirananda, I tried to tell him how I was feeling. He didn't answer directly but urged me to do regular *sadhana* (meditation).

"You will be like a flower, opening up gradually, one layer at a time," he said.

Days later, I found myself sitting in my room in the attic of the large West Philadelphia Victorian I shared with several other people. (We were an interesting mix: undergrads and grad students, a handful of older working people in their thirties, plus a few drug-using hangers-on.) I was looking at the color portrait of Viirananda I'd placed on my desk and was trying to meditate. I felt silly. Who am I kidding, pretending to be a yogi! I thought. I soon stopped trying. From time to time I would gaze at the picture, feeling I was failing someone, though whom I couldn't say.

In the spring of '72, not quite two years after my first contact with Ananda Marga, I left Philadelphia and drove out west with a stranger whose ad for a ride share had been posted on a bulletin board at Penn. The trip passed uneventfully, and I was left off near Albuquerque, where my ex-boyfriend Tim was living. I showed up at his door without so much as a phone call. He didn't seem terribly thrilled to see me, maybe because he was living with the same woman who'd become his girlfriend at Penn after we had broken up. Even so, Tim agreed to let me stay in his spare bedroom. It was filled with all kinds of junk, and I was able to reach the bed only by climbing over the boxes piled all around it, but I didn't care. At least I had a place to stay.

One afternoon, I decided to look up the local Ananda Marga center. The "Margiis" (Ananda Marga members) welcomed me in, and if they felt at all put off by my appearance—wild, permed hair topped by an intricately beaded, multi-colored cap; an African shirt full of strong purples, oranges, and yellows; and overalls—they didn't let on. They asked me to stay for dinner. First, we meditated (thankfully, I still remembered my mantra), then ate in near silence, everyone chewing brown rice sprinkled with *gomasio* slowly and mindfully. It was all very peaceful. After dinner, I sat out in the tiny back yard and read pamphlets about meditation, asanas (yoga postures), and fasting and its benefits— and resolved to start practicing regularly.

I tried to meditate on the lumpy bed at Tim's, but the cluttered room didn't really lend itself to spiritual practices. And because things were getting tense between Tim's girlfriend and me, I knew I couldn't stay there much longer anyway. A week or two later, I somehow met up with some lesbians; when they heard I needed a place, they invited me to stay with them.

I was the only non-lesbian in the household, but they didn't seem to mind. It certainly didn't prevent me from joining in on the fun—and there was lots of it to be had. There was always a Carole King album on the turnstile, always some grass to smoke, and my attempts at meditation soon came to an abrupt end. I even started thinking like my housemates, looking at any men we would run into while waiting in lines to buy ice cream or see a movie, as if they were members of a different species.

The women had friends who had a farm in the hills above Taos, and I accepted an invitation to stay for a few weeks. I loved it up there. The women showed me how to milk the goats, and I helped in the fields. I continued to be the only straight one in the group. Maybe I'd have tried being in a lesbian relationship, but no one seemed interested in starting one up.

One evening in late May, a few of us decided to take some LSD. I hardly gave a thought to the bad trip I'd had in

Philadelphia, thinking that out here on the farm, everything would surely go well. I started to get high just as the moon was rising—full, enormous, the biggest I'd ever seen. Within it, I saw a huge fetus, just like the one in the movie *2001: A Space Odyssey*. As I stood there, transfixed, I wondered if I was going to have a baby. Or was that fetus me, being reborn to a new life?

As I wandered around the moonlit fields, everything as bright as day, a strong longing for God overtook me. A few days earlier, I had been offered what I'd thought of as the chance of a lifetime: to move in with a Native-American woman in Taos and learn weaving. But now I wasn't sure if that was what I was meant to do. Maybe I should go back to Philadelphia and move into the Ananda Marga center, I thought. Then I prayed for a sign.

Something prompted me to meditate. I sat down cross-legged in the field, closed my eyes, and saw the face of a Margii I knew back in Philadelphia. He was smiling, his face full of light, eyes half-closed as if in meditation or a state of bliss. Then he opened his vividly blue eyes, and a ray of light shot out of one of them as he gazed at me, nodding. The slow, wise way he nodded made me sure I had gotten my answer.

I left for Philadelphia the next day. Having almost no money, I hitchhiked in a state of grace alone all the way from Taos. Even though I had a close call with one or two of the men giving me rides, I felt untouchable, as if God were carrying me across the country in his hands, depositing me safe and sound back East (but not before, on the second or third day, bestowing upon one of my rides, a middle-aged, balding man, the blessing of my presence in his hotel room, sitting opposite him in a hot tub with a beatific smile upon my face, as if one of the sisters of mercy from Leonard Cohen's song.)

Although I didn't immediately move in with the Margiis, I started going to group meditation every week. It wasn't long before they told me about their guru and showed me his picture. The guru wasn't Dada Viirananda, as I had originally thought, but Shrii Shrii Anandamurti. The Margiis called him Baba (which meant "father"), and it was clear they had great reverence for him. Even the fact that he had been in jail since 1971 on charges of having ordered the murder of several former followers didn't dim their enthusiasm. The Margiis saw him as a political prisoner—in jail, they said, because of his strong stance against casteism and other entrenched ideas in India.

One fall evening, I was sitting in the meditation hall of the yoga center (which was called a *jagrti* or "place of awakening") on Regent Street in West Philadelphia. *Dharmacakra* (group meditation) had just ended. I asked one of the Margiis, Vikram, a bearded, likeable guy who was always playing guitar, about the *Baba Nam Kevalam*[6] phrase affixed to the wall. It was made of bright, artistically crafted letters, and I thought it was pretty.

"That's really nice," I said. "Who made it?"

"We all worked on it," Vikram replied. "We put it up for Baba's birthday and decided to leave it there."

"When's Baba's birthday?" I asked.

"The full moon in May."

The full moon in May! The realization hit me like a bolt of lighting and I started to cry. Vikram and the others looked at me and then at one another with puzzled looks on their faces. Through my tears, I told them about that night in Taos when I had prayed to God for guidance. That had been Baba's birthday. He'd been there, taking care of me all along.

That night, Baba became my guru, too.

When Ananda Marga arrived in the States in the early seventies, Philadelphia was one of the first cities to boast a fully functioning unit. After the first wave of initiations, those which took place in that little room at Penn, a dada came to Philadelphia from

---

[6] *Baba Nam Kevalam:* Ananda Marga translations of this Sanskrit phrase include "Only the name of the Beloved" and "Love is all there is." Margiis chant *Baba Nam Kevalam* before meditating.

India to care for the newly created flock. His name was Ramesh Gupta. We called him Rameshji.[7]

Dada Ramesh was quite different from Dada Viirananda. Instead of wearing orange robes, he dressed normally; instead of sporting long hair and a beard, he had short hair and a small mustache. And Rameshji wasn't a renunciate; he was married and lived with his wife and their little girl in a cramped apartment in West Philadelphia, not far from the Regent Street jagrti. He also had a job.

Rameshji, it turned out, was one of a fast-disappearing breed of family *acaryas,*[8] or teachers. In the earliest days of Ananda Marga in India, the first acaryas were all family men. The *sannyasiis,*[9] the renunciates who wore orange robes and took vows, came later. Since we were all new to Ananda Marga, the fact that Dada was a family acarya didn't seem at all strange to us. It was only later, as more and more whole-timers arrived who were monks in the usual sense, that we realized that Rameshji was not the norm.

We all had the greatest respect for Dada. Despite his humble and quiet way of speaking, his words seemed to be infused with the kind of spiritual energy born of rigorous spiritual practice and insight. Along with a few of the local Margiis, Rameshji ran a yoga drop-in center at Temple University. Classes were held there, and Dada also saw people individually, initiating new students and giving higher lessons to those who were already Margiis.

When someone is initiated into Ananda Marga, they are given an introductory meditation technique called *"Nama Mantra,"* or they can be given the "first lesson" (the first of six). In the early days, most people, including me, were initiated with *Nama Mantra.* The dada would give the student the first lesson when he thought the student was ready. There was no prescribed time

[7] In India, adding "ji" to the end of a person's name or title indicates respect and affection.

[8] *acarya:* "One who teaches by example." (Ananda Marga's transliteration. More commonly transliterated as *"acharya."*)

[9] Sanskrit or Hindi transliterations typically involve only one "i" when that vowel is encountered; in Ananda Marga we often used two. Hence *sannyasii* instead of *sannyasi,* and so on.

for this; it depended upon the student and his or her progress. Usually, the same acarya who initiated someone would give that person higher lessons. At first, because didis (female teachers) had not yet arrived in the States, dadas initiated women as well as men. Once didis came, women were initiated and given lessons only by didis, and men, by dadas.

Because Dada Viirananda was no longer in the States, Rameshji gave me my first lesson. He also gave me a spiritual name. If you wanted a spiritual name, you got one; it was one of the things that symbolized a spiritual rebirth and a new identity. Mine was "Liila" and meant "play or sport of the Lord." I loved my new name—and my new identity.

Some months after I had returned to Philadelphia, I was sitting on a bus on my way to the drop-in center to get my first lesson, reading *Autobiography of a Yogi* by Paramahansa Yogananda, which I'd taken to carrying around with me. I never tired of looking at Yogananda's picture on the cover, at the large, luminous eyes that looked out at the world with so much compassion and love. Yogananda's account of his experiences and relationship with his guru had touched me deeply. I was looking forward to getting my first lesson. It would be an important first step in becoming more like him, I thought.

I got off the bus, my anticipation growing as I entered the building—along with the certitude that this was going to be an important day, even a momentous one. I took the steps down to the basement and entered the center. Rameshji got up from his chair as I came in and greeted me with hands folded in *namaskar*.[10] We went into the room he used for giving lessons, and I sat opposite him on the rug. We meditated for a few minutes. Then he began to describe the meditation process and

---

[10] *namaskar:* A spiritual greeting meaning, "I salute the divinity within you." While saying *namaskar*, the person puts his or her hands together, brings them up to the center of the forehead, then down to the chest.

gave me my new mantra—the *Ista Mantra*, which would lead me to the goal of union with the divine consciousness.

When the lesson ended, I could hardly speak. I felt myself transported to another world. While I could see that I was still in this one, it had been radically altered and shimmered with a spiritual glow I had never before experienced. Everything, even the everyday objects on Dada's desk—the pens, the papers, even the desk itself with its chair slightly askew—seemed imbued with significance. I said goodbye to Rameshji, left the room with my hands folded in namaskar, and floated up the stairs and out into the street. I felt myself transformed.

Rameshji also gave me my second lesson, during which I received another mantra, the *Guru Mantra*. Unlike the *Ista Mantra*, which was repeated during meditation, the *Guru Mantra* was to be uttered internally before every action. By repeating this mantra, I would ensure that the "little I" (the "I" connected with my ego) would not identify with the action or reap its fruits. Instead, everything would be given over to the Divine. By perfecting the second lesson, I would free myself from karma, the cycle of action and reaction. Reinforcing this cosmic ideation before every action would ensure that I would no longer form new karmic reactions, or *samskaras*, which bind people to the world.

Around this time, Dada Yogeshananda arrived in the United States. Replacing Viirananda, he now had the responsibility of supervising all the Ananda Marga units and projects in New York Sector,[11] which included not only the United States, but also Canada, Mexico, and the Caribbean Islands.

---

[11] Ananda Marga divided the world up into nine sectors: Cairo (Quahira), New York, Delhi, Berlin, Hong Kong, Suva (Australasia), Manila, Nairobi, and Georgetown. Within each sector were regions. Each region was then divided into dioceses and each diocese into *panchayats*, a term borrowed from Indian political terminology.

I was impressed right away by Yogeshananda's seemingly boundless energy and enthusiasm and the long hours he spent in meditation. Despite the fact that he had never before been out of India, Dada seemed to have little trouble adjusting to a culture so vastly different from his own. He related well to the American Margiis, and his wonderful sense of humor, along with an uninhibited and disarming laugh, helped smooth his way.

Weeks passed. I learned more through the talks the acaryas gave, classes at retreats, and by reading all the Ananda Marga books I could find. I experienced feelings of profound peace and bliss not only while meditating, but also while chanting *Baba Nam Kevalam* and dancing *kiirtan* (devotional chanting often accompanied by dancing) with my hands held up and eyes closed, swaying to the music.

I began to feel that I had found my true family. Out of the myriad spiritual paths and gurus gaining popularity at the time (Guru Maharaji, Meher Baba, Rajneesh, Zen Buddhism), I had been guided to the one that was right for me. While other spiritual paths maintained that the mundane world of the senses was an illusion, Ananda Marga declared it to be a relative truth. I soon discovered that Ananda Marga had not only a developed spiritual philosophy and a series of practices based upon the ancient science of *Astaunga Yoga,*[12] but also a unique social philosophy known as PROUT, or Progressive Utilization Theory. Margiis celebrated birthdays, too. When mine came around, they gave me a cake, sang happy birthday, and put a red dot between my eyes. I was touched because my brothers and I had rarely had birthday parties growing up.

In short, Ananda Marga's philosophy far surpassed anything I had ever come across or, I was convinced, ever would. To me, it was a perfect blending of the spiritual and social. I felt no need to explore other spiritual groups and teachers; I was sure I

---

[12] *Astaunga Yoga:* "Eight-limbed yoga," based on the Yoga Sutras of Patanjali, an ancient Indian sage. (Another common spelling for this system of yoga is *Ashtanga.*)

had found the best. Other Eastern paths, whose devotees strove only for their own spiritual enlightenment, appeared selfish in comparison. As a member of Ananda Marga, I would not only work on my own spiritual transformation, but would help the world while doing so.

I had my first thoughts of becoming a didi not long after I had been given my second lesson. I was sitting in the meditation room of the Regent Street jagrti after a particularly long and deep meditation, during which I'd had intimations of living at the time of Christ in a previous life, seeing date trees, the streets of old Jerusalem worn away by the feet of countless passersby, and the rough-hewn robes worn by Jesus and his disciples as clearly as I now saw the *puja* table[13] with its picture of Baba in front of me. I lost all track of time as I continued to gaze at the table and the luxuriant greenery of the plants surrounding it.

A thought came to me from somewhere deep within: *You can become a didi, you know. . . . You can become a didi!*

The idea thrilled me. I had not yet met any didis, but I knew about them. In Ananda Marga magazines, I'd seen pictures of Indian ones, dressed in their robes. Covered head to foot, they looked like nuns, except that their habits were orange, the traditional color of robes worn by renunciates in India. Right then and there, I promised myself that I would one day put on the habit and become one of them.

When I shared this desire with Yogeshananda, he told me I should work first as an LFT ("Local Full-Timer," someone who works full-time for the organization but has not yet become an acarya, or a "whole-timer"). I went to the Sectorial Office in Wichita to do as Dada advised; then, when the office moved to Denver some months later, I moved right along with it. I was so busy (Dada had appointed me as editor of the Ananda Marga newsletter for the sector), that I gave little thought to what I had told him.

---

[13] *puja* table: A small table upon which are placed pictures of the guru, incense, and so on. (*Puja* means "worship.")

One evening several months later, Yogeshananda called me into his room after dharmacakra and, without any preliminaries, asked, "Are you ready to go to training?"

I felt as if someone had thrown a bucket of cold water over me. "I . . . I don't know, Dada," I finally managed to say. "How will I get the money for my ticket?"

"The money will come."

"What will I tell my parents?"

Dada smiled, his eyes twinkling. "Why don't you tell them you're going to Israel?"

Israel! That resonated with me. I'd often dreamed that once I became a didi, I would get posted there.

Then the smile left Dada's face. He grew serious and a stern tone entered his voice as he said these final words: "Your mother is Baba. Your father is Baba."

I stumbled out of the room, my mind reeling. But why? Didn't I want to go to training? Hadn't I been the one to tell Dada I wanted to go? After all, it wasn't his idea! I went upstairs to my room and flopped down on my sleeping bag.

I'm not ready to go to India, I thought. After all, I haven't thought about this for ages! And what would I say to my parents?

I felt my eyelids growing heavy. I had one last thought before succumbing to deep sleep: Baba, please help me decide. I need some sign to know what to do.

I had a dream.

I am sitting in a circle of devotees. We are all sitting in sand, up on a dune. Baba is also there, sitting in the middle of the circle, but lower down, on sand firmly packed and smooth. He is speaking. I can't hear what he is saying because I am struggling to keep my balance in the loose sand. Suddenly I have a realization: why don't I just stop struggling and let myself slide down? So, that's what I do—slide down the dune until I am on the same level as Baba, on the firmly packed sand. The sense of relief I experience is almost overwhelming.

Now I can hear what he is saying: "So, you will need to struggle to realize we are all one entity. But you will struggle and you will realize we are all one entity." His voice rings with power. As his words vibrate in the still air, Baba gets up and begins to walk around the circle, comes nearer, and then stops in front of me. He reaches out with his hand as if to touch me. My mind races and I think: Is he going to touch me? Is he going to put me in samadhi?[14] Baba takes his finger and presses my ajina cakra, the point between the eyes. I lose all sense of my body. I am limitless light, brilliant and infinite, expanding outwards.

I woke up, my whole body vibrating, as if every cell were suffused with light and joy, and marveled at the dream. Although Baba hadn't told me to go to training, the fact that he had visited me was confirmation enough. Later that morning, any doubts I was still holding on to evaporated when Prakash, the president of Ananda Marga in the States, came into the office with a large white box. "It's from Arpita," he said in answer to my inquiring look, and placed the box on my desk. Arpita was Prakash's wife and an excellent seamstress, but as I hadn't been expecting anything, I was mystified. With great anticipation, I opened the box—to find an orange shirt, something like an acarya would wear. I took it out with shaking hands. As I held it up, tears came to my eyes. First, there had been the dream, and now, there was this! I had my answer. I knew with absolute certainty that I would go to training and become a didi.

After that conversation in his room, Yogeshananda spent more time with me, giving me my third and fourth lessons. He also saved me from the one brief attraction I had almost fallen prey to. One evening, during one of the LFT meetings we had at the Denver office, I had ended up sitting in the jagrti basement with an LFT named Vikram. It seemed like we had so much in common. For one thing, we discovered that we both played guitar and loved to sing, and we ended up doing both.

---

[14] samadhi: A state of bliss; the merging of the individual consciousness into universal consciousness.

(I particularly loved his rendition of Bob Dylan's "Knockin' on Heaven's Door.") As we talked about our lives far into the night, a sense of magic seemed to steal into the cellar and surround us, and I started to wonder if I was really meant to be a didi after all. Afterwards, we went upstairs to the meditation room. Dada was still up, sitting with some Margiis. He looked at me intently, then at Vikram, and said, "You know, Liila is almost ready to go to India and become a whole-timer." As he said the words, I could feel Vikram stiffen beside me. By early the next morning, he was gone, on his way back to California and his LFT work— along with the threat he had represented.

Chapter 2

I Arrive in India

It was July, 1974, and I was in Reading Terminal Station in Philadelphia about to board a train to New York. At long last, I would soon be on my way to India and the Ananda Marga training center. I had gotten a job taking care of people with disabilities to earn part of the money for my ticket. Ananda Marga members, including Mangala, the woman I'd met at Penn almost four years earlier, had donated the rest. Mangala had recently left for the training center herself, and I was looking forward to seeing her there.

Before boarding the train, though, I still had one more important thing to take care of: saying goodbye to my parents. As I approached the waiting area we had agreed upon, I caught sight of them and felt a pang: they looked so old. My mother was in her sixties and wore her hair in the bouffant style, dyed nearly black and as hard as a helmet with all the hair spray she used. Her large dark-framed glasses dominated her face. Thanks to conscientious dieting and an ulcer, she looked thin in her Jackie Kennedy-style sleeveless white dress with blue trim. My father was over seventy and, to me, had always looked old. His heavily lined face was dominated by his nose, which seemed even larger than when I'd last seen him. As I got to where they were sitting, he gazed up at me with melancholy, rheumy eyes magnified by thick bifocals.

I sat down and we talked. Or tried to.

"We're going to miss you, Marsha."

"Don't worry. I'll write."

Then we fell silent. There we all sat, feeling uncomfortable. I was feeling that they didn't understand me; they were likely feeling confused and sad, maybe wondering why things were turning out as they were. (*What did we do wrong with her? Why is she leaving us to go to a yoga group, of all things?*)

"The weather's nice," my mother finally said. "You'll have a good trip." My father, his expression bleak, didn't say anything.

This is awful, I thought. Here I was, leaving them for what they knew would be a fairly long time, and still, there were no feelings expressed. It had always been that way in our family. In a way, though, the fact that we never talked about things in any deep way was making it easier for me to leave. At least I wouldn't have to try to explain what I was doing and why!

The time came for me to board my train. We exchanged hugs. As I walked away, an impulse seized me, and I turned around to run back and hug them a second time. They seemed surprised at this outpouring. But my parents didn't know what I did: I wasn't going away for just a few months, but quite possibly for the rest of my life. I hadn't been able to bring myself to tell them.

The first four years of my life were spent in West Oak Lane, a modest neighborhood of row houses in Philadelphia. We moved out of the city to the leafy suburb of Elkins Park shortly after my fourth birthday, soon after my father opened a hardware store in the neighborhood.

The move was a step up for my parents, both of whom were from working-class backgrounds and had never gone to college. Compared to most other couples at the time, they had started their family unusually late. By the time I was born in 1949, the youngest and the only girl, my mother was thirty-nine and my father was in his mid to late forties.[15]

My father Maximilian, or Jack, as he sometimes called himself, was an immigrant who had arrived at Ellis Island (or perhaps it had been Philadelphia; we don't know for sure) as a boy. He emigrated from Ukraine with his mother and sister after his father, who had gone to the States a few years earlier, sent for the family. Things weren't destined to go so well for Maximilian in the new country. His father died relatively young (having gotten a fish bone stuck in his throat causing an infection, the story went), and my father ended up having to take care of the whole family, particularly the younger siblings born after the family's arrival, even putting his brother Bernie through medical school.

A mostly unsmiling, hard-working man of few words, my father spent six days a week working in his store and would have worked all seven, if it hadn't been for the blue laws.[16] Occasionally he would flout the law and stay open. "We're *Jews*," he'd say. "Why should I have to close on Sundays?" At dinnertime he would come home, sit down in the kitchen and finish eating within minutes, then get up to walk back to the store. "Time to return to the salt mines," he'd say, going out the back door.

The only time my father would loosen up a little was on Sundays, when we sometimes had company. Sitting at the dining room table, he would have a beer or two and tell a few stories of his childhood. His favorite one was about the pogroms visited upon the shtetl outside Kiev where his family lived. When Cossacks came riding in looking for Jews, the villagers would run over to his house and hide in the basement along with my father and his family. There they would remain until the sound of the Cossack's horses thundering overhead had faded. My father's grandfather,

[15] I'm not sure what year my father was born. His driver's license has his birth date as July 15, 1904. His death certificate lists his birth date as July 15, 1901.

[16] The blue laws restricted activities or sales of goods on Sunday to accommodate Christian Sunday worship. In the fifties and sixties, it was illegal for businesses to be open on Sundays in Pennsylvania.

the story went, had been conscripted into the tsar's army as a teenager and had served with distinction, so the Cossacks left his house alone. My father would relate the story in a jocular tone, almost as if he'd been telling a joke.

Then there was the one about the boat journey over to the new country (a story that I remember but my brothers do not). My father was crowded into steerage along with his mother and sister and masses of other people. Conditions were poor. Against regulations, people sometimes lit the kerosene or wood-burning stoves they'd brought along to cook. One day a stove ignited a fire, which spread quickly. Thankfully, it was put out in time, and the boat arrived safely days later.

I was afraid of my father. Although he had a softer side, it rarely showed. (Sometimes it did when he would lie down on the living room carpet after Sunday dinner and listen to music on the radio. Whenever songs from *Fiddler on the Roof* came on, he would tear up, no doubt thinking about his boyhood village.) Although not usually a physically violent man, red-hot anger churned right beneath the surface. Feeling myself on dangerous ground, I tiptoed around the house, so his anger wouldn't erupt and engulf me.

My mother Mina was a child of immigrants, her mother having emigrated from Poland and her father from what was then Austria-Hungary. Mina was one of six children. Lou and Rhoda were older, Danny and Lorraine younger. And then there was Dorothy, another younger sister. She had died in childbirth from a cerebral hemorrhage years before my birth, and held an almost mythic place in our family's psyche. The faded framed picture of a woman with near-perfect skin, large and dreamy eyes, and an abundance of dark hair piled up on her head in the style of the day, dominated the chest of drawers in my parents' bedroom. There was talk of her having been the real beauty of the family.

For my mother, appearances were everything, so much so that she was known for changing the labels on our clothing. After buying things at Artie's, a local store known for its inexpensive clothes, she would replace the labels with ones from Lord and Taylor (though where she got those remains a mystery).

Having a horror of dirt and disorder, my mother would spend hours cleaning an already spotless house. Often I would come home from school to find the house taken apart, the carpets rolled up, and my mother down on her hands and knees, scrubbing. Or I'd find her in the kitchen with the dishes out on the table and her head inside the cabinets, wiping them down. When I talked to her, she'd mumble an answer with her head still in those cabinets, even if I had something important to tell her. When guests came and sat in our living room, my mother would jump up after they stood up to leave the room, run over to the sofa cushions, and fluff them up. When we kids tried to lie down on our beds during the day, she'd shoo us off. "Don't lie on the bedspread," she'd say, "you'll wrinkle it."

Normal childhood messes were frowned upon. Unlike at my friends' houses, there were no cheerful piles of books or magazines scattered about (the only books in our house were a set of out-of-date World Book encyclopedias), no toys or drawings in progress or jigsaw puzzles lying half-completed on spare surfaces. When my friends visited, we were relegated to the basement. So I rarely invited friends over and spent most of my free time at their houses, where we were allowed to draw on paper or chalkboards, play in sandboxes, or eat and leave some crumbs.

Our house was an emotionally cold place. It was as if each of us—my mother, my father, my two brothers and me—while sharing the same physical space, had our own orbits that rarely intersected. Early on, I learned to keep my feelings to myself.

Three days after saying goodbye to my parents, I was at JFK Airport, along with another soon-to-be trainee named Janet. We had spent the last few days rushing around buying some last-minute items: a toilet bag, a toothbrush, a few bottles of shampoo, and some water purification tablets. I had my ticket in hand and was towing a light blue hard-case Samsonite suitcase behind me. Janet, whose spiritual name was Jayamala, was lugging her own Samsonite suitcase, identical to mine, but black.

I was feeling good about our preparations. Only one thing bothered me ever so slightly. As we got in line to check in, I said, "Do you think we need to worry about money pouches?" We'd planned to save money by buying some cloth and making a few, but had run out of time.

"Nah!" Jayamala said, waving my remark aside.

She was right. This was not the time for worries. We boarded the plane with hardly a glance behind. I was free. Not until that moment did I realize how many things in my life I'd long been wanting to leave behind—not only my Jewish identity, which I had found limiting, but the whole overly materialistic American culture—and the mixed-up college girl who had been trying to find happiness in drugs and sex.

After a largely uneventful flight, we landed in Delhi and took a train to Calcutta,[17] our first stop on the way to Benares and the training center. Riding in a taxi from the train station at dawn, we had our first glimpse of the city. It was shuttered and still, with battered shop signs of garish colors written in the lyrical, artful-looking Bengali script and large posters of actors and actresses from Indian movies plastered on peeling walls. Through the gloom, I could make out huddled shapes of various sizes sleeping on pieces of cardboard and others dressed in mud-colored rags sleeping on concrete. Some were on sidewalks; others were curled up in shabby doorways. Those who had the cardboard were the lucky ones. I had been prepared to see desperately poor people, but the sight of it all was a shock.

We stayed a few days with an older Margii couple. They were well off, and their cool, quiet apartment offered refuge from the

---

[17] Throughout the book, I use the names of Indian cities by which they were known at the time: Calcutta, Bombay, and Madras—instead of Kolkata, Mumbai, and Chennai, as they are called now. The city of Benares is also known as Varanasi.

teeming streets. They had a refrigerator, which I soon learned was a luxury in India. We were given *dahi* (made from milk and similar to yogurt) and slices of mango. Since mango was not readily available in the States at the time, this was the first opportunity I had to try it. I found its taste transporting—and exotic. Just like India, I thought.

A few days later, we boarded an evening train to Benares. We were looking forward to the weeks and months we would spend learning and meditating, anticipating the peace and quiet to be found in the training center. The train was crowded and none too clean. At least we had reservations. We also had sleeping berths, which turned out to be flat, hard boards that had to be let down when it was time to sleep. We sat on our seats, closed our eyes, and meditated briefly, trying not to look conspicuous. When we finished, we opened our eyes to find people opening round, silver containers that contained puris, *sabje* (vegetables), and milk sweets. It was dinner time. One family offered us some of their food, and we took a few puris. But we declined the vegetables, concerned they might have onions and garlic in them, forbidden foods considered unconducive to spiritual practice. A few of the men spoke English and asked us where we were going.

"We're tourists," we said. "We're going to Benares."

"Are you going to visit the temples? Our Varanasi temples are famous, you know," one said with pride. We nodded but didn't say anything. We couldn't tell them what we were really doing in India, or where in Benares we were going. The Indian government frowned on Ananda Marga. If we were discovered to be Margiis, we would be deported.

Finally, it was time to sleep. Everyone readied themselves, putting down their berths and arranging blankets. As I watched men in their spotless white kurtas and dhotis and women in their colorful saris making their way to and from the latrine, I wondered how they managed to stay so clean in such dirty surroundings. Jayamala and I took turns going to the latrine. On the way, I nearly stumbled over people sleeping in the aisles;

those without reservations sat and slept anywhere they could. It was filthy in the latrine, and I had to hold my nose.

We'd been told that thieves were clever in India, so in order to avoid something being stolen, we decided not to sleep. We placed our small red bag with our money and passports under our legs for safekeeping and took turns watching it.

All through the night, as the train pulled into and out of stations, the platforms were bustling with people and with vendors hawking all kinds of food. *"Chai, chai,"* called out men in khaki-colored uniforms and caps, carrying little earthenware cups and battered aluminum teapots black with soot. *"Garam chai!"* Others sold puris and potato and cauliflower *sabje,* or peanuts in paper cones made from old newspapers. Some of the people around me woke up and bought something; most slept on.

As I sat watching the bag and struggling to stay awake, I wondered what time it was in Philadelphia. Would the Margiis in the Regent Street jagrti be sleeping or meditating? I thought of the meditation room, of the *puja* table surrounded by its plants—and of that momentous day when I'd sat there and decided to become a didi.

The shouts of vendors as the train pulled into yet another station brought me back to my surroundings, and I looked at my watch: only a few hours to go. Moments later, we were on our way again. The rhythmic swaying of the train with its wheels clicking on the rails and the sounds of passengers snoring conspired against me. Despite my best efforts, my eyes began to close, my head drooped, and I dozed off.

I started and jerked awake, immediately sensing that something was wrong. A quick glance her way told me that Jayamala was asleep. I looked for the bag and was relieved to find it still there at my feet. But it looked different, emptier, somehow. I opened it, fingers trembling—to find that our passports and money were gone. Frantically, I dug through the bag to be sure. Gone! Both passports and all our money except for a few rupees—money collected for the cash-strapped training center—all gone!

I woke up Jayamala with the news, and we sat mutely through the last few hours of our journey, defeated by our stupidity. Why hadn't we taken the time to make those money pouches?

When the train arrived in Benares, so early in the morning that there was only a light tinge to the edge of a still-dark sky, we dragged our ridiculously heavy suitcases alongside us in a drizzly gray dawn. Outside the station, we found rickshaw drivers waiting for customers. We motioned to one, although the rickshaw (black and yellow, with a high back and cracked and peeling seat attached to a bicycle) seemed far too small for two people with Samsonite suitcases. We hesitated for a moment before climbing on, the driver precariously placing our suitcases next to our feet on the small ledge. I held on to the handle of my suitcase, its size seeming more absurd than ever, and grasped one side of the rickshaw with my free hand.

We consulted our directions, then managed somehow to make our destination understood. The driver got on his bicycle and, much to our amazement, was able to start pedaling, despite all the weight he was pulling. As he splashed and careened his way through the rainy streets, we spotted people sleeping in doorways, covered head to toe in cloths like mummies, trying to escape the drizzle. When we reached the large wooden door at our destination, we paid the driver with our few remaining rupees and struggled off with our suitcases.

We opened the door and went in. I was surprised by a lovely garden, with plants on either side of the pathway leading to the building where the training center was. Despite the early hour, I could make out the reds, whites, and oranges of hibiscus, frangipani, and ornamental gingers (flowers I didn't yet know the names of but would soon learn). We dragged our suitcases up some stairs to the training center. As I climbed the last few steps, I could barely make out a figure taking shape in the haze of drizzle and the dim light of dawn, a young Caucasian woman in a white sari standing on the verandah and moving towards us.

"Namaskar," she said, drawing her hands together. "Liila and Jayamala, I presume. I'm Balavatii. This way." We followed her through a doorway and into a room with young women, just girls, really, sleeping on blankets on the concrete floor. Some of them looked painfully thin. A few woke up as we came in, including Mangala. She propped herself up on an elbow and asked if we had brought the money. Still in shock about what had happened, I was taken aback and mumbled something about telling her later.

Later that morning, two Indian dadas in their orange robes arrived to give classes to the trainees. We told them our story and were relieved not to be scolded. They listened, nodding their heads, then retired to a small room. We could hear them discussing our fate in low, even tones. As we sat there waiting, I could hardly keep my eyes open. I longed for sleep.

One of the dadas, the extremely thin, soft-spoken one with black hair flowing down his back, came out to tell us we would have to return to Calcutta and go to the American Consulate, report our passports stolen, and get them replaced. Another pang of guilt hit me as I listened to him. His large, gentle eyes, larger because of his emaciation, seemed to rebuke me for my stupidity.

"There is no money for tickets," he told us. "You will have to go to the local Benares government and borrow your fare back to Calcutta. Some Margiis will help you when you get there."

Jayamala and I looked at each other, shocked. How could we borrow money from "the enemy"? (That was what any government in India was to Ananda Marga.) If they found out who we were, we would be deported. If we weren't so tired, though, the idea of borrowing money from the local government by convincing its officials we were merely ordinary tourists would have filled us with excitement. As it was, contemplating such a step made us feel only more exhausted.

Anxious to look like tourists, we dressed carefully before heading to the government office, Jayamala looking neat in khakis and I looking presentable enough in navy slacks. We left the compound we had entered just a few hours earlier and hailed another rickshaw.

"At least we don't have those stupid suitcases to lug around with us," Jayamala said as we climbed on. Our situation was absurd to the point of disbelief, and I found myself wondering if I was still in New York, dreaming all this up. Sleep deprivation and culture clash were conspiring against me, and I felt out of my body, as if looking at myself from a great distance.

The honk of a taxi whizzing by perilously close to our rickshaw brought me back to myself, and I looked with amazement at the variety of people and vehicles around me: bicycle rickshaw drivers, people on motorcycles, black and yellow motor rickshaws spewing smoke, taxis, the occasional black Ambassador car, laborers pushing loads in front of them on long wooden trolleys—all jockeying for position on the narrow road and trying to avoid hitting the cows meandering across it, as relaxed as if they were lolling about in a field of grass.

The rickshaw driver deposited us on the jam-packed street in front of the government building. We made our way past the sidewalk food stalls and people engaged in various apparently bureaucratic tasks, sitting cross-legged at typewriters with reams of official-looking papers next to them (right there on the sidewalk!), and headed to a clerk behind a grill at a window looking out to the street. He told us which room to go to, and we went in the building, found the stairs, and headed up to the second floor. Men hurried past us, many of them carrying bulging folders. The high ceilings caused the din of footsteps and voices of people shouting back and forth down the halls to echo. The noise made my head hurt.

When we got to the room, we explained our situation to a clerk and waited. I felt like I was sinking into my chair. The sense of unreality returned, and I struggled to keep my eyes open. The clerk came back, motioned to us to follow him, and led us to an inner office. The man who greeted us looked important and had a presence about him. He smiled and asked us to sit down, introducing himself as Mr. Sharma.

"Now, tell me what happened," he said as he settled into his chair. "Oh, yes, before you do, would you like to take tea?" I glanced quickly at Jayamala. As trainees, black tea was forbidden to us. "Yes, thank you," I heard Jayamala answer, much to my astonishment.

Mr. Sharma called in a clerk and ordered tea, then asked us to tell him our story. Jayamala gave him our half-fabricated account and asked for a loan.

"Madam, that is terribly unfortunate," Mr. Sharma said. "Surely, someone must have warned you that we have some very clever thieves in India. Many specifically target foreigners."

"Yes, we have friends who have been here," I said. "They warned us and told us to get money pouches. But we ran out of time before our flight to get them."

The clerk brought in a tray with three small glasses of tea. Mr. Sharma took a glass then had the clerk bring the tray over to us.

"Please, take tea," he said. We each took a glass. I brought mine to my lips and pretended to take a sip. Jayamala actually sipped at hers; then her hand trembled, and she spilled a little on her khaki pants. She mopped it up quickly with her handkerchief, her face red.

"Yes, each of you must get something to put your money and your new passports in, once you get them," Mr. Sharma said. "We have them available in India. They go around your neck and are worn under your shirt." We promised him that we would.

After a few more questions, Mr. Sharma cleared his throat and said, "On behalf of the Varanasi government, I am happy to tell you that we will extend a loan of six hundred rupees."

Thank you, Baba! I thought, making a supreme effort to remain composed. If Mr. Sharma only knew who we were!

"Thank you," we said in unison.

"No mention, please."

Mr. Sharma explained how long the loan was for and how we would go about repaying it. Later that evening, we boarded a train to Calcutta. (As if it were meant to reveal her infraction, Jayamala never managed to get that tea stain out of her pants!)

Early the next morning, our train pulled into Calcutta, and we hired a rickshaw. This one, unlike those in Delhi, had no bicycle, which meant the driver would be on foot, pulling the rickshaw behind him. I had noticed before that all the rickshaws in Calcutta were like that; thankfully we hadn't had to use one. But now we were compelled to. Rickshaws were the cheapest mode of transportation besides buses. A bus was out of the question because of our luggage (buses were far too crowded for that) and we couldn't afford anything else, so we had no alternative. That didn't stop me from feeling terrible about it, though. I kept thinking, How can I even consider doing such a thing—letting a human being pull me as if he were a donkey!—even as the man we had called over (scrawny and barefoot and dressed mostly in rags) helped us pile our luggage on. Once we were situated, he took off running, clanging his bell.

When we got to the home of the Margii couple we had stayed with before, we gave them the letter one of the dadas had written about our situation. We each took a bath, then tried to meditate, but mostly dozed with our heads drooping. After a meal of chapattis and vegetables, we lay down on the rug for a nap. I fell asleep immediately and had a dream.

I am sitting with Baba. We are in a log cabin in the woods. It is late afternoon, and sunlight is streaming in the windows. Baba is seated on a chair, women devotees from the training center surrounding him. He says something tender to each but does not speak to me.

In a small voice, I say, "Baba, don't you have anything to tell me?"

"Oh, you're all right," he says and waves as if to dismiss me. He turns away, resumes talking to another trainee, and then turns back to me.

"You're very dirty, aren't you?" he says in a firm but loving voice.

Dirty? . . . I'm dirty? . . . I'm dirty! My panicked mind shouts. I stumble out of the cabin and into the woods, weeping, then into another building where I find my Samsonite suitcase. I take out a dress I used to wear in my hippie days, a red and yellow Indian dress with little mirrors all over it. I struggle to put it on, but I get my arms all twisted up in its sleeves. I give up and toss the dress aside, then look down and see that I am fully clothed—in orange.

I woke up sobbing. The afternoon sun slanted into the windows, lighting up a patch of the richly colored Oriental rug on which I had been sleeping. The image of the Indian dress twisting in the dream as I had struggled to put it on swept across the screen of my mind. With it, I found myself thrust back into a painful episode I thought I had gotten over once and for all.

It had all started late one afternoon in the summer of 1970. I was heading to a rock concert outside of Philadelphia, going with a group of people I didn't know very well. I decided to wear my Indian dress with the mirrors on it; I thought it looked good on me. Before we all piled into the car, one of my companions passed around some little pills. For a moment, I hesitated. I didn't do acid much, and it wasn't a good idea to trip in the company of relative strangers. But I wanted to fit in, so, ignoring the inner warning, I put out my hand. A pill dropped into my palm, and I popped it into my mouth.

I was in line to buy a drink when I started to feel the effects. They weren't good. Panic surged in me as I quickly spiraled down into the dread of all trippers: the bummer. I knew I needed to do something, but what? I couldn't tell the people I was with. They were all older—seasoned acid users who would surely taunt anyone inexperienced or weak enough to have a bad trip.

I knew that Sarah, a nurse and the only non-drug user out of the eight of us living in the big house we shared in West Philadelphia, was on staff that evening in the "trip tent," a place where people having bad trips could go and get help. Was I actually thinking of going there and talking to her? The panic not only wasn't going away, it was getting worse, and I knew I needed help. But to go to the trip tent and see Sarah? How uncool was that! And what if some of my companions saw me there? Then they'd know I was freaking out. To be seen at the trip tent would be the worst thing for my reputation I could think of.

I found myself drifting over to the tent, spotting Sarah in her white nurse's uniform. She looked like a fat insect of some sort, with a huge abdomen and bug eyes encased in glasses. Her uniform symbolized the straight world, the world of officialdom, the world to which I had never belonged and was determined I never would. Struggling with dread mixed up with terror, I glanced over my shoulder to be sure no one was watching, and went in.

Opening my mouth, I tried to talk. Multicolored words came out and hovered in the air in front of me, but it was as if I were speaking a foreign language. Sarah had no idea what I was talking about, never having had a drug-induced hallucination, the experience of thinking something, then seeing or hearing it. Her eyes were flat and dead as she looked at me.

I lay down on the floor of the tent, feeling terror welling up even more strongly. My heart began to beat rapidly, like a caged animal trying to free itself from the prison of my ribs. Then, as the fear of being discovered in the trip tent by my companions became overwhelming, I got up to leave. Too late! I saw some of them approaching and tried to hide, but they (or was it my hallucinations of them?) started to laugh. "Hey, look who's in the drug tent!" they chortled. "What's the matter, can't handle the trip?" Their derisive laughter followed me as I struggled to my feet and stumbled out into the night, alone.

I don't know how long I wandered around. Everywhere were people pointing at me and laughing. Everyone could see right into me and knew me for what I was: a quaking piece of jelly on a bad trip, a caricature, a fake.

Some deep, primal urge for self-preservation welled up from somewhere. *Get out of here!* a voice shouted. *Go home!*

Stranded without a car, I did the only thing I could think of: I went out to the road and stuck out my thumb.

A car full of teens careened to a stop. They took one look at me and sped off.

The next car that stopped had no one else in it but a middle-aged driver.

"Where are you going?" the man asked.

"Philadelphia," I said, my voice barely a whisper.

"I'm going in that direction," he said. "Hop in."

I knew it was risky, but what choice did I have? I opened the door and got in.

"Whereabouts in Philly are you headed?"

"Near the University of Pennsylvania," I managed to answer and gave him the address.

He took pity on me and delivered me right to my door.

I trudged up the flights of stairs to my room in the attic. I lay down but couldn't sleep. Early the next morning, I sought out Rob and Ginny, the two therapists who lived in the house. As pale morning light began filtering into the large window in their room overlooking the street, I told them what had happened. They tried to help me.

"You feel bad right now because you're still feeling the effects of the acid," they told me. "Every feeling is magnified. You'll feel better in a day or two."

But what they said didn't really help. I began to think I didn't really know who I was. I felt as if I had to go somewhere and be taken care of. Rob and Ginny took me to the University of Pennsylvania Hospital, and I signed myself into the psych ward.

The next morning, I awoke to find my mother, father, and brothers, surrounding my bed and gazing at me with frowns on their faces. I felt like a specimen on a lab table. Anger welled up. Who told them I was here? Saying nothing, I turned my head away from the burden of their concern and went back to sleep.

I had no faith in the therapist they assigned me to. I could swear he was afraid of me. A thin and nervous man with mousy, thinning hair, he averted his eyes whenever we were together, and his hands trembled. I told him about my interest in Zen and meditation and insisted on keeping the necklace of wooden beads I had brought with me.

I stayed on the ward for three days but left abruptly when I witnessed a fellow patient, a quiet, mild-mannered woman who had been in my therapy group, go on a rant. They threw her, screaming, into a brightly lit, cell-like room with pads on the walls, placed her in restraints, and locked her in. I'll be like her, I thought, if I don't get out of here right away.

A few months later, when I started outpatient psychotherapy at Penn, my new therapist allowed me to read the ward therapist's diagnosis of my condition and the notes he had written. "Diagnosis: Latent schizophrenia. Patient spouts platitudes about Eastern religion, Zen."

Jayamala stirring beside me brought me back to the present. Then the images of the Baba dream came flooding back into my mind, and once again, I heard his unsettling words: "You're very dirty, aren't you?" I thought about the drugs I had taken in college and all the sex I'd had. Baba's right, I thought. I *am* dirty. But before I could sink any further into despair, I recalled how the dream had ended: I hadn't been able to put on my old clothing and had been dressed in orange. There's bound to be lots of purification to undergo in training, I thought—maybe even suffering. Maybe I'll try to return to my former life, but in the end I'll finish training and become a didi. I felt comforted, at least a little bit.

A few days later, we went to the U.S. Consulate. We were hoping to get new passports right away but found out that it wouldn't be so fast or easy. So we had to stay in Calcutta for a while. Jayamala and I couldn't stay any longer with the Margiis (we were wearing out our welcome), so we packed our bags and with the financial help of the Calcutta dadas, moved to the YWCA. Then both of us succumbed to dysentery. I wasn't as sick as Jayamala so ventured out to buy food and medicine.

Whenever I went out, I was pursued by beggars, many of them children. Swarming around me, they cried out, begging for rupees. Some held out battered and blackened tin cups. Others, their milky-white eyes sightless, held out their palms. Some had no hands; others swung themselves along the ground, their stumps of legs useless. Whenever I gave some of the ragged children a few rupees and bananas, the crowd would grow larger and threaten to swallow me up, and I had to flee. I felt helpless in the face of all this need and despair. (Later I would be shocked to learn that although some child beggars were crippled because of polio, which was all too prevalent in India at the time, others were that way because they had been deliberately mutilated, mostly by criminal gangs, to make them more pitiable when soliciting donations.)

Most streets were narrow and filthy. Along with skins of papaya and banana and other trash, there were mysterious red stains that seemed to be everywhere. I also saw spittoons filled with the red substance, which turned out to be from chewing betel nuts. The nuts were sold in tiny *paan* shops, where the proprietors sat cross-legged and wrapped up the nuts in green beetle leaves to make small packets, adding white lime paste and all kinds of spices and herbs. Every man in Calcutta, it seemed, chewed the packets and spat out the crimson juice. When the monsoon rains came, rivers of filth flowed down the streets. The weather was breathlessly hot; day and night, sweat sat on my skin like a swaddling cloth.

I'll never forget the first time Jayamala and I took a bus. We shoved our way on and spent the trip smashed up against other passengers, staring, disbelieving, as we careened madly along, narrowly missing cows and laborers hauling crates on their long wooden contraptions. The bus was so crowded it seemed we might capsize any moment. Some of the passengers never even managed to get inside; instead, they held on to doorways and windows.

When we got to our destination, we had to push our way through the crush to get off, and I lost a sandal in the process.

Those first few weeks, it seemed that all I saw was dirt and beggars. But slowly I began to see my surroundings in a different light. I became aware of subtleties, again noticing that the kurtas and dhotis of the men were always dazzlingly white. I admired the colorful saris and the grace with which the women walked. Entering a store or crossing a street, I caught the musty scent of incense in the air. Boarding a bus, I saw the tiny *puja* that the bus driver had arranged above his seat, a picture of Shiva with a fresh garland and sticks of incense burning beside it. Flower garlands were sold in the streets, some made of vivid orange marigolds, others of sweet-smelling frangipani flowers, still others of tiny star-shaped white flowers, which I couldn't identify but which smelled almost excruciatingly fragrant. India, it seemed, had some beauty after all, and I soon came to regard it as my true home.

After we had been in Calcutta a while, Jayamala and I were feeling out of place wearing pants, so early one morning, we went shopping. Pausing outside of several identical-looking shops, we were unsure as to which one to enter, until one of the shopkeepers caught sight of us and waved us inside.

"You want sari?" he asked. "I give you good price." The tiny shop was packed with them. We fingered a few, but since we knew it would be impossible to teach ourselves how to wear one (we'd learn later, in the training center), we pointed to some skirts that had caught our eye. The merchant asked us to have a seat and offered us tea (which we declined—no need to pretend here!), then showed us some skirts. Like the saris, they came in a variety of colors. Some had ruffles; others had straight hems. We could choose from cotton, polyester, or silk. As renunciates, we were forbidden to wear silk as it was considered aristocratic (and also was produced by taking life), so it would have to be polyester or cotton.

"Cotton's cooler than polyester," Jayamala said. I agreed.

We settled on two white ones each. Looking similar to the skirts we'd worn as LFTs in the States, they felt familiar and somehow comforting to us.

We started wearing them the next day, along with the long-sleeved cotton shirts we'd brought with us. We felt good in our new skirts, but as soon as we went out on the streets, people began staring at us and would turn to each other and gesture, speaking rapidly in Bengali. Maybe it was because we were foreigners, we thought, but noticed that other foreigners weren't looked at the same way. "And," I reminded Jayamala, "no one stared at us like that before!" It was indeed puzzling.

A few days later, we went to Sunday dharmacakra at the Central Office, the global headquarters of Ananda Marga. As we entered the meditation hall, one of the dadas, a blush visible beneath his dark skin, came up to me and said, "Sister, you're not properly dressed."

"Not properly dressed? What do you mean?" I asked. We were completely covered, head to toe.

"You are wearing a petticoat, which is worn only under a sari," he replied, then turned and walked quickly away.

Jayamala and I looked at each other wide-eyed, the realization sinking in that as far as Indians were concerned, we were wearing underwear! We bolted for the latrine, where we hid until we could leave without being seen. Then we rushed back to the YWCA with our faces red and put our pants back on.

At long last, the day we had been waiting for arrived. We went to the American Consulate and got our new passports. That evening, as we boarded a train for Benares, our passports safely hidden under our shirts in our new pouches, we were confident this trip would go much better than the last.

Chapter 3

Training

This time Jayamala and I arrived at the training center without incident. As there was no real starting and ending time for courses, we just began when we got there. Like most of the trainees, we had six-month tourist visas, but we'd already used up more than a month getting new passports. Because it was known to be nearly impossible to extend a tourist visa, we plunged right into the schedule, hoping to make up the lost time.

Every morning we were up early, usually before dawn. As we readied ourselves for spiritual practice, we would hear chanting coming from temples in the city. I would sometimes stand outside on the landing, listening in the dark, as the sonorous sound swelled and increased in intensity as more temples joined in, until it was as if I were surrounded by a timeless sea of sound at once thrilling and haunting. We, too, started our practices with chanting, which was followed by meditation and asanas, then breakfast. Morning classes were given by Gaganananda, the tall, emaciated dada who had told Jayamala and me to go back to Calcutta. (From conversations with other trainees, we learned that he had been robust and healthy mere months earlier but now suffered from constant dysentery. So the money we had

35

failed to deliver wouldn't have helped him gain weight. That greatly relieved our feelings of guilt.) Noon sadhana (meditation) followed morning class, and there were more classes after lunch. After they ended, we had a brief period of free time, followed by evening meditation, yoga postures, and dinner.

The dadas conducted classes on several topics, but I soon learned that we wouldn't be learning how to teach meditation and give mantras; those classes would come later, in Calcutta, when we would finally become acaryas. Instead, the dadas instructed us on Ananda Marga spiritual and social philosophy. It had been the social philosophy, PROUT, which had appealed to me early on, and I was enjoying learning its finer points.

We also studied basic Sanskrit and memorized countless *slokas*, or verses from sacred texts. *Sa tu bhavati dharidraha, Yasha asha vishala, Manasii ca partistute, Ko rithavan ko dharidraha,* we'd repeat, over and over ("He is indeed poor whose desires are limitless. If one has contentment, then who is rich and who is poor?"), then start in on another.

Then there were the "conduct rules." There were lots them, and we had to memorize and occasionally repeat them in front of the dadas: rules for workers or acaryas and more rules for *avadhutikas*, who took a special oath from Baba, wore all orange, and performed a special type of meditation. (We all hoped to achieve that lofty status someday after becoming acaryas.) One rule for avadhutikas was *Avadhutika must not laugh loudly*. Many of the rules were, like this one, ungrammatical or contained "Indian English." Still, we learned them that way, and I thought it lent them a kind of charm. A fair number of them had to do with food: *One must not take food touched by a mean-minded man,* was one. *Avadhutika must not take food while seeing one take non-vegetarian diet,* was another. Rules which were to have a great impact on my life were these: *No relationship will exist with worldly family* and (seeming to contradict the former) *The avadhutika must not give any chance to her ex-worldly family to see her in any place except jagrti.* At the time, I was only too happy to leave my worldly family behind. There was also a series of less-important guidelines called "Social Norms." There were forty of them having to do with all kinds of situations. *Don't talk standing before someone who is then eating* and *You should not engage in private talk in train or bus,* were two of them.

Most important, though, were the Sixteen Points, a series of practices, including following all conduct rules (*Non-compromising strictness and faith regarding the sanctity of conduct rules*) that we were to perform daily. They included meditation four times a day, yoga postures twice, daily full bath, half bath (to be done before eating, meditating, and sleeping)—and even service to plants and animals (*bhuta yajina*): no matter how hungry we were, at every meal we would set aside a small piece of chapatti or a handful of rice and throw it out to the birds once we had finished eating. (The Sixteen Points for us female trainees really only totaled fifteen because one of the points didn't apply to us: *Males should pull back the foreskin.* Though it was never stated, we supposed it was done by men while bathing.)

Far from considering all these rules burdensome, I loved them. For the confused person I had been before finding Ananda Marga, it was comforting to have these strict guidelines, these dos and don'ts. I wouldn't need to think about what to do in any situation I might face in the future. All I had to do was follow the conduct rules. It made life so simple—like having a detailed map.

Our daily routine involved a fair number of mundane, time-consuming tasks. We spent a lot of time washing our bodies and clothes, the floors, latrines, and bathing areas. We had to draw all our water from a well. Doing so required going down the stairs to the well, pulling up a bucket of water, emptying it into the bucket we had carried down with us, then lugging it back up the stairs, water sloshing out all the while. The supply of buckets was limited, and shouting matches sometimes broke out over who got to use them for what.

Even bathing had its own prescription. One was to do it in a squatting position, first pouring a tinful of cool water on the navel region (to cool down the *manipura cakra*[18]), then on the back opposite the navel, then from the top of the head down the spine. Once that was complete, the bather was free to soap herself up.

After bathing and before drying off, there was the bath mantra to perform. In ideal circumstances, the bather would face the rising sun and chant a fairly long Sanskrit *sloka*. It was to be recited three times, with hand movements. Performing the bath mantra at dawn facing the rising sun provided health benefits, we were told, by means of the rising sun hitting drops of water on the body. If the training center had been out in the country, maybe we would have been able to do it that way. As it was, we had to make do performing it facing the bare light bulb in the bathing area.

Trainees who had just arrived had highly coveted soaps and shampoos from home. When the Herbal Essence shampoos and their cousins ran out, we had to use Lifebuoy, a red-colored Indian bath soap (not to be confused with the American bath soap of the same name), and Sunlight, a yellow bar soap for washing clothes. Neither was particularly effective.

We used nylon-bristled brushes to wash our clothes. We rubbed soap on our saris and petticoats, scrubbed and pounded them on the ground, and finished by rinsing them in a bucket. The bright white of our new cotton saris quickly dulled to a muddy brown color. We countered this by using *niila*, a blue substance which was supposed to whiten garments when you applied it and hung them out in the sun. It worked up to a point, but all our saris ended up with a decidedly blue tinge.

Since the well water was suitable only for washing, we had to get our drinking water from a faucet located in the home of the family living downstairs. We would carry up the drinking water a few buckets at a time, and pour it into one of several large reddish brown clay jugs we kept for the purpose. Going to the

---

[18] *manipura cakra:* According to yogic philosophy, there are seven *cakras* (pronounced "chakras") or energy centers in the body. The *manipura cakra* is the third and is located at the navel.

family made us feel uncomfortable, though, so we kept our trips down to the bare minimum.

We took turns at chores. The concrete floor of the large room where we ate and slept was washed daily. We learned to clean Indian style, squatting down on our haunches while scrubbing, then moving crabwise, still on haunches, to another area until we had covered the entire surface. Sweeping the floor took place even more often. We used a short broom made from grasses for the purpose. It didn't have a long handle like the brooms most of us were accustomed to, so sweeping was also done on haunches.

Cooking was a major task, but did not involve shopping. Because we almost never ventured beyond the gates of the compound, we didn't do our own; instead, we had vegetables brought to us by one of the male trainees, a young Indian whom we called "Vegetable Dada." Two or three times a week, he'd ride into our compound on a beat-up, old-fashioned bicycle, with vegetables in sacks. There wasn't much variety. He mostly brought potatoes, eggplant, and a gourd-like vegetable with pale green skin. Cauliflower, being more expensive, was provided only for the very occasional festival day.

All cooking was done on a small stove that consisted of a tin cylinder with a hole midway down, plus sawdust for fuel. Once we got it going (itself not an easy task), we cooked chapattis. Every morning and evening, we would cook stack upon stack of them. (The first time I tried to make a chapatti, it resembled a map of Australia; with practice, I soon got good at making round ones.) Each trainee was asked how many she wanted, and everyone, unless feeling ill, ordered several. So the cook would often prepare fifty or sixty, fighting the smoke from the sawdust fuel, eyes and throat burning.

We all ate with our right hand, as was the custom in India. I liked it. It gave me more of an experience of my food. Whenever I did use a fork, which was rarely, the feeling of metal in my mouth felt strangely artificial. But adjusting to the diet proved far more difficult. Most of us from outside India lost weight, including me. (While meditating, I often found myself visualizing a jar of crunchy peanut butter instead of concentrating on my mantra. Sometimes the peanut butter would change into a bowl of creamy yogurt.)

We slept on the floor on grass mats and blankets. Pillows were deemed unacceptable for yogis, but some didis, especially once out of the training center, would fashion a kind of pillow from their sari or other clothes and put it under their heads. I, however, had no trouble being pillowless, having never slept with them growing up. My mother had thought them bad for the neck. (Once, when I was in elementary school, a friend came over my house and, thinking they were pillows, almost split her head open on one of the hard bolsters my mother had put at the head of my bed.) Back then, I had felt deprived. Now, I felt grateful. What would my mother have thought if she had known she was preparing me for life as a *yoginii?*[19]

As challenging as all these physical adjustments were, they paled in comparison to the arrival of "SPT," or *Seva Pita Training*.[20] It was a one- or two-week period (I don't recall which) that each trainee had to undergo involving a variety of physical hardships. A trainee was allowed to take a bath but could not use soap, shampoo, a comb, or toothpaste. The diet was even more limited. SPT trainees ate only once a day (or was it twice?) and had to cook their own meals outdoors, on their own fires. Only boiled, unsalted foods were allowed. Male trainees on SPT had to go out into the streets and beg for their food, in keeping with the long-standing tradition of monks in India. Each would extend his bowl and hope for a donation of rice, flour, or if especially fortunate, some vegetables; all the while maintaining silence, save for chanting the traditional *Hari Om Tat Sat* ("The Lord is the Supreme Truth"). Since begging on the streets was for male trainees only, our female SPT trainees chanted *Hari Om Tat Sat* not to people on the streets, but to the trainee who was cooking that day. She would then give them some raw vegetables and uncooked rice.

---

[19] *yoginii:* Female yogi.

[20] *Seva Pita Training:* Training that serves the ancestors (*seva:* service; *pita:* father, ancestor).

Surely, I thought as the time for my SPT approached, I'll prove myself equal to the task. What's a week or two without combing your hair? I wouldn't be alone: Jayamala and two or three others would be doing it at the same time. Soon after starting SPT, though, the scope of the challenge became clear as my sari lost any semblance of whiteness, my hair became knotted and tangled, and I lost even more weight.

One day around noon, we were outside preparing our fires. We were going to try something new: making chapattis on the open flames. We missed the stacks of chapattis we were used to eating, so one of us had gotten the cook to give some us some flour. There was one hitch, however: we weren't allowed to use the cooking gear used to prepare them. It was Jayamala who came up with the solution. "Listen. We'll make balls of dough, flatten them out with our hands, then place them on the coals."

We all thought it was a great idea and set about getting our fires started. Mine, however, was giving me trouble. It kept going out. After an interminable time, it finally caught and started to burn. The other trainees were well on their way to having their little chapattis done while I was just getting started. No matter. There was no need to rush. I had plenty of time.

Except that it started to rain. Feeling a drop on my arm, then another on my face, I looked skyward. When I saw the thick dark clouds that were moving in, I couldn't believe it. It doesn't rain this time of year! I thought—but the fire I had labored so hard to start was already going out, hissing as the rain fell. The other trainees grabbed their mostly cooked chapattis and ran to shelter. As the rain increased in intensity, extinguishing my fire completely, I collected the half-cooked, ash-streaked chapattis, followed the other trainees inside, and ate what I could.

Our numbers waxed and waned; someone finished training, another trainee arrived. At any one time, there were about ten or twelve of us, which was a lot considering our accommodations.

The women I remember best were the ones who went through most of the training with me. There were four of us from the United States: Mangala, Prashanti, Jayamala, and me; from the Philippines, Tripura and Kalyanii; from Australia, Balavatii; and (surprisingly) only two from India, Rachana and Mohinii.

While we shared ideology and spiritual practices, we were all very different; cultures and temperaments saw to that. There were optimists such as Tripura, a solidly built young woman who always seemed to be smiling. She loved to sing. Whenever she got a chance, she would play guitar while we chanted *Baba Nam Kevalam* and danced kiirtan, or she'd sing hopeful songs *(I believe for every drop of rain that falls a flower grows . . .)* while sitting cross-legged and strumming with eyes closed, her voice gathering strength and power. Tripura tried to smooth over others' disputes, and whenever she encountered difficulties, she would shrug them off. Hers was a sunny personality.

Our resident blissful personality was Mangala. She had a slow way of smiling that seemed to increase the blissful expression on her face, as if she were lit up from within. Her blue eyes and blond hair made you think you were gazing at a veritable spiritual goddess. When she sat in meditation, a small smile played at the corner of her lips, as if she were listening with rapt attention to some wonderful music playing within. She was known to have a special relationship with the Guru.

The resident comic was Mohinii, one of the Indian girls. She was very young and somewhat spoiled; I suspected that her family was wealthy and she was used to having things her way. She told me once that her father had been very close to Baba and that she'd grown up around Baba, even sitting on his lap. We agreed that Mohinii was somewhat "cheeky" (a word Indians often use to refer to a naughty child) and liked to do things that were just on the edge of being frowned upon. The discipline and conduct expected from trainees was difficult for her, and she was always complaining about something. One of her favorite phrases was "No logic, no reasoning, but the *complaints* of order," which was her paraphrasing of the conduct rule, *No logic, no reasoning, but the compliance of order.* I suspected she was tolerated precisely because she was Indian; the dadas who gave us our classes had likely known her since she was a child.

Mohinii was the one who first introduced me to the Hindi word *"jootha"*.[21] "That's *jootha!*" she said one day when a trainee dropped one of our few tablespoons down the latrine. After it was retrieved, washed off, and boiled, she still wouldn't use it.

"But, Mohinii," someone said, "when you boil something, it kills all the bacteria. It can be used again."

"No, you can't," she countered. "It's *jootha* now. You can't use it again." Science was no match for the concept of *jootha*. For us, the loss of a precious spoon, properly rescued and returned to usability by boiling, was more unbearable than the fact that it had been in the latrine. For Mohinii, however, it would forever give off filthy vibrations.

Prashanti was our cantankerous trainee. Tall, thin, and pale, with glasses and mousy brown hair, Prashanti was fussy and fastidious and seemed much older than her years. She was often argumentative and would fight over buckets or bicker about small things, acting as if she were keeping a scorecard in her head of points won and lost. But she also had a sweet side; under its influence, her face would take on an angelic aspect, and her pale blue eyes would look out at you with an innocent appeal.

And then there was Balavatii. She was three or four years younger than I, just twenty or twenty-one, but seemed older, more certain of herself and where she was going. She was a serious student and strict with her practices. She'd be absorbed in

---

[21] *jootha:* Polluted (not to be confused with the word *joota*, which means "shoes"). In India, toilet paper is often not available in latrines in public places. Instead, what you find is a faucet near the ground and a plastic mug. After using the latrine, you fill the mug and clean yourself using water and your left hand, then get some soap from a bar of soap with your right hand and wash both hands. The left hand, therefore, is considered to be in a permanent state of *jootha*. Indians often eat with their hands but only use the right one.

chanting whenever we did group kiirtan, her off-key voice rising above everyone else's. Despite her strictness, she had a good sense of humor and a dry Australian wit. She bore difficulties lightly, even the serious illness she came down with, when she developed severe dysentery and her weight dropped precipitously. Despite her numerous trips to the latrine, Balavatii never complained, and her strict adherence to the schedule never wavered. She kept right on doing her half baths and meditation, even when we could see her hip bones starting to protrude and her skin starting to stretch thin across her face. When her skin took on a translucent, other-worldly quality, the dadas got her a wooden cot to get her off the unforgiving floor, and she started doing her sadhana lying down. Finally, when it was impossible to tell if she was meditating or dying (she lay there for days, unmoving, her hands folded on her stomach), she was taken to a hospital. She got better slowly but continued to have health problems for a long time afterwards.

Balavatii's stone-like determination was at one point the only thing that kept me at the training center. A few months after Jayamala and I had returned from Calcutta, I decided I wanted to leave. No one thing stands out in my mind as the reason: culture clash, hunger, the hardness of the concrete, the mosquitoes (there were so many in the evening that everyone did their meditation looking like sitting ghosts, with cloth draped over their motionless heads), homesickness, and guilt about leaving my parents without telling them the truth—all must have played a part.

Balavatii had the key to the trunk where all our passports and tickets were, but she refused to give me my documents. "I'm not going to open the trunk. You're not leaving. No one is leaving," she informed me. (If I'd had more awareness at that point, I might have gotten alarmed. Just what is this organization? I might have thought, but didn't.) No amount of pleading would get her to change her mind. By watching her, I tried to figure out where she kept the key, but she never let on. So I stayed. We never talked about it again.

I was also experiencing bouts of depression. I soon learned that you take yourself with you no matter where you go. The dark moods that had plagued me throughout my high school and college years adjusted quite well to my new surroundings. I managed to beat them down most of the time, burying them under the avalanche of meditation, classes, cleaning, cooking, and memorizing of *slokas*. The routine kept me mercifully busy, but depression still managed to sneak up on me at quiet times. Sometimes I fought it off; at other times, it pulled me down. In its grip, I would lie on my blanket, unable to do anything. To think of moving on and climbing out of the pit seemed to require an expenditure of energy beyond my capacity.

Whenever one of these episodes overtook me, everyone left me alone. I often wished someone would come over to where I was lying, my face turned to wall, and offer some kind words or a comforting hand on my shoulder. But no one ever did. At the time, I thought the other trainees were trying to respect my privacy. Now, I'm not so sure. Now, I realize there was a kind of hardness in Ananda Marga, a ruthless attitude towards one's own body and feelings that made you avoid showing compassion to someone in pain.

After a while, the dream I had in Calcutta (or rather, my interpretation of it—that I'd have to undergo suffering and a kind of purification) proved prophetic. While nearly everyone lost weight, the problems I developed were unique. The first thing that happened was painful boils began to erupt all over my body. The first one appeared on my leg. When that one began to clear up, I got another. One developed in my armpit and another on my breast.

Dada Gaganananda thought they were a reaction to the extreme heat. Someone else theorized that it was the green chilies I sometimes ate with my rice and dahl (lentils). "Then why isn't everyone from outside India getting them?" I asked. No one had an answer. But I thought I knew their cause: they were my impurities coming out. After all, I had been forewarned by that dream I'd had in Calcutta!

No place on my body, it seemed, was immune. When the boils got to my private parts, it was time for action. I was sent to a doctor whom I had insisted be a woman. She examined me, then clearing her throat and looking at me severely, issued her diagnosis. "You have venereal disease," she said.

I was silent for a moment. Venereal disease?

"I've been in training to be a yogic nun for the past five months," I replied, trying to keep the outrage out of my voice and pointing to my white sari (traditionally worn only by nuns or widows). "There's no way I could have that."

"The tests will show that I am right," she said.

I'm not sure why I agreed to the tests. Maybe I wanted to prove she was mistaken. By the time I reported to the doctor's office to get the results, the boils had all but disappeared. She waved off the negative results, as if to say that I might not have venereal disease this time, but next time I would. Maybe she had seen a lot of American movies and assumed that I was sexually active, even as a nun.

In any case, I was shocked to experience what seemed like prejudice. All the months I had been in India, I hadn't experienced anything like that. However, upon reflection, I realized that the training center, its own world with its own rules, didn't really count as being in Indian culture. Classes were given in English, and those of us from outside India were in the majority. We rarely left the compound, and when we did, it was only to visit the dadas' training center outside the city to celebrate festivals together. That visit to the doctor was my only excursion to the outside world while I was in training.

My next physical trial was to come in Calcutta, but its cause was in Benares. One afternoon, after sweeping the floor of the training center, I glanced down towards the well and noticed a plastic pipe on the ground with water coming out of it. Assuming that the pipe came from the faucet where we got our drinking water and having a raging thirst, I picked it up and drank my fill. Prashanti saw me.

"Liila, why did you drink that water?"

I stared at her blankly. "That water was coming from the well, you know," she said.

Soon after that, Jayamala and I left the training center to finish our training in Calcutta. I felt the first symptoms of what I thought was hepatitis in the Calcutta hotel room we were staying in while attempting to extend our visas. I woke up feeling achy and noticed that my stool was chalky white.

We called Central Office and spoke with Dada Pareshananda, who sent a doctor to examine me. The doctor thought I had the flu, which he claimed was going around, and prescribed a long list of medicines.

"There's no way I'm going to take all of that stuff," I told Jayamala. She went out and got the one medicine I had agreed to, a liquid tonic.

Two days later, my eyes turned yellow and so did my skin.

"You have jaundice," is what the next doctor I was sent to by the dadas told me. He gave me some little brown pills in a yellow and brown bottle.

Whichever it was, jaundice or hepatitis, I spent weeks recuperating in the didis' small apartment in Calcutta, lying on a thin rug in the heat (even though it was December, it was still quite warm during the day), a fan blowing hot air over me, my hair full of lice, with barely enough energy to drag myself to the table for my meals of boiled vegetables and plain chapatti. Kamala, a Margii woman who spoke little English and whose daughter Rachana was in training with me, cooked my meals and tended to me as if I were her own daughter. I liked her soups more than the oily and over-cooked curries everyone else was eating. She put coriander leaves in one of them and I loved the taste. *"Mai dhaniya bahut like karta hai,"* I told Kamala in my broken Hindi, and asked her to put them in everything. I was reduced to finding such little bright spots to help get me through the maddening tedium of the long days. In the end, though, my illness served a positive purpose: the Indian authorities agreed to extend my tourist visa by two months.

When I was well enough, the dadas sent me to Madras to get some experience in the field. I was to assist the local didi in the Ananda Marga children's home there.

When I got there, Madras was in the grip of a water shortage. Taking a bath became more difficult than ever. A half bath wasn't a problem; I was already adept at taking one with just a single mugful of water. I would soon become similarly adept at taking a full bath with half a bucket of water.

The fifteen or twenty children in the home varied in age. The youngest were three or four; the eldest were teenagers. I was shocked the first time I witnessed the local didi beating the younger children, something she did on a regular basis. I couldn't believe what my eyes were telling me. How could someone who did sadhana and followed Baba's ideology do such a thing? In time, I would find this not to be uncommon in Ananda Marga children's homes in India.

Food was in short supply in the children's home. Rice and chapatti, some dahl, and a few vegetables made up the children's diet. One evening, I took some of the older girls to the home of an American couple I had met in town. We'd been invited to dinner. I was as surprised as the girls were by the size of the house. It was so big, so luxurious compared to our simple, cramped accommodations, where the children slept side by side on the hard floors of little rooms.

"Have a look around," our hostess said. The girls took in everything with wide-eyed wonder. As we entered one unoccupied bedroom, Vandana, the eldest, took me aside and whispered, "Didi, why are the lights and fan on in this room? No one is in here!" Having no good answer for her, I felt ashamed of my fellow Americans.

Next we went into the gleaming, well-equipped kitchen. The girls gaped at the large refrigerator, as did I, not having seen one in months. Our hosts were in the kitchen, preparing the meal.

They had carrots out and were chopping off and discarding the ends. The girls' faces registered shock.

We left the kitchen and sat down in the living room. "Didi," Vandana said, "they were throwing out good food! We could make a meal out of those carrots. Maybe we can ask for them. We never get to eat carrots."

Our hosts had carelessly cut off one or two inches of perfectly good carrot and had tossed those pieces in the trash. How was I to explain that they'd always had enough to eat and had no idea they were wasting food?

My face burned with shame. That American couple, with their lights and ceiling fans left on in empty rooms and the perfectly good food they had thrown out, starkly symbolized the wasteful culture I had gladly left behind.

Chapter 4

A Jewish Didi Unleashed: Egypt and Israel

By March, I was back in Calcutta. My time in India was drawing to a close, and soon I would be receiving my first posting. I wouldn't get the chance to see Baba before leaving India, though. He was still in jail, where he'd been for the last four years.

I'd already received my acarya name, Malatii, from the dada who had given us classes in Calcutta. (Although Dada had given it to me, the teaching was that all acarya names came from the Guru, and that's how I took it.) From now on, I would be known as Acarya Malatii Brahmacarinii.[22]

"What does Malatii mean?" I had asked, nearly trembling with excitement.

"It is the name of a small flower that has a very beautiful smell," Dada had replied.

I struggled to hide my disappointment. I felt deflated. A flower! I was expecting something more dynamic, revolutionary

---

[22] *Brahmacarinii:* One who practices celibacy. Also, one who ideates upon the Supreme Consciousness.

even. I thought of Balavatii's new name, Vishaka, which meant "Unconquered." Now, that's a name! I thought.

There was no such disappointment with my first uniform. I put it on carefully over my sari, buttoned the jacket, and tied the white belt around my waist. With shaking hands, I placed the veil on my head. Once I had buttoned it beneath my chin, my transformation was complete. I was no longer Marsha, no longer even Liila. I was Malatii, Baba's worker.

After I put on my uniform, I went to the Central Office to receive my posting. As I entered the room where Pareshananda, the Office Secretary,[23] sat surrounded by papers at his large desk, he caught sight of me and his face lit up.

"Malatii, congratulations!" he said, his eyes twinkling. "I suppose you want to know where you've been posted?" I nodded, almost holding my breath.

"You'll be going to Cairo. You'll be the first didi in the Middle East!"

I thanked him, then left the room, my mind in a whirl. Ever since that conversation with Dada Yogeshananda back in the States, I'd been hoping to be posted in Israel one day. Cairo definitely wasn't Israel, but at least it was in the vicinity.

When I told Vishaka my posting, she looked at me in a funny way and asked, "Does Dada Pareshananda know that you're Jewish?"

It was a fair question. The Yom Kippur War had taken place less than two years earlier, and a high level of distrust and animosity now existed between Egypt and Israel. I remembered hearing somewhere that Egypt was on the lookout for Zionist spies. Maybe I would be mistaken for one.

"I'm not sure," I answered.

---

[23] Office Secretary: In Ananda Marga, we would often capitalize the names of positions within the organization, often using them to identify a person without using his or her name. Throughout the book, I mostly capitalize these positions (despite the fact that in ordinary usage, they would not be capitalized) in order to help create the world of Ananda Marga for the reader.

"Let's go and tell him."

We found Dada still sitting at his desk. He reacted to the news by gazing at me in silence, his eyebrows furrowed, a troubled look on his face. Then the look vanished and he smiled.

"No problem!" he said. "In fact, it will be *good*—a Jewish person bringing our universal ideology to the Middle East!"

So the posting remained—not that I needed to worry about being recognized as Jewish in my uniform!

A month later I was in Cairo, anticipating my first real experience as a didi fulfilling Baba's great mission. The initial sights and sounds were not unfamiliar. There were crowds on the streets and throngs at the bus stops. Day after day, I would fight my way onto an already over-packed bus, which threatened to capsize as it squeaked and rocked its way down the dusty streets. In that way, Cairo resembled Calcutta. As in Calcutta, here, too, were heat and humidity. Most days would find me dabbing away at the sweat on my face with my handkerchief. I was unable, though, to do much of anything about the rivulets trickling down my body, too well-clad as it was in my nun's dress. None of that mattered to me, though. *One should be ready always to accept all the sufferings as rewards and become the ideal son or daughter of the Cosmic Father,* went the conduct rule. To suffer such physical discomforts for the mission was a privilege, I reminded myself.

A few dadas had gotten to Egypt before me. Narendra, from the Philippines, had already established a jagrti in an apartment building, and it was to that address that I first reported. Narendra was very young, his smooth round face only beginning to show the first traces of a beard. He had a sweet and charming demeanor and played guitar. People, most of them young men, flocked to our classes, jamming themselves into our small meditation center after packing themselves into buses to get there. Some were in jeans and T-shirts; others wore the traditional *gallabiya*, a flowing ankle-length white robe.

They loved our singing and chanting. We provided them with an outlet previously unavailable in their lives and had come with the kind of universal message that appealed to youth everywhere. It was an exotic message, too, wrapped as it was in incense smoke, Sanskrit chants, and orange robes.

One weekend we held a retreat in Giza near the pyramids. The buildings we rented were boxy and totally unremarkable. Even so, the pyramids lent everything an air of mystery. At night they loomed large in the moonlight, casting shadows upon the sand, and our chanting had an ancient quality. For those few moonlit hours, we were cast into a state of utter timelessness, thrust as we were into a magical world where the present and ancient past seemed to merge.

The men who came to our meetings didn't quite know what to make of me, and some cast quizzical looks my way. Here I was, a woman in the role of a spiritual teacher, almost unheard of in their spiritual tradition! Even so, most treated me with respect. Very few women came, though, and those who did rarely attended regularly because most of them didn't have the freedom to do what they pleased. I was allowed to teach meditation only to women and so had few initiations, in contrast to the large numbers initiated by Narendra. Whenever we had dharmacakra, the men formed long lines on their side of the room, but there would be only two or three women on my side. This frustrated me.

One of my initiates who did come regularly was Subira. A student in high school, she came to nearly every meeting and even stopped eating meat, which, she confided to me, was quite difficult to do in her home, where meat was served at almost every meal. I could only imagine what it must have been like trying to explain it to her mother. (Her father was away on a business trip, so at least she didn't have to explain it to him.) She also told me that the radio was constantly blaring songs when she tried to do meditation. Despite all the obstacles, she kept at it, practicing twice a day.

I began conducting yoga classes at her home, in an extra apartment that her family used for guests. Spacious and fabulously decked out in the Arabesque style with multi-colored Persian rugs, and full of traditional furnishings such as large, ornate gold vases and wall-hangings with reds and golds predominating, it made quite a contrast to the drab, crowded apartment her family lived in.

After a month of classes, Subira starting dropping hints that something wasn't quite right. "It's my father," she said. "I don't think we can continue to do this after he gets back."

One particularly humid afternoon, I went to her home, and there he was. He confronted me in the hall, a short, stocky man with a hard look to his face. Pointing a stubby finger in my face, he accused me of brainwashing his daughter. "We are *Muslims*," he growled. "We don't need another religion!"

My efforts to explain that yoga was not a religion were fruitless. What was even worse, he had been in India and had read about the imprisonment of Baba. He repeated to me some of the sensational stories he had found in the newspapers. My own words in defense of my guru could not get through his stony exterior.

"Leave my house," he shouted, "and if you should ever see my daughter in the street, I want you to walk right past her as if you do not know her. You are not to say a word to her. Get out!"

He nearly threw me out the door. Before he slammed it behind me, I caught a glimpse of Subira's shocked, hurt face behind him, appearing shrunken and beaten by his words.

That was my first experience of Muslim men in authority. It would not be the last.

Subira's father wasn't the only Egyptian to regard us with suspicion. With the general wariness towards outsiders and the outsize fear of Zionist spies that was common at the time, almost anyone who was a non-Egyptian got a second glance.

A few months after my arrival, we organized a food distribution in our neighborhood. In Cairo, as in India, the rich and poor often lived side by side, with shacks and shanties growing up around and almost touching multi-story apartment buildings and gated properties. Not far from our apartment building was one such area.

One Saturday, we prepared large pots of *ful medames* (large beans) and bought a generous supply of the whole wheat pita bread that was invariably eaten with it. The three of us, Mohan (the other dada who was posted in the Middle East), Narendra, and I, lugged the steaming pots of beans and bags of bread out to the spot we'd chosen and set ourselves up. As we began doling out heaping platefuls, people began to gather: men, smiling tentatively, and children, their laughing eyes flashing in grubby faces—but no women.

Mohan began to take pictures, and a sudden commotion ensued. The crowd grew agitated, and without warning, police arrived. One of them seized the camera; others grabbed Mohan by the arms and lead him away.

Narendra and I returned to the yoga center discouraged and bewildered. We'd been doing something good, giving out food. And what could possibly be wrong with taking pictures?

As the day wore on, we learned that Mohan had been arrested solely because he had been taking photos, which foreigners were not allowed to do. After hours of interrogation, he was released along with his empty camera; the film had been confiscated, and Mohan had been warned never to take another picture in Egypt again.

Not long after, our time in Egypt came to an abrupt end. One afternoon I was summoned to the front door of the jagrti by a heavy and insistent pounding. When I opened it, three burly men came in uninvited and stood in a row, shifting their weight from one foot to the other. For some reason, their hands stand out in my memory: they were rough-skinned and beefy, as if the men did construction work on the side. Not meditators, I thought. Even so, I folded my hands and greeted them with namaskar.

"Passports! Bring us your passports!" one barked.

Feeling almost assaulted by his words, I called Narendra and told him what they wanted. We exchanged worried glances, then retrieved our documents and handed them over. The men hardly looked at the first couple of pages before snapping them shut and handing them back.

"You have forty-eight hours to leave Egypt," one intoned. Then they left, slamming the door behind them.

We stared at each other, shocked. Narendra's earnest face was cloudy with concern, his eyebrows drawn together. "They have no right to do this!" he said. "We'll fight it. I'll go to the Foreign Ministry tomorrow and find out what's going on."

Even as I murmured something in reply, I found myself starting to rejoice inside. Recently I had been thinking, What good can I do here? I knew that the idea of a female spiritual teacher was ludicrous to most Muslims, and I'd been longing to be posted somewhere else, especially since the incident with Subira's father. At the same time, though, I'd been trying to accept it all, believing everything happened for a reason. Less than a week earlier, I had spent an entire day meditating in the dusty little basement apartment that I used mostly for sleeping, located as it was far from our downtown center, in one of Cairo's poorer sections. By the time I finished, night had fallen and I had reached a place of surrender. If I'm here, I thought, there must be a reason for it. I'll do the best I can.

And now, here it was a mere day or two later, and we were being told to get out of Egypt! What a cosmic joke on me! Isn't it true that when you give up a desire for something, I said to myself, you often end up getting it? I knew that Narendra and I would be leaving Egypt, and there was nothing anyone could do to prevent it.

Narendra certainly tried. He went to the Ministry of Foreign Affairs, from one minister to another. He never found out who had issued the order to have us deported, only that it had come from high up in the government. We were sure it had something to do with the Indian government and the state of emergency that had been declared just a few weeks earlier: Ananda Marga was one of the organizations banned under the Emergency, and India and Egypt had close diplomatic ties. Perhaps it also had something to do with the pictures that Mohan had taken and the paranoia over spies. What would they have done if they had known I was Jewish? Maybe they would have arrested me!

As it was, the authorities granted us an extra day to get ready. Fortunately, Narendra and I both had one-way tickets to Frankfurt. We packed in a hurry and gave away whatever we couldn't carry to our students, who, muted and sad, came to the center one last time. One young man said, "We don't know what we will do without you." Others echoed his sentiments. A few had tears in their eyes.

"Just keep doing your meditation," Narendra said. "We'll be back someday."

They didn't look at all cheered by his words. Narendra exchanged hugs with a couple of them and then they were gone.

Dada had a couple of special possessions he wasn't sure what to do with: two skulls that he'd had sitting on his shelf. For Ananda Marga yogis, skulls held special significance as a reminder of the transitory nature of all life, that one day, a practitioner's body would be nothing but bones. Narendra couldn't leave them with any of his students; none of them were ready for that. He could have packed them, but he had heard that foreigners, especially people from countries like the Philippines, could expect to have their luggage searched by German customs officials.

He ended up throwing the skulls out the taxi window on our way to the airport. My last memory of Egypt is of those skulls bouncing along the highway as we sped away.

We touched down in Frankfurt early the next morning. It was the first time either of us had been in Germany. Compared to our recent experiences, we found that everything ran with an almost military precision. The comfortable train we got on after leaving the airport clicked along quietly and was air-conditioned.

A precise voice announced each stop, and instead of having to share a seat with other passengers and their packages, I had one entirely to myself. It was all in such stark contrast to Egypt and India that I felt like I had landed on another planet.

We were met at the station by some German Margiis who had come to take us to the jagrti. As the car took off, I looked out the window. In contrast to the streets of Cairo, these seemed eerily sterile and antiseptic, nearly empty and devoid of life. I wondered where all the people were.

When we got to the jagrti, the Margiis were preparing to have breakfast. After washing up and doing a few asanas, Narendra and I joined in. We sat down to fruit, yogurt, muesli, and thick slabs of black bread—a much heavier breakfast than what I'd grown accustomed to over the past year.

"What was it like working in an Arab country?" one of the Margiis asked me. "Wasn't it hard to find people to initiate?" "For me, it was," I replied. The women were sympathetic. They were happy I was there; I was one of the first didis they had ever seen.

One of the LFT sisters (Margiis referred to each other as "brothers" and "sisters" because we looked upon ourselves as members of a global family) approached me with something white in her hands. "Here, Didi, take this," she said, handing me a sari of satiny cotton, the kind which didn't wrinkle easily and had a good weight to it. She had noticed that mine was worn and no longer white. I felt grateful. "Thank you," I said. "I'll put it on right away." She smiled and did namaskar in reply. I remember being struck by her blond hair and especially by her beautiful sky blue eyes. She couldn't have been more than eighteen or nineteen, and I was sure she would be a didi one day. Our paths were to cross again some years later in an extraordinary way.

It was midsummer and the sectorial retreat, a spiritual gathering open to all Margiis from Berlin Sector, would soon be underway. It was taking place in Germany, so Narendra and I went to the retreat site with the Frankfurt Margiis. On the way, I found myself wondering where I would be posted next. Surely not back to Cairo!

At the retreat a few days later, I was lying on my sleeping bag, taking a brief rest before evening meditation and mulling over the news I'd been given that morning. Dada Hiranayananda, who was the SS (Sectorial Secretary) of Berlin Sector, which meant he was the overall in-charge of the work in Europe, had told me I'd be staying in Germany. For some reason, it just didn't feel right. What a strange reaction! I chided myself. You should be happy to be posted in a Western country. Just think of all the sisters you'll get to initiate! But I couldn't shake the feeling that I didn't belong in Germany.

I wondered if my reaction had anything to do with anti-German feelings. All I had associated with Germany previously had been Holocaust tales of horror. I thought back to the boycott of Volkswagen Beetles in the fifties that many American Jews had participated in. I'd been very young, but I could remember looking upon any VWs and their owners I had come across with a mixture of suspicion and hostility.

I recoiled from the possibility of such prejudice. Maybe it's because everyone here seems so well off and everything runs so smoothly, I told myself. Who would feel a need for meditation? But I knew that wasn't true. I had already figured out that the sense of isolation people had in Germany was not unlike that of Americans and made Germans good candidates for spiritual practice.

My musings were interrupted by a soft knock on the door.

"Didi?" I heard a voice call out. "Dada Yogeshananda is calling you."

I thanked the Margii brother and quickly made my way to where Dada was staying, feeling an immediate upswing in my mood. I was always happy to see Yogeshananda. The last time had been in India when he had come to visit us in the training center. "You're all half the size you were when you left," he'd said, laughing, offering us peanut butter and other goodies he had brought along.

Now, Dada had even greater responsibilities than his role as the Sectorial Secretary of New York Sector. After Indira Gandhi declared the State of Emergency, all whole-timers in India had gone underground, including the General Secretary (GS) of the organization. Yogeshananda was now Acting GS. I couldn't think of anyone better suited to the task.

Welcoming me into his room, Dada indicated that I should sit down opposite him on the floor. We both sat on blankets, in easy pose, our legs crossed.

"Get your things ready. You are going to Israel!" he said, eyes twinkling, a mischievous half grin on his face.

I felt a surge of excitement. "Really?"

"Yes, really! You are posted to Israel as DS (L)[24] for Tel Aviv."

"Dada, you knew all along I would get posted to Israel, didn't you?"

He threw back his head and laughed, pointed at me, then laughed some more. Like me, he remembered that conversation back in Denver.

I arrived in Jerusalem in the fall, after having gotten a new passport. (Everyone had agreed that having Egyptian stamps in my passport was not a good idea when applying for an Israeli visa.) On the flight from Frankfurt, I watched a group of Orthodox Jews standing in the aisle praying, swaying back and forth in long black jackets and large black hats. They're praying for the Messiah to come, I thought. If only they knew that he's already here! I could hardly wait to get to work and bring the good news of Baba and his philosophy to the people of Israel. At the time, there was no doubt in my mind that once the Israelis had come to know about Baba, they'd see him as the Messiah. We all thought of him as the savior of the world.

I was met in the airport by Mohan, the dada who'd been detained by the police in Egypt for taking photos. We went up

---

[24] DS (L): Diocese Secretary (Ladies).

to the Mount of Olives, where our jagrti, a gleaming white stone building in the Arab style, was located. Mohan had rented it a few months earlier. Although now posted in Baghdad, he spent time in Israel whenever he could: Working in Baghdad was proving close to impossible; he couldn't work openly as an Ananda Marga teacher because of the hostile attitude of the Iraqi government.

I soon met our Arab landlord. "Welcome, Didi," he said, his dark, leathery face breaking into a smile as he extended his hand. Didis and dadas frowned upon shaking the hand of the opposite sex. I didn't want to put Ahmed off, though, so I took his offered hand, all the while promising myself to explain the hand-shaking thing to him later on. Ahmed was friendly and hospitable, and it wasn't long before he invited me home to meet his wife and children. They lived nearby in a building similar to ours.

I loved our center. Up on the Mount, the atmosphere seemed purer than in the city below. Sunrises and sunsets were spectacular and meditation was good. An American LFT sister named Vinita was working with me. We got along well. Enthusiastic and possessing a cheerful personality, she was also pretty, with almond-shaped eyes, a smooth oval face with a smattering of freckles across her nose, and a dimpled smile. People liked being around her. She was already thinking of becoming a didi, and I encouraged her. Mohan also attracted people. He was dreamy-eyed and had long, well-cared for hair that he was fond of brushing. The Margiis were drawn to his charismatic personality, guitar playing, and devotional singing. And there was Nurit, an Israeli Margii who had been one of the first Westerners to meet Baba in the years before he was arrested. She liked to tell the story of how she had met a dada while traveling on a boat from Africa to India. At first, she had been suspicious of him and his accounts of Baba. "I'd been warned not to trust the men on the ship," she said. But then he gave her one of Baba's books and she became intrigued. After they arrived in India, Dada took her to meet Baba. We listened with rapt attention to her stories since none of us had met Baba yet.

A few months after my arrival, attendance at our dharmacakras began to dwindle. Since the Jewish Margiis lived down in the city, getting to the jagrti was proving difficult for them. Most didn't have cars and traveling to-and-fro on the only available public transportation up to the Mount, an Arab bus, made them feel uncomfortable. (I didn't have a problem with it; the Arabs would smile in a friendly way whenever I boarded the bus. Maybe they thought I was a Muslim myself, despite the strange color of my dress.)

We desperately wanted to stay on the Mount; after all, we had come to Israel for all Israelis, both Jewish and Arab. We saw ourselves as a means of bringing the two communities closer together and fostering understanding between them. Eventually, though, the reality of the situation forced our hand. Most Margiis were Jewish and ever fewer were coming. We would have to move.

We had been told that rents in the city proper were higher and decent accommodations more difficult to find. That turned out to be true. The first place we moved to was cold, uninviting, and dark at all times of day. We felt that we had not only come down physically from the Mount, we'd descended from a place of light and beauty to one in which the spirit seemed to flicker fitfully like the candles we used to try to brighten the place up. Our numbers shrank as even more of our members drifted away.

After a few months in that house, the next place we found was a third-floor apartment, chosen because of the cheap rent. It was located in an ultra-orthodox neighborhood; to the residents, we must have appeared to have come from another world. Every day they would stare as I walked down the street in my orange nun clothes with my students in tow—in the midst of men with their characteristic *payes* or side curls, black coats and felt hats; and women in wigs pushing baby carriages. In warm weather, the sound of our drums, guitars, and chants of *Baba Nam Kevalam* traveled far with the windows open. The neighbors regarded us with suspicion at best and animosity at worst. We were their worst nightmare: an organized religion trying to convert the Jewish people to another faith.

We, of course, didn't see it that way and explained to all who would listen that yoga was not a religion and that anyone from any religious background could practice it. "Meditation will deepen your experience of your faith," we'd say. "We're not trying to convert anybody." Some people believed us. Many did not. We would talk about "one truth, many paths," but many of us were convinced that Ananda Marga was the only real way to it. Maybe people detected an underlying attitude on our part that at least some of us were guilty of: *Once they begin meditating,* it went, *they'll experience the real truth and will stop practicing their senseless rituals.*

One afternoon I was confronted in the street by a middle-aged man, his face contorted. "What are you people doing in our country?" he shouted, his voice thick with anger and a strong Polish accent. "Stop trying to convert us! Go back to where you came from!" Before I could say a word, he drew his lips together and spit came flying out of his mouth and landed on my chest. I took out my handkerchief and wiped it off as best I could, then went on my way. One should accept all sufferings as rewards, I reminded myself yet again.

Soon after that experience, I had another one that really threw me for a few days. Late one morning, not long after we moved into the Orthodox neighborhood, an unexpected visitor came to the jagrti. I was in my room, a mostly unfurnished space the size of a large closet, when one of the Margiis knocked on my door.

"Didi," she said, "someone is here to see you."

I hadn't been expecting anyone, but people dropped in all the time, so I didn't think anything of it and opened the door.

"Marsha?"

I couldn't believe my eyes. Standing there with a look of utter confusion on his face was my cousin Richard, the son of my mother's younger sister. What could he possibly be doing here?

"I was in Jerusalem on business, so I thought I would look you up," he said.

I mumbled something in reply, then began getting over my daze and suspected that my parents had asked him to check on me. He came in but just stood there looking around, not sure what to do. There was no chair to offer him (there was only a straw mat, which was covered with the paperwork I'd been working on), and I made no movement to get one. He stared at me as I stood up and adjusted my veil. We stood facing each other for a few minutes. I couldn't think of anything to say.

"So, how have you been?" he finally said.

"Fine."

Another minute went by. Finally, shrugging his shoulders, he said, "Well, I'll be going, then," and left.

I sat down amidst my papers in a state of shock. It was as if my old life had reached out with its tentacles and tried to pull me back. But I reminded myself that there was no way it could. I was no longer Marsha, a mixed-up Jewish girl from the suburbs of Philadelphia. I was Baba's daughter and worker and part of a great mission.

I left the room and went into the meditation hall. There, I realized that Richard must have seen the *puja* table with its picture of Baba and the *pratiik*, the Ananda Marga symbol. The *pratiik*, consisting of a swastika and a rising sun within a six-pointed star, was especially hard to explain to Israelis, of course, given the association of the swastika with the Nazis. Margiis knew that the six-pointed star was an ancient symbol, having made its first appearance in the Far East, even before Judaism. With its upward- and downward-pointing triangles, it symbolized the balance of the inner spiritual life and the outer life in the world. And we knew that the swastika[25] (in the center of the star) had not been invented by the Nazis, but was itself an ancient Tantric

---

[25] swastika: A Sanskrit term which we described as meaning "to be dedicated to the good"; "*su*" meaning "good," "*asti*" meaning "to be," and "*ka*" symbolizing the creative principle.

symbol representing the uncoiling of the kundalini[26] energy at the base of the spine that leads to spiritual liberation. Besides, as anyone could see, our swastika wasn't like the German one; Hitler had taken the symbol and put it on an angle.

It was a tough sell, though. After some particularly unpleasant experiences (more than once, a new person had come to the center, only to take one look at the *pratiik*, have the blood drain out of his or her face, turn, and bolt out the door before we could say anything in its defense), we agonized as to whether we should display the *pratiik* in the meditation room or bring it out only during group meditation.

"Didi, we need to be sensitive to the people here," a Margii sister said after one of these incidents. "Israel is unique. You can't have people walking in and seeing a Jewish star and a swastika displayed together."

"Yes, I understand," I had answered. "But it's our symbol and it's important. It's nothing to be ashamed of. We just have to explain it to them. Then they'll understand."

Now, I wondered what Richard had thought of the *pratiik*. I bet it scared him off, I thought. Kind of serves him right for barging in like he did. Still, I didn't quite feel like myself for a while.

We had that jagrti for less than a year and were in the process of moving again when Yogeshananda visited Israel briefly. He told me that a new didi, just fresh out of training, would be coming to join me. I received the news with mixed feelings. On the one hand, there was plenty of work to do and it would be great to have another didi to work with. And I had to admit I'd been lonely, even in the midst of all the Margiis, so it would be nice

---

[26] kundalini: The cosmic energy symbolized as a coiled serpent lying dormant at the base of the spine. Through a series of exercises involving postures, meditation, and breathing, a practitioner can raise the kundalini energy up through the *cakras* (energy centers) to the top of the head. This brings about samadhi, or merger of the ordinary self into the eternal self, the goal of yogic practices.

to have a peer. But I just couldn't understand the organizational reason for having another didi come to a country as small as Israel. My posting was DS (L), Tel Aviv. What would hers be?

"Didi Mohinii will be an extra DS (L)," Dada said. "Technically, you'll be responsible for different areas of Israel, though you'll work closely together." This wasn't going to be an official posting, he went on to explain, because everyone from Central Office was still underground due to the ongoing Emergency. I thought it was strange. There weren't any extra DS (L)s anywhere else in the world. Didn't they think I was doing a good enough job?

Feeling bad that we didn't have a center to welcome the new didi to, I was relieved that we at least had somewhere to stay. A Margii sister was hosting us for the time being in her place on the outskirts of Jerusalem. Damayanti, an artist originally from the States, lived alone most of the time. Her home was filled with sculptures and weavings and had a rural, peaceful feel to it, nestled as it was in groves of olive and fig trees. I was sure Mohinii would like it.

When I met Mohinii at the airport, I was convinced I'd seen her somewhere before, but couldn't figure out where. Maybe it was because Mohinii was quite tall and looked down at me while talking, but something in her manner immediately struck me as arrogant and disdainful. She didn't take well the news of no jagrti.

"How long have you been working in Israel?" Mohinii asked, looking at me with her haughty pale blue eyes.

"Around a year and a half," I said.

"Almost two years! And you still don't have a jagrti? What have you been doing all that time?" I explained as patiently as I could that we'd already had three centers, but that just seemed to give her more reason to think I was incompetent. Here she was, ready to plunge into the work, and there was no place to work out of.

And so it went. We argued almost from the minute we met. Our squabbles soon grew heated and loud, shattering the peace of our surroundings. Damayanti began to avoid us. Whenever the three of us ended up in her living room together, she would glance at us nervously, looking drawn, then turn her eyes away. "Damayanti," I said one day, "I'm sorry for all of this. We'll move out as soon as we can." Relieved, she nodded and thanked me.

About a month after Mohinii's arrival, we moved from Jerusalem to Tel Aviv, renting a ground-floor apartment in a complex in the neighborhood of Ramat Gan. An Elite chocolate factory was a stone's throw away. Day and night, a sickly sweet, perverted chocolate smell permeated the air. I loved chocolate, and giving it up had been difficult for me. (I hadn't had any since the day in Cairo when I received the poorly mimeographed notice from Central Office that it was to be off-limits. I had just gotten back to my dusty apartment and was eating a chocolate bar when I read the notice. I ended up reading it two or three more times before I could really believe it, all the while mournfully finishing up what I thought to be the last chocolate bar of my life. Later on, chocolate would be the substance I would turn to during times when I was "clashed out" as we said in Ananda Marga. I'd eat it secretly, feeling tremendously guilty all the while.) But I wasn't at all tempted by the smell of what they were concocting in the factory. We tried in vain to mask the odor by lighting incense. Then there was the constant squeak and grinding of a machine there. It would start up long before our morning meditation and would still be going as we got ready for our evening practices. Clearly, the apartment wasn't suitable, but the rent was cheap, so we stayed.

Mohinii considered herself quite the devotee and had the trances to prove it. Meditating with the Margiis after kiirtan, she would often call out "Baba!" then fall over and moan, or spin around like a top, her limbs circulating around with her head at the center. The first time I saw her do this, it brought back a vivid memory: a retreat in the States before I had left for training. There had been several Margiis crying out, others falling into trances, and one woman spinning. Yes, I realized now, that had been Mohinii.

Immersing herself eagerly in work, Mohinii went to various towns and kibbutzim for talks and initiation, happy for an outlet for the energies that had been pent up during training and the time without a jagrti. She soon started dressing in a style that she felt was more in keeping with the kind of country Israel was. "I think it's negative *pracar* to go around looking like a Christian nun in a Jewish country," she would say. "And it's very hard to do anything in a kibbutz wearing a skirt." She began wearing white pants while on tour.

On top of that, though, one Sunday before dharmacakra, she came out of her room with a small Arab scarf, a *keffiyah*, on her head instead of the cap and veil. I stared at her in shocked silence. With that scarf, dyed orange and wrapped around her head and tied in front, she looked more like a cleaning lady about to scrub a floor than a didi about to lead group meditation.

"Didi, what are you doing with that thing on your head?" I asked, suppressing a laugh.

"I think this is more appropriate for the field than a veil," she answered, her pale blue eyes looking down as if daring me to challenge her.

"I know the impression the veil gives here," I said, holding my ground. "But you can't just change the uniform without permission."

"Well, I'm going to. If I tried to get permission, it could take forever."

She was right about that, especially with the Emergency still going on in India. She handed me an identical orange scarf and asked me to change. I thought about it. Even stranger than two didis with scarves wrapped around their heads would be one with a scarf and one with a veil. I decided to go along with it. At least we'd be presenting a united front to the Margiis.

So, as our Margiis drifted in for dharmacakra, there we sat, two didis looking for all the world like twin cleaning ladies. I wasn't happy with the situation and was sure the Guru would not approve. Baba, give me sign, I prayed during meditation. Let me know what you think.

A few days later, I was walking to the bus stop on my way to Jerusalem, with my veil stashed in my suitcase. I had the scarf wrapped around my head but wasn't about to be caught dead wearing that thing once with the Jerusalem Margiis. It was around noon, and as I hadn't yet done my midday meditation, I decided to do a quick fifteen minutes before catching the bus. Looking around for someplace suitable, I spotted a grassy area to the right of the road, sat down, and was just getting settled when I caught sight of a slovenly dressed man with long gray hair, walking towards me and muttering to himself. Sighing, I prayed he would pass by. Instead, he stopped in front of me, grinned, and exposed himself. I leapt to my feet, grabbed my bag and, glancing now and then over my shoulder to be sure he wasn't following, ran back to the jagrti. Once there, I took the scarf off and flung it into a corner.

I'd gotten my sign, all right—loud and clear.

Chapter 5

I Meet the Guru

Shrii Shrii Anandamurti was a fascinating and complex personality. He was also a figure who inspired controversy. In 1971 he was arrested and charged with sanctioning the kidnapping and murder of six former disciples. During his imprisonment, he went on a long fast to protest a poisoning he claimed had happened to him in jail. After a trial in which he was acquitted of two of the seven charges against him, Anandamurti was released on bail in 1978. Eventually, he was cleared of all charges. Ananda Marga has always maintained that although in jail on criminal charges, Anandamurti had really been a political prisoner, held because of his bold stance against entrenched ideas such as casteism and communism.[27] Indeed, the communist government of West Bengal, the state in which our organization had its international headquarters, was known to be virulently anti-Ananda Marga.

The government of Indira Gandhi also looked upon Ananda Marga unfavorably, suspecting it of insurgent activity and inspiring violence. Anandamurti's concept of the rule of the

---

[27] Anandamurti was critical of both capitalism and communism and was known to have said, "Capitalism makes a man a beggar, and communism makes the beggar a beast."

sadvipra, a cadre of selfless spiritual leaders who would gain power and govern through a benign dictatorship (a key principle of PROUT), likely contributed to the government's concern. Then there was the subgroup within Ananda Marga called VSS, or Volunteers for Social Service, whose members wore uniforms bearing a striking resemblance to military dress. The government suspected it of being the paramilitary wing of Ananda Marga, complete with caches of secret weapons.

In 1975, while Baba was still in jail, Gandhi declared the State of Emergency and arrested hundreds of political opponents. Ananda Marga was named as one of four "paramilitary" organizations that were declared illegal; in an editorial in the *New York Times* on July 28 of that year, T.N. Kaul, the Indian ambassador to the United States, referred to Ananda Marga as "a subversive group parading under a spiritual garb."[28]

The Emergency lasted for twenty-one months. It was a difficult time for Indian Margiis and whole-timers alike. The folklore of the organization is replete with stories of how didis and dadas went underground and not only survived the Emergency but went on with their work, how mysterious events connected with the Guru had kept them out of trouble.

My first face-to-face meeting with Baba took place in 1977, the year the Emergency was lifted and Morarji Desai, who himself had spent time in jail during the Emergency, was elected Prime Minister. Although Ananda Marga was allowed to resume functioning, the Indian government still imposed restrictions, a major one being that all foreign nationals identified as members were to be deported.

Once the Emergency was lifted, word got out that it was possible to visit Baba in jail. Most non-Indian Margiis had never met the Guru; every day, more and more of them were arriving in

---

[28] T. N. Kaul, "In Which Reasons for the State of Emergency Are Explained and Defended," *New York Times*, July 28, 1975.

India from all over the world despite the possibility of deportation. Mohinii had been one of the first to go. I was anxiously awaiting my chance and was making plans. But there were one or two obstacles to contend with: I had no one to travel with and little money. I certainly wasn't going to let such trifles (as I considered them) stand in my way. Since I had traveled alone before without encountering any major problems, I figured I didn't really need a travel companion. As soon as Mohinii got back to manage things, I began figuring out how to get to my destination. Flying was far too expensive, so I would have to be more creative about it.

A Margii brother who had recently gone to India suggested traveling by boat from Haifa to the Greek part of Cyprus. "Once in Cyprus, you can take another boat from the Turkish part of the island to Turkey," he said.

I knew the rest. When I got to Turkey, I would travel overland by bus from Turkey to Iran, Iran to Afghanistan, Afghanistan to Pakistan, and then finally on to India. But there was a gigantic flaw with the plan he was suggesting. It had only been a few years since Turkey had invaded Cyprus and seized the north, resulting in the partition of the island, and no one was allowed to cross the border from the Greek South to the Turkish North.

When I objected on this basis, he said, "But you *can* cross over. The Greek guards aren't supposed to let anyone cross, but it's pretty easy to convince them to let you. I did it. It wasn't hard. Really."

"Are you sure?"

"No problem!" he said, waving his hand in assurance. "It'll be easy for you."

Convinced (but also ignoring an inner voice urging caution), I promptly booked a seat on the ferry from Haifa to Cyprus. Surely, I told myself, the reluctance I was feeling was due to a lack of experience traveling by boat—and that shouldn't be a big deal. After all, it would only be an overnight trip. Baba would take care of me.

Two days later, it was getting on towards sunset as I got on the ferry. I was pleasantly surprised at the substantial size of the craft. It had lots of amenities and wasn't at all the little dinky thing I'd imagined. Good, I thought. Less likely to sink! I wandered around for an hour or two, feeling superior as I watched passengers consuming large quantities of food and alcoholic beverages and buying all kinds of junk in the gift shops. Then I went in search of the seat I had booked in the steerage compartment, which turned out to resemble a small auditorium. Most of the seats were already filled. Not wanting to have to step over sleeping bodies in the dark, I had only a small snack to avoid having to use the bathroom. I did my fourth meditation of the day and then settled down for the night. The day had been a hectic one, so despite my cramped quarters, I had no trouble falling asleep.

A few hours later, something jerked me awake. I looked around, feeling confused. Vaguely aware of a strange sensation in the pit of my stomach, I felt something lurching and pitching violently. For a moment, I couldn't remember where I was, but when it happened again, I came to full awareness: I was on a boat, and the sea which had been so calm when I had gone to sleep was now roiling and churning and tossing the boat around as if it were a toy. Groans from passengers in varying stages of sea sickness were coming from every corner of the compartment. Feeling compelled to help them somehow, I started to get up but quickly abandoned the idea when I felt my own stomach begin to turn over.

By spending the next several hours not moving any more than the boat did, I managed not to get sick and felt a bit smug about it. It's because I'm a yogi, I thought. I'm in control because I ate so little before going to sleep. I was sure those first-class passengers I'd seen eating and drinking would be the sickest.

When the morning finally arrived, it was calm and sunny. As the ferry neared the shore, I walked through the upper decks and came upon passengers staggering out of their rooms, clothing askew, their faces pale and drawn, circles under their eyes; and crew members furiously mopping up the splattered corridors. As the ferry docked, I looked out over the Mediterranean, the sun glinting and sparkling upon its azure waters. I took a deep breath. It was good to be out in the open air.

Unlike those poor first-class passengers, I was feeling fit—and hungry. After celebrating the victory over my stomach by breakfasting on some of the fruit, cheese, and bread I had brought with me, I approached the next stage of my journey with a confidence as serene as the morning. When I got to the border between the Greek and Turkish areas of the island, I approached the Greek police and, showing my passport, asked to be let across to the other side.

"I'm sorry," one of them said, "but no one is allowed to cross the border."

"But I have a friend who did it—" I began, but was quickly interrupted.

"No, no one, *no one* is allowed to cross this border!"

I then launched into my story, telling the policeman about this person who had sworn to me that he had crossed the border, that I'd gone through the trouble of taking a ferry because of it, and so on.

The policeman listened with his arms crossed and legs apart.

"I want to go to India," I said, finishing up my story. "Once I get to Turkey, I'll go overland, by myself."

Sometimes people would be moved by my courage, guts, or (in retrospect) foolhardiness when they realized that I was traveling alone. But it wasn't foolhardiness to me at the time; I felt that I was being protected by the Guru. I wasn't afraid to travel alone through the Middle East, through countries I had never been before, even as a woman, because Baba was there with me, guiding and helping me. It had been that way ever since that time in Taos, New Mexico—years ago, when I had known nothing about him.

But it didn't seem like Baba was going to get the policeman to do what I wanted. The man wasn't at all moved by my situation.

"I'm sorry. You cannot cross this border," he said and turned away.

It was close to noon and getting hot. As I left the border station, a feeling of heavy exhaustion settled over me; the previous night spent guarding my stomach and getting little sleep was catching up with me. I was at a loss as to what to do. Maybe I should meditate, I thought, but where? Just then I spotted a small grassy area to the left shaded by a few trees. It seemed a perfect place. I went over and sat down under one of the trees and closed my eyes. Soon I was lost to the external world.

Gradually, I became aware of some people shouting. At first, I ignored them; after all, a few shouts were nothing to someone adept at meditating in noisy, chaotic places like train stations in Calcutta and Bombay. The din quickly grew in intensity, the voices growing shriller, with hysterical ones joining in.

What are those people making such a fuss about? Annoyed at having my peace disturbed, I opened one eye to check it out—to see rifles pointing at me from all sides! Guards, gesturing with them, were shouting, "You! Get out! Get out or we shoot!" They trained their guns on me—and took a few steps forward.

At first, I couldn't believe what I was seeing. My eyes widened. *Rifles?. . . RIFLES! My GOD, they're going to SHOOT me!* Heart pounding, I scrambled to my feet and was out of there, fleeing for all I was worth back to the sun-drenched, fly-ridden spot I had been standing in before. When the commotion died down, I was told that my grassy meditation spot was in the "no man's land" between Greek and Turkish Cyprus, a kind of Mediterranean DMZ. Had I not moved, I would likely have been shot.

My stubbornness—and my determination to finish my sadhana no matter what—had almost done me in. It was as if, once I had discovered the inner world, I began to deny the reality or importance of the external one. My lack of understanding (and arrogance, I realized much later) had almost gotten me killed.

It was clear that my trip was going to take a lot longer than expected, but I wasn't about to give up. Since I couldn't get into Turkish Cyprus, I ended up going to Rhodes, traveling there on a thankfully calm sea, and spent a week waiting for a boat to southern Turkey. Rhodes was a delight of blue skies, picturesque buildings, stone-paved narrow alleys, and friendly people. I was glad to be in one place for a while, and it was nice to do some sightseeing. Although limited by lack of money to long walks through villages, I felt satisfied; usually, I had no time for such things.

Once in southern Turkey, I caught a bus to Ankara, boarded another to Tehran, then got on yet another to Kabul. That part of my journey also did not prove uneventful.

I remember it being evening, with the lights dimmed on the bus. I had just settled down to do some meditation when I fell into a strange state somewhere between waking and sleeping, between meditation and dream. I found myself wondering what I would do if I should ever come across a serious accident scene. I had taken a course in first-aid several years earlier but didn't remember much. In this dreamy state, I vowed to take another one the first chance I got. Then I fell into a deep sleep.

Sometime later, I was jolted awake. The bus had come to a stop, its interior ablaze with lights. Cries and shouts were coming from outside. Most of the passengers had gotten off, and the rest were on their way out. I spotted a young Englishman I'd spoken with earlier.

"What's happened?" I asked.

"Seems there's been an accident."

An accident! I could hardly believe it. I grabbed my flashlight and raced outside.

It was serious. Another bus was lying on its side, and some men were attempting to extricate the driver, who was wedged inside the crumpled front of the vehicle. From the waist down, his body was bathed in blood. I turned my face away. From the hills rising up on both sides of the road, I heard screaming and moaning. I took my flashlight and went up one side, seeing people scattered about with varying degrees of injury. One man was doubled over. He didn't look so bad. I trained my flashlight on him and was thinking about how I could help when he sat up suddenly and removed his hands from his abdomen. He had a huge hole in his stomach, and the whites of his intestines were clearly visible against a background of vivid red blood. Turning away in shock, I left him and wandered around in a daze.

The bus driver sounded the horn, letting the passengers know he was about to leave. Some of us pleaded with him to take some of the injured to Kabul. He refused. "You must to understand," he said in his broken English. "This is Iranian bus. I can no stop here. I not allowed. I get in trouble."

Some of the younger passengers threatened to lie down in front of the bus, but in the end, we all got back on, and the driver pulled away, honking to clear the road. Why hadn't I taken another first-aid course? I berated myself. For some reason, it didn't occur to me that any knowledge I might have gained (not to mention having no supplies) would have been almost nothing in the face of such a terrible accident. But I didn't see it that way. Instead, I felt guilty that I couldn't help.

I had always felt that way. Whatever I was able to do, it was never enough, and when I found I couldn't do anything, I felt consumed by a painful sense of regret—and guilt. I was a didi, and I was supposed to help people. That was my reason for being on earth: to help. I was only dimly aware that I felt that way because I lacked an intrinsic sense of self-worth. I was no good unless I could serve others. Unless I was helping others all the time, I didn't deserve to be alive.

By the time we reached Kabul, I'd had enough of traveling overland. I decided to fly to Delhi, even if I had to spend most of the money I had left. Then I would take a train to Patna, where Baba was. Still consumed by guilt, I decided to fast to honor all those people I had been unable to help. I would not eat for the two days it would take to get to Patna—and Baba.

Patna, a city poor even by Indian standards, was the capital of Bihar state, itself one of the most impoverished and backward in India. Even so, because Baba was there, it was a place more beautiful to me than anywhere else in the world. When I got off the train, I felt like getting down and kissing the dusty ground. The desire to see Baba was so strong that I wanted to rush right over to the jail. Like all Margiis, though, I would have to get official permission to meet him, and since it was late in the afternoon, I would have to wait until the next day to apply.

When I arrived at the Ananda Marga office, I learned from others that getting the permission was not a straightforward task. While some Margiis had to wait only a day or two, others had to endure several days of being bounced from one official to another. Some officials seemed to like us and quickly signed our papers; others were notorious for creating delays. It seemed to depend on the mood of the particular individual encountered. There were stories of Margiis being turned away simply because they had caught someone having a bad day. I prayed this would not be my fate.

Early the next morning, I went to at the government office and began filling out my application. Besides filling in the usual information like name and passport number, we had to answer some unusual questions. *Describe your relationship to Shrii Shrii Anandamurti,* was one of them. *Who is Shrii Shrii Anandamurti?* was another. I was prepared for these questions, having already heard that many Margiis approached them like a creative writing exercise, offering "He is my father," "He is God," or "He is *Parama Purusa*" (Supreme Consciousness) as answers. I answered in much the same way, handed my application to the official, then watched as he stamped and added it to just one of the several piles of papers and aging brown binders stacked high on every available inch of space on his desk. Surely, my application would disappear into this ocean of paperwork, never to be seen again!

Thankfully, it didn't turn out that way. After a few days, I received permission to visit Baba, along with some Israeli Margiis who had arrived in Patna around the same time I had. (Unlike me, though, it hadn't taken them weeks to reach India. They had arranged the money to do the sensible thing: fly!)

The day I was to meet Baba, I was up early, as were the Israeli Margiis. After we completed our morning sadhana, we had a light breakfast and hurried over to the jail.

Patna Jail was an imposing and impenetrable red brick structure with barbed wire and shards of glass on top of its walls. Incongruously, right in front of it was a flower market with a multitude of fragrant *malas* (garlands) displayed on mats. There were *malas* of red and yellow marigolds, creamy frangipani, and the tiny, fragrant, star-shaped white flowers I still didn't know the name of. We bought garlands for Baba. I chose one of puffy orange marigolds. (Had I known at the time that the name of those tiny flowers was jasmine and, even more importantly, that my name, Malatii, actually meant "jasmine," maybe I would have bought one of those garlands!)

We waited outside the jail, fidgeting with our clothes and holding our garlands. I had also brought a bottle of little white sugar balls that I wanted to leave with Baba. He would give the sweets to visitors coming after us as *prasad* (blessed offering, usually food, given to disciples by their guru). I'd been told that Baba had a whole row of sweets in bottles under his cot and that he always opened one and distributed sweets whenever he had visitors, so I figured he would need more.

We were mostly silent, thinking about what we were going to say to Baba and imagining what he might say back. I had waited years to meet my guru and was flooded with a whole series of emotions. There was excitement and longing—and some fear mixed in as well. Would he be happy to see me?

The door opened and we were led inside to the superintendent's office. Everyone had to wait there before meeting Baba. Rumor had it that the superintendent himself had become a devotee, liked Margiis, and treated them well. We knew, however, that he had to be careful: being too open about his sentiments could cost him his job.

We were asked to produce our passports and fill in some papers. Just as we were finishing, the superintendent came in smiling, hands folded in namaskar. I immediately liked him.

"So, you're going to meet Baba," he said. "Is this your first meeting?"

"Yes, sir, for all of us," I said.

"Good! Baba will meet you now." He bowed and left us.

A mustached little man dressed in a khaki uniform came up to us. Right away, I realized who this was—the "little jailer" I had heard so much about. Talkative and good natured, he was also someone who could be bribed. In exchange for a bribe of several saris, he had once allowed an ex-worker, a dada who had left the organization, to get in for an unauthorized visit with Baba. (Baba had promptly thrown the visitor out. "Get out! Get out!" he was reported to have shouted. "Do you know how many bad things you have done? I allow only good people to visit me!")

"Namaste! Namaste!" the jailer was exclaiming. "You're about to meet Baba. Wonderful! Come with me." When we got to a large steel door, he took out one of the biggest keys I had ever seen and inserted it into a huge keyhole. The door swung open, then shut with a clang behind us, and the jailer led us along narrow stone corridors, making one turn after another, chattering away all the while. "Didi," he said, "Do you like Indian food?" I nodded. "What kind of curry do you like? Do you like roti?" Food was the last thing I wanted to talk about. I murmured something in reply, trying to stay in a contemplative mood by repeating my mantra.

Then there we were, in front of Baba's cell. There wasn't a door with a lock. There wasn't any door at all. Instead, a light-colored blanket hung over the entrance. I felt waves of bliss coming from the room, as if we were about to enter not a jail cell, but a temple. The Israeli Margiis were in front of me, and they suddenly got shy. "You go in first, Didi," they urged, hanging back. I hesitated for a moment; then, leaving my sandals outside, I went in and did *pranam*.[29] I heard the others come in quietly. They, too, did *pranam*.

---

[29] *pranam:* A respectful greeting when meeting one's guru. In Ananda Marga, men perform *pranam* by lying prostrate with arms extended, palms down; women do it crouching with arms extended.

We got up and sat in a row in front of Baba. The cell was plain, with only a few garlands draped on its walls. It was indeed a holy place, a shrine. Baba was lying on a wooden cot, dressed all in white. There was an ethereal feeling about him. He had very light skin, and a sweet spiritual vibration was pouring out of him and over us.

We gave Baba our garlands. He held each one to his forehead, closing his eyes. Then he handed them to his assistant, a young man who was standing to one side, and asked us our names and where we were from.

"Acarya Malatii from Israel, Baba," I said. One by one, the others gave their names and said that they were also from Israel.

"Ah, Israel, Israel!" he said, touching our heads lightly with his forefinger. "Israel is a small country, but it is *not small.*" He repeated his remark, looking at each of us.

"Israel is a small country, but it is *not small.* Do you understand?" We nodded, transfixed, our eyes never leaving his face. Baba spoke softly, yet his voice echoed with power. "The Israelis are a strong people, a hard-working people," Baba said. "They have transformed the desert!"

One of the Margiis asked about the Arab-Israeli conflict.

"They are brothers," Baba said. "The Jews and the Arabs are brothers. They have forgotten this fact. But I remember. I remember this fact." He paused for a moment then said, "Yes, it is very hard to build a bridge. But once the bridge is built, it is very easy to walk across it." Baba moved his forefinger and middle finger back and forth, like legs walking. "Left, right! Left, right!" he said. We laughed. We were so happy. We were finally with Baba, and he was telling us that one day, Arabs and Israelis would live in peace. Nothing could be better!

I shifted a little, knocking over the jar of sweets I had brought with me, then grabbed it in a panic before it could fall to the ground and shatter. Trying to recover my composure, I said, "Baba, I've brought you some *prasad.*" Baba glanced at the jar and exclaimed, "That is my duty. Let me do my duty!"

He gestured to his assistant and said, "Jar Number Five." I looked down and saw the row of jars under Baba's cot, filled with all kinds of sweets: some contained little white balls, like the ones I had brought; others were filled with lumps of different kinds of crystallized or unrefined sugar like *mishri* and *gur*.

The assistant gave Baba the jar he had requested. "I can't open this," Baba said. (He was weak from his liquid fast, which had lasted several months.) He handed it to me and said, "You open it." I did so, then passed the jar carefully back to him. Baba took out handfuls of little white balls, then poured the sweets into our outstretched palms, one after another, and asked us to eat. I took care not to eat all of mine, determined as I was to carry some back to share with the Margiis in Israel. For a timeless moment, the only sounds were of us chewing our sweets and of Baba, rubbing his hands together and making a "Mmmmm" sound as he watched us, beaming.

"Time is up," Baba said.

"Baba, can we do *Guru Puja?*"[30] I asked. He nodded—and my heart leapt. We knelt on our knees and held up our hands, closed our eyes, and sang. It was so sweet. Countless times I had sung this Sanskrit prayer kneeling on my knees in front of his picture, and now, here I was, actually doing it in front of him.

When we got to the last line, *Tava dravyam jagat guru, tubhya meva samarpayt* (all these things of yours, Guru of the world, I offer to you in complete surrender), we moved forward into the *pranam* pose, our heads down and arms extended. After a moment, I heard the others get up. A thought came into my mind. Why get up? I think I'll just stay here.

"Get up, Malatii," I heard Baba say firmly but lovingly.

I got up. Baba gestured to his assistant for our garlands, put each one to his forehead while closing his eyes and uttering a

---

[30] *Guru Puja:* Offering to the guru. Ananda Margiis perform *Guru Puja* after finishing meditation by singing a Sanskrit verse three times while kneeling and holding their hands in front of them in offering. It ends with a *pranam*.

blessing, and handed them back to us. I took mine and held it carefully. As we were leaving the cell, I turned around to get one last glimpse of Baba. He was smiling with his hands folded in namaskar.

"We will meet again! We will meet again!" he said.

Chapter 6

The Second Visit

We were indeed to meet again. I went back to the government office, filled in another application in much the same way as the first, and got permission to visit Baba a second time. On the designated day, as the early morning sun was slanting against the prison walls, I was standing alone by the gate, waiting to be let in. Everything seemed bathed in a kind of rare clarity, washed clean of dust, and pure as if just sprung from the womb of creation.

I was the only one scheduled to visit Baba this morning and would thus have him all to myself—a rare stroke of luck. Most Margiis, if they were able to spend the time to do so, were able to visit Baba more than once, but few got to see him all alone.

Before going to the jail, I had checked in at the Ananda Marga office just to be sure that everything was ready for my visit. Rupeshanandaji, Baba's PA (Personal Assistant), had greeted me with a question.

"Malatii, your last name: Goluboff. That is not a German name, is it?"

"No, Dada."

"Good," he said, not explaining his query. "Now, go and meet Baba!"

Not needing any encouragement, I went out to the street and waved down a rickshaw wallah.[31] As he pedaled rhythmically, my thoughts turned to Dada Rupeshananda—and the question he had asked me. I wondered about it for a minute or two, then dismissed it as something not worth bothering about.

After all, Rupeshananda was someone who inspired confidence. I had always liked and respected him. I remembered the time when we had first met. He'd been visiting the States and had come to the Philadelphia jagrti. I was a new Margii and had just gotten my spiritual name.

"What is your name, sister?" he asked me.

"Liila, Dada."

"Ah, Liila! There is only one *liila*, and that is the Lord's *liila!*" he said, laughing.

Though short and thin, Rupeshananda had the air of a powerful sadhu or ascetic about him and could be firm as well as affectionate when need be. But his laugh was what you remembered. It seemed to come from deep inside him, so that you had to join in, even if your mental state had been dark just moments before. He was like bright sunlight, I thought. He had spent a lot of time with Baba and seemed to illuminate everyone around him. I remembered him telling me once what it was like to listen for Baba's call even if he was in the middle of doing his *pranayama* (breathing exercises). "If I heard Baba call," he said, "I would just leave my *pranayama* in the middle of an inhalation, jump up, and go to him." Then he laughed that wonderful laugh.

Rupeshananda was still seeing Baba in jail every day; he was, in fact, the only one allowed to visit Baba on a daily basis.

I waited outside the jail for what seemed a long time. Finally, a guard opened the gate and motioned me in. He took me to

---

[31] wallah: A person in charge of, employed at, or concerned with a particular thing or function; such as book wallah for bookseller or ticket wallah for the person in charge of the ticket counter.

the superintendent's office and told me to have a seat and wait. He could see that I was an Ananda Marga worker because I was in full uniform. Most workers (except for Indian ones) went to the jail in civilian dress because they didn't want the Indian authorities to know their status in the organization, but I figured they already had my name from my first visit and could prevent me from entering India in the future whether I was a worker or not, so why not wear my uniform? I considered wearing it an honor, an orange badge of courage.

I put my *mala* of reddish orange marigolds, still enclosed in its protective wrapping of leaves, on my lap. As I did, the image of the flower market in front of the jail and of the beggars, mostly children, milling around it, came to mind. Dressed in filthy tatters, they had implored me with outstretched hands or stumps where hands should have been as I'd purchased my garland. It was so hard to know what to do when confronted with beggars. Some said that Baba didn't want us to give them money because that would only perpetuate the institution of begging. Mostly I gave them fruits: bananas, chicos (which were very sweet and looked like perfectly round potatoes), or guavas.

Growing concerned that the morning was wearing on, I glanced at my watch. I shouldn't worry about the time, I told myself, I should think about what I'll say to Baba once I get in. Maybe I would tell him about the challenges of working in Israel.

Thinking of Israel brought Mohinii to mind. Unlike her, I didn't think of the uniform as a challenge. When she had returned to Israel after visiting Baba, Mohinii told us she'd discussed it with him. "I told Baba it was difficult to wear it in Israel," she said. In fact, she had used the same words with him that she'd used with me: "It doesn't help to look like a Christian nun in a Jewish country." (I had to hand it to her—she certainly had nerve talking that way to Baba!) "But Baba didn't agree with me," Mohinii went on. "He said, 'Who told you that you look like a Christian nun? You tell them who you are. You tell them you are an Ananda Margii!' Then he told me I had to wear the full uniform."

I had felt a secret satisfaction at that. Now, not only would Mohinii have to put on the veil instead of that silly orange scarf, she would also have to wear a sari; even the skirts we sometimes wore were a no-no (not to mention her white pants!).

Thinking about Mohinii's mistake only brought to mind my own. The biggest one had to have been introducing the *pratiik* too quickly to Israeli newcomers. Maybe I would talk to Baba about that. I also had something special to ask him that only he could answer.

I looked at my watch again. It was almost eleven o'clock. Where could the superintendent be? I couldn't get in to see Baba without him. And if he came too late, I might not get to see Baba at all because he would be doing his midday meditation. It was known that even in jail, Baba adhered to a very strict schedule.

Finally I heard some people coming. In came three men, two guards in their khaki uniforms and the superintendent. They passed me on their way to another room and gestured to me to follow. I entered a room with a large oval table and was told to sit down opposite them.

I was puzzled. The superintendent's manner was brusque and rough, totally different from my first visit. The other men stared at me almost malevolently, traces of sarcastic smiles on their lips. The superintendent gave no indication that he recognized me, nor any apology for being late. Instead, he said, "You see, we're all ready to have you meet Baba, but he is not ready to meet you." He paused as if to see what effect his words would have.

I took a sharp breath. "What do you mean?" I demanded. "I have permission. I saw Dada Rupeshanandaji this morning, and he told me to go and see Baba. There must be some mistake."

The superintendent greeted my words with silence then leaned forward. "Baba told me that he is not prepared to meet the person with your name," he said. "We can't make Baba meet you if he doesn't want to meet."

Everyone in the room was staring at me, no doubt speculating as to what sordid thing I could have possibly done (a worker in uniform, no less!) to cause Baba to react that way.

My earlier confidence evaporated and was quickly replaced by fear—and shame as well. What could it have been? My mistakes in the field? Maybe all that stuff I did in college? Thoughts of the ex-dada who had bribed the little jailer with saris in order to meet Baba came to mind. Baba had had him promptly thrown out. That was the only person Baba had ever refused to see. And now, me! Why?

I fought down tears of panic. The men surrounding me seemed to be enjoying the spectacle. Then the superintendent dismissed me, his voice rising with anger.

"You'll have to leave now," he shouted. "Go, leave this instant!"

My eyes blinded by tears, I stumbled out of his office and was let out of the jail, the gate clanging shut behind me. Indian Margiis waiting outside for news gathered around me. They mistook the tears streaming down my face for tears of joy.

"Didi, did you see Baba?" they asked. "What did he say to you?"

"They wouldn't let me see him," I stammered.

"Why not? Why not?" they demanded.

Turning away without answering, I was running now, in a total panic, dimly aware that I had experienced this anguish before. The dream! I suddenly remembered. The dream back in Calcutta when Baba told me I was dirty! Could that be why he didn't want to see me—because he thinks I'm dirty? But everyone who comes to see him has gotten to see him. Why not me?

I had only one rational thought: to call Rupeshananda. He would fix it. He would tell them it was all a mistake. It *had* to be a mistake!

I ran to the railroad booking office across the street and asked to use the phone. Hoping against hope for a problem-free connection, I dialed the number and got my wish. Rupeshananda answered.

"Ah, Malatii. Have you visited with Baba?"

Attempting to keep the hysteria out of my voice, I spoke faintly. "No, Dada. They told me that Baba doesn't want to see me."

He was silent for a moment. "Oh," he finally said. "They must have thought you were that dirty German boy. Do you still want to meet Baba?"

"Of course, Dada," I said, my voice small and shaking.

"Wait in front of the jail. I'm coming right away."

Moments later, Rupeshananda zoomed into the compound on his orange motorcycle, raising up clouds of dust and smiling reassurance. He hopped off and entered the jail. Before I knew what was happening, I was being waved in. But I was no longer alone. Another Indian dada had come to the jail. We would be seeing Baba together.

Moments later, we were standing outside the large padlocked door that led to the cells. The little jailer let us in and then we were standing in front of Baba's cell. We pushed aside the blanket and did *pranam* in front of Baba, then sat in front of his cot.

Baba was lying down, dressed all in white. Light was pouring out of him. He appeared confused and was muttering something. I lifted up my garland, wishing to place it around his neck, but stopped with my arm in midair. A sudden panicky feeling overtook me as my mind shouted: He's lying down! How am I going to get it over his head? Then, as if hearing what I was thinking, Baba smiled sweetly, lifted his arm, and helped me place the garland around his neck.

Baba and the dada, Santosananda, began speaking in Bengali. My Bengali being rudimentary, I understood little of what they were saying. Dada massaged Baba's arm as they spoke. There was something so intimate about the two of them that I felt almost like a voyeur.

A powerful desire to massage Baba's other arm then arose in me. Much to my amazement, Baba moved it closer, as if he were reading my thoughts, twisting his arm in a way that looked almost painful, with his palm facing up. It was as if he wished to get it as close to me as possible. I longed to convey all my love by massaging it, but what had transpired in the superintendent's office was like a raw wound, and I couldn't overcome the fear that Baba would reject me, would snatch his arm away and shrink from my touch.

As I stood there frozen with indecision, Baba began to speak in English.

"Yes. Yes, to err is human." Santosananda looked confused. Baba looked at me, as if he wanted me to help explain the meaning.

"To err . . . to make a mistake," I said.

"Yes! Human beings have so many faults; they make so many mistakes," Baba said. "To err is not bad, but not to do anything to correct one's faults, *that* is bad!" He repeated his words. "To err is not bad, but not to do anything to correct one's faults, *that* is bad!" Then he playfully tapped us, first Dada and then me, lightly on the head with one finger, as if to give his words more emphasis.

"Human beings have so many imperfections," he continued, growing more animated. "But as you struggle against your imperfections, you will gain more and more speed. You will become more and more perfect. And the state of perfection is the state of absolute motionlessness, the state of bliss."

Dada and I were silent for a moment, taking in his words.

"Baba," I asked suddenly, "what should we do about the beggars?"

I was aghast. I hadn't planned to say that. It was as if the words had come out of nowhere. Baba closed his eyes, a look of tremendous suffering crossing his face.

Extending his hands palms out, as if he were pushing my remark away, he said, "Please don't talk about the beggars. It gives me too much pain."

"Baba," I said, "will you come out when PROUT is established, or do you want—"

"Yes!" Baba exclaimed, getting up on one elbow and interrupting me. "When PROUT is established, I will be very happy because all my children will have belly-full meals. You lead the way," he said, looking at me. "You establish PROUT."

Moments after we had left Baba's cell, I asked Dada what he had been discussing with Baba. "I was telling him about some mistakes I made in my field," he answered.

I took a sharp breath as the import of Dada's words struck me. Mistakes! Just what I'd been thinking of telling Baba about while waiting for the superintendent to come!

Some of what had happened now became clear. Baba knew what both of us had been thinking. He had the same message for both of us, so he'd arranged for us to see him together. That way, there would be no need for him to repeat himself. After all, he was fasting and had to conserve his energy.

After I left the jail, I saw Rupeshananda. "So why did Baba say he didn't want to see me?" I asked. "Was it something about my name?"

"He thought you were that dirty German boy you were telling me about," Dada said.

I put two and two together. A few weeks earlier, I had told Rupeshananda about a certain German boy, a hippie-looking character who'd been attempting to get permission to see Baba at the same time I had been. Dirty and barefoot, with long matted locks and carrying a small flute, he'd looked like he hadn't had a bath in at least two weeks and smelled like it too. He told me that he had arrived in India weeks ago and had been traveling around, sleeping in railroad station waiting rooms. "Now, I've just come to Patna and want to see Baba," he'd said. He can't possibly be a real devotee, I had thought at the time. Otherwise, he wouldn't have traveled around for weeks before coming to see Baba. A real Margii goes straight to the Guru, like a bee to nectar.

When I told Rupeshananda, he agreed that the German shouldn't be allowed to see Baba. Days later, when my last name was cleared for a visit, Rupeshananda, who had never heard my last name, thought it was the name of the boy I had warned him about. Then he told Baba that a boy named Goluboff had gotten permission to see him and suggested that he not be allowed because he hadn't been doing practices. Baba must have agreed. What a tragic comedy of errors! Still, Rupeshananda must have realized his mistake. After all, that very morning, he had asked me about my name. For some reason, he didn't share with Baba (surely, not on purpose?) the fact that the person with the name in question was a didi and not a boy, German or otherwise.

Maybe I had spared Baba from seeing someone unsuitable, but cosmically speaking, who was I to decide suitability? It was a case of what we called instant karma: my small-mindedness had been immediately reflected back on me, causing me great distress and the pain of rejection.

(It wasn't until years later that I fully understood why I had felt such sheer panic at being told that Baba didn't want to see me. It was because, for me, Baba wasn't only a spiritual father. He was also a kind of substitute father figure onto whom I projected my experiences with my own father. Even back then, it wasn't lost on me that Baba in some ways physically resembled my father, with his stern face and the dominating black glasses with thick lenses. And then there was Baba's anger. I was terrified of arousing it, just as I'd been afraid of provoking it in my father. Most of us feared Baba on some level, but the fear I felt was sometimes overwhelming. When told that Baba didn't want to meet me, the rejection and the panic close to terror I had felt had been compounded because the experience was familiar: my own father had rejected me in the past, and now my new father was doing the same.)

The superintendent was mortified and apologized over and over for his behavior. Although I told him it wasn't his fault ("You were just doing your job," I said), I did feel some satisfaction at his embarrassment. He was determined to set things right, though, and showed me a copy of the letter he had written to the authorities requesting that they allow me another visit. "Due to this mix-up," it read, "this didi was unable to visit properly with Baba as her mind was disturbed." Despite his best efforts,

I was not granted another visit, even though I stayed in Patna for another couple of weeks. After a while, it became unseemly to keep trying, so I left for Istanbul and a new posting—Acting SWWS (Sectorial Women's Welfare Secretary) of Cairo Sector. I was "acting" because only Indian workers were assigned the higher positions—a clearly discriminatory practice that should have given me pause, but didn't. (Despite all the claims of universalism in Baba's speeches and writings, there was a definite pecking order in Ananda Marga, with the Bengali-speaking dadas at the top (Baba was Bengali) and most didis and Westerners near the bottom.)

The fact that Baba interrupted me when I asked him if he would come out of jail when PROUT was established held great meaning for me. I was convinced it was not by chance that he'd done so.

I had been about to ask him, "Do you want us to do something?"—the word "something" being code for a course of action I had been thinking about for weeks before going to see him. It was a radical step to help get Baba out of jail, to get the attention of the world focused on the imprisonment of our guru on false pretenses. Four Indian dadas had already done it and had drawn some notice, but mostly just in the Indian media. If I were to do it, I'd be the first Westerner as well as the first woman to take the step.

Using gasoline, I would set fire to my body and immolate myself. I would do it somewhere in the Middle East, in either Israel or Istanbul. I spent long hours planning this and got to the point of typing the letters I would send out to newspapers and public officials right before carrying it out.

By committing the act of self-immolation, or voluntary death by fire, I would not be committing suicide, like some depressed person who sees no way out. Far from suicide, self-immolation is an ancient tradition which has sometimes been carried out to draw attention to cruelty or injustice. By doing it, I would be following a tradition of protest practiced for hundreds of years, particularly by Hindu and Buddhist monks. Since both religions maintain that the soul (the true self) survives death and incarnates into a new body, the act of self-immolation may destroy the body but cannot annihilate the true self.

If carried out, my plan would surely horrify Westerners, who, it seemed to us, erroneously identified with their bodies as their true selves. But I wanted to shock people. By doing so, I would bring world attention to the injustice being committed against Shrii Shrii Anandamurti, whom we regarded as the world's greatest living spiritual master.

First, though, I needed to be sure that was what Baba wanted; I would take no action without knowing I had his approval. So I was going to ask Baba in code. I knew he would understand what that "something" meant. But I didn't get to finish my sentence. Baba cut me short, telling me that he would be very happy when PROUT was established and that he wanted me to take the lead. It couldn't have been clearer. He had other work for me to do.

Not long after my arrival in Istanbul, we received word that a German didi would be coming. Her name was Uditi. I knew her; she was the LFT sister I'd met in Frankfurt after I had been deported from Egypt, the one who had given me the sari. I'd often thought of her when I wore it. She had become a didi just like I had thought she would, and I was looking forward to spending time with her. Then, after helping her to get settled in Istanbul, I would go elsewhere in the sector.

However, only days after hearing about Uditi's posting, we got some more news by telegram. A didi and dada, both German, had committed self-immolation in Berlin. We didn't know who they were at first, but I knew deep down that the didi had been Uditi.

As it turned out, I was right. We heard later that Uditi had visited Baba just days after I had. She must have been contemplating the very same thing. Like me, she must have formed a plan as to how, where, and when; like me, she hadn't wanted to take action without Baba's consent.

What I remember us all finding out was that an LFT sister had visited Baba along with Uditi and reported that when they had gone in to see him, Uditi already knew she had been posted to Istanbul. But still she asked, "Baba, where will I be going next?" According to the LFT sister, Baba motioned Uditi to come closer. She bent her head down to him (Baba was lying on his cot), and then he whispered, "Berlin." Berlin was the place she had planned on doing it, so she must have concluded that she had his approval.

The self-immolation of Uditi and Loknath (the dada) took place at rush hour in front of a church in a busy area of Berlin. It was widely covered in newspapers and magazines all over the world, complete with pictures of their half-burnt corpses. There were also pictures of the large posters they had set up at the church beforehand, which explained that they were taking this action to bring the attention of the world to the continued imprisonment of Prabhat Rainjan Sarkar (Baba's given name). Eventually, a total of eight didis and dadas committed self-immolation. "They are the torch of my New Year's *Vanii*," Baba said about them later, after delivering his New Year's message, which read in part, "The light of one lamp lights up innumerable lamps."

Uditi's action affected me deeply, and I was not myself for some time afterwards. She and I had both planned the ultimate sacrifice. We had both asked Baba for permission. My request was denied; hers was granted. She was supposed to come to Istanbul, where I was working. It was like we were linked. I wasn't all there; part of me felt like I had gone with her, while another part of me continued inhabiting the space she was meant to be in. For some time, I wasn't quite in my body. Everything felt unreal, as in a dream, as if I'd been brought back from the brink of death and had survived, without the fact sinking in yet.

A week or two afterwards, I had a vivid dream.

It is late at night. I am a passenger in a car that stops and picks up Uditi. She loads a large drum of gasoline into the back seat, then gets in. We travel together in silence to her destination. The car stops and Uditi hands me her orange uniform and white sari, neatly folded. Without a word, she leaves the car, taking the gasoline with her.

My peripheral involvement with the self-immolation events in Ananda Marga was very powerful for me, and I sometimes contemplate it even today. Would I have really doused myself with gasoline and lit the match? Back then, I was absolutely sure I would have if Baba had indicated that he wanted it of me. Back then, whatever he would have asked of me, I surely would have carried out. Now, I find myself wondering: if he had asked me, for example, to strap explosives to my body and blow myself up in the midst of West Bengal's Communist government officials, would I have carried out his wishes? Hamas suicide bombers are convinced that they will be rewarded for their martyrdom; they will go to paradise to be attended by dark-eyed virgins. In much the same way, I was convinced at the time that by immolating myself, I would achieve samadhi, the state of divine consciousness, in which it no longer matters if you have a body—if that had been what he wanted me to do.

Those outside the movement might have only contempt for someone who would knowingly send a young girl barely in her twenties to a fiery death. We saw it differently. Although I don't believe Baba *told* Uditi to commit self-immolation, we believed that Baba was omniscient and knew what Uditi was contemplating, and we were fully confident that he knew as well the state of her soul and its relationship to the Divine. We were all convinced that Uditi was very close to liberation, and that was why Baba had allowed her to do what she longed to do for him. Her work on this earth, we told each other, ended with that last final act of devotion, and her last tie to this life was burnt up in the flames. With that, she attained *moksha* or liberation, the goal that we all worked and meditated for.

As for me, Baba knew that I wasn't in the same spiritual ballpark as Uditi. Despite my willingness to do it, spiritually, I wasn't at all ready for such a step. My service to him lay elsewhere.

It was a matter of obedience to his will; I had too much karma, too many *samskaras* left. I still had work to do.

That's what I believed then. Today, I'm just grateful to still be here.

Chapter 7

Sexism Within and Without

No one got posted to replace Uditi, so I stayed on in Istanbul, in the apartment the dadas had rented. Located in the basement of a building located near Taksim Square in the center of the European side of the city, the jagrti was dark at all times of day. The low rent and location, however, more than made up for its drawbacks. Across the street was a small shop where we would run out to buy fresh white *ekmek* (bread) and occasional feta cheese for breakfast. The friendly shopkeeper liked to quiz me on my Turkish whenever I went in.

"Didi, count for me," he would say while holding up his fingers. *"Bir, iki, üç, dört,"* I would mumble. If I managed to get up to *on* (ten) without making any mistakes, he would clap his hands and chortle, *"Çok güzel,*[32] Didi! *Çok güzel!"* his dark face breaking into a wide smile.

I remember venturing out alone one morning to an open-air market to buy carrots, armed with several newly acquired Turkish words, thanks to the shopkeeper and a few of the Turkish Margiis. Small and nondescript, the market consisted of a handful of

---

[32] *Çok güzel!*: Very nice! Very good!

vendors who had their produce out on wooden platforms and were standing around smoking. I went up to one of the vegetable sellers, who was endowed with the kind of bushy moustache sported by so many Turks. There didn't seem to be any carrots, but I asked him in Turkish anyway, thinking he might have some in the big sacks next to his table. The man nodded while making a "tsk"ing sound.

Great! He's got some, I thought, standing there and waiting. The man didn't make any move towards the sacks, so I repeated my question. He nodded and made the same sound as before. I waited. Again, nothing happened. Well, he's definitely got carrots, I thought. I wonder why he won't give me any. Maybe he doesn't like foreigners or something. Summoning the courage to ask a third time, I said, *"Havuç var mı?"*

"Yok! Hayır!" he shouted, flailing his arms.

I backed away, surprised at the sudden outburst. First he says he has carrots and then he says he doesn't. Puzzling! When I got back to the jagrti, I recounted the incident to Satish, a young Margii who'd been helping me with my Turkish. Before I could finish my account, he started laughing.

"What's so funny?" I demanded.

"Didi, when a Turkish person makes a gesture that looks like a nod to you and makes a 'tsk' sound, they mean, 'No,' or 'No, I don't have any'!"

He kept laughing. Another experience of cross-cultural confusion! At least I wasn't caught out on the streets in my underwear this time.

Living with me in the Istanbul jagrti was an Indian dada who was posted as head of RAWA, the Renaissance Writers and Artists Association, yet another suborganization within Ananda Marga. RAWA Dada, as we called him, was a refined and delicate-looking person with finely chiseled features, a sweet smile, and an even sweeter disposition. He liked to cook; even though our diet consisted primarily of white bread and bulgur, we occasionally had enough vegetables for him to perform near miracles with the few ingredients we had. Dada helped me fashion a room of sorts by sectioning off one area of the large living room with a curtain, so living there was reasonably comfortable.

But I knew I'd be staying in the dadas' place only temporarily. My goal was to get an apartment for didis and sisters. (Didis and dadas weren't supposed to live together anyway. We would do so only out of necessity whenever we came to a new place.) So I saved every Turkish lira I could. Some of the Margii sisters donated money; other funds were raised through a yoga class I was teaching for some wealthy middle-aged women.

When I had enough money for the required three months' rent and went looking for a place, a young Margii sister whose spiritual name was Kalindii accompanied me. She was from a Jewish family and was one of my most enthusiastic students despite the active opposition of her father. Kalindii would sometimes lie to her parents about where she was going so she could come to our programs. (I remember the time her father followed her. He stormed in, a squat, angry little man who reminded me of Subira's father in Egypt, grabbed his red-faced daughter by the arm and led her out the door, slamming it behind them. Unlike Subira, however, Kalindii wasn't intimidated by her father's opposition and kept right on coming.)

Kalindii spoke little English, but fortunately for me, she did know French. The French I had taken in high school and college proved adequate. Together, we went out on several apartment-hunting excursions, but nothing seemed quite right. The apartment would invariably be too expensive, too small, or too far from the center of town. After weeks of searching, we finally found one that seemed perfect, a third-floor apartment with a living room large enough to accommodate my students. I was ready to plunk down a deposit when Kalindii spoke up.

"Didi," she said, "Let's wait. I have a funny feeling about this place. Something isn't right about it."

"What could be wrong? It's not expensive, and it'll be easy for everyone to get to."

But Kalindii was adamant. "Let's wait a bit. I want to ask people around here some questions."

I was anxious to get a sisters' jagrti and was tired of living with the dadas. But in the end I gave in, and it was a good thing I did. It turned out that the apartment building was in Istanbul's red-light district, and all the other flats in the building were occupied by prostitutes!

Around this time, a new SS dada, Sanjogananda, came to Istanbul. All the Margiis had been waiting for him for weeks and were excited by his arrival, having heard a lot about him. Sanjogananda proved to be quite an imposing figure. Powerfully built, he was tall even by Western standards and had a loud, echoing voice that matched his size.

A few days after his arrival, Sanjogananda and I sat down to discuss the progress of Ananda Marga in the sector. We had jagtis and projects in Israel and Istanbul. The work in other countries wasn't going so well, however. No workers had gone to Egypt since Narendra and I had been deported. The partition of Cyprus had made things difficult for us there as well. We had accomplished little on the island, apart from establishing one small center in Nicosia (or Lefkosa as the Turks called it) in the Turkish part. Sanjogananda thought that Cyprus had potential. "I'm interested in doing some work in the Greek part," he said. "We need to open a jagrti there. I'll need your help to get some funds together to support a worker and a center." He then asked me to give him all the money I had. "You can always stay here until we get more money to get your sisters' jagrti," he said.

As acting Sectorial Women's Welfare Secretary, I was technically on par with Sanjogananda as far as responsibilities went, but sectorial secretaries, being men, always pulled more weight than didis in comparable positions. And at that point, I didn't want to think in terms of didis versus dadas or brothers versus sisters. I wanted to cooperate with Dada; since we didn't have a center in the Greek part of Cyprus yet, I considered the needs of the organization as a whole to be more important than my own. I decided to give Dada the money. As it turned out, though, Sanjogananda never did open that jagrti. And not long after that meeting, I became homeless.

It was around eight o'clock on a drizzly autumn evening. I'd been in Izmir, and having just arrived in Istanbul, I got to the jagrti and let myself in. RAWA Dada was on tour elsewhere, and Sanjogananda was nowhere to be found. I bathed and went into the meditation hall to do my sadhana. As I lit a candle and prepared to sit, I heard the front door open, and there was Sanjogananda, standing in front of me with a frown on his face.

"You know, you can't stay here anymore," he said. "Baba has told that didis and dadas are not to stay in the same place. It leads to immorality. You will have to leave." He didn't seem to care that we had been making this adjustment out of necessity for months now—or that I had no jagrti because I had given all my money to him.

"And where do you suggest I go, Dada? It's getting late, it's raining, and thanks to you, I have no sisters' jagrti to go to."

He shrugged. "You can stay with some sister," he said, turning to go to the kitchen. "And leave your key. You can't come back here."

Such a harsh experience of male chauvinism in Ananda Marga should have bothered me more than it did. While I had encountered such attitudes in the organization before, this was the first time I'd been adversely impacted. But far from engaging in any kind of analysis, I only took refuge in what was becoming my most oft-repeated conduct rule (the one about accepting sufferings as rewards), repacked everything I'd just unpacked, grabbed my umbrella, and left. I had no idea where to go. You couldn't just arrive unannounced at people's homes: most of my students were school girls still living with their parents. I imagined myself showing up on Kalindii's doorstep, ringing the bell, explaining my plight to her pugnacious father, and having the door slammed in my face.

Debating what to do, I walked around the darkened streets for an hour or two, looking over my shoulder every now and then. Istanbul wasn't a place to be wandering around alone at night! Finally, I went to the home of an older woman I knew, not a Margii but a sympathizer. She took me in for a few days. Then I called others, staying here and there for a day or two, until my classes and groups in other towns took me elsewhere.

We never did get a sisters' jagrti. For months afterwards, whenever I had classes to teach or initiations to do in Istanbul, I would stay with Satish and his elderly mother. I had a place in their cramped apartment next to a massive ancient dresser in a dimly lit room. There was just enough space to sleep and do my yoga postures and meditation.

About a year after I had been forced to leave the jagrti, a Filipino didi named Shivapriya arrived in Istanbul. (I'd met her before. She had been the first didi to be posted to the United States and had given me my fifth lesson right before I had left for training.) We pooled our meager resources and rented a small place far from the city center. It was another basement apartment, even darker than the dadas' was. Unheated and icy during the winter, it was so damp that its walls dripped with moisture all year long. We couldn't hold yoga classes or meditation sessions in such a place and used it solely for sleeping and eating. The cold made it barely suitable even for that. Getting up in the middle of the night to go to the bathroom was so unpleasant that we made every effort not to.

Staying in that terrible apartment guaranteed that I wouldn't forget what Sanjogananda had done. Knowing that he was someone not to be trusted and who used people to his own ends, I was sure I'd find a way to get even. One day, I thought, I'll catch him doing something outrageous—and I'll report him.

It wasn't long before I got my chance. Satish came back one day from a trip to Ankara and said, "Didi, remember Akasha? He's opened a yoga center in Ankara."

(I sure did remember Akasha. He was the young Filipino dada who had worked with us in Istanbul but had left the organization because he had gotten into a relationship with a Turkish woman. She was a yoga teacher who was older than Dada and had a kind of mystique about her. Dada Chitananda, who had been the first SS in the sector, had tried to convince Akasha to end the relationship. A kind man, Chitananda had given Akasha some time to do it, but he'd refused. The day came when Chitananda had no choice but to tell him that he would have to remove his uniform and could no longer be considered an acarya. I was in another room when it happened. I heard shouting and ran in, to find Akasha with his fists up. "Who do you think you are?" he was yelling at Chitananda. "You can't tell me what to do." He then swung at the much older Chitananda and hit him, grabbed a suitcase, threw some clothes into it, and left.)

"I saw Dada Sanjogananda there," Satish continued, "in Akasha's yoga center. Akasha is wearing his uniform again and people are calling him 'Dada.' He told me that Dada Sanjogananda gave him permission." Sanjogananda, it seemed, had gone to Ankara to set up some classes and give some initiations. He had ended up meeting Akasha, just happened to see him sitting on a park bench or something, and lacking a place to stay, had moved in with him.

I was filled with elation at Satish's words. This was just the kind of thing I'd been waiting for! Sanjogananda—with no official authority to do so—was allowing an ex-acarya to act as one in good standing, just so he could have a place to stay. This was the worst type of hypocrisy, a serious infraction of acarya discipline by any standard, and I was going to report it to the Central Office.

I carefully composed a letter to the General Secretary, then went to the post office and sent it, sure of its explosive impact once it reached him. I never received any formal acknowledgment from GS or Central Office that my letter had been received. However, I did hear from Sanjogananda the next time I saw him.

"How dare you write to GS Dada and complain about me!" he roared. He vowed to teach me a lesson I wouldn't soon forget.

I wasn't intimidated. We'll see about that, I thought.

Throughout my time in Ananda Marga, there were occasional experiences that left me disillusioned and depressed, that confronted me with the reality of the world I was trying to transform, and sometimes made me begin to wonder if it was all worth it. Coming across a personality like Sanjogananda within the organization was one. Getting to know the situations of two women, Nesrin and Natalie, was another.

I got to know Nesrin when I spent some time in the little center we had near the town of Lefkosa in the Turkish part of Cyprus. In this tiny village of a handful of small stone and concrete houses, there was little besides weeds growing in a barren, sun-baked landscape. I taught English to the children after they returned from school, and conducted yoga and health classes for the women.

Attendance at our weekly meditations was sparse, but there were a few regulars, including Nesrin. Trim and animated with short dark hair, she would arrive early every week and was often the last to leave. Nesrin was a good student and asked deep, insightful questions with an air of intense concentration. Unlike other women of the area, she had a job, spoke excellent English, and seemed completely independent.

One evening, Nesrin was subdued after meditation and appeared strained. After the other women left, I made some herbal tea. She was silent as I brought the steaming mugs over to the table. For a few minutes we sipped our tea quietly together.

"Didi, this is probably my last week here."

I looked up in surprise as she continued. "I don't think I'll be able to come anymore. My husband is returning."

A dark, threatening presence seemed to enter the room. I suddenly thought of Egypt, of Subira and her returning father.

"You see, my husband would never let me come here," Nesrin said. "I've only been able to because he has been away on business. He'll be back in four days."

Another Muslim man returning from a business trip, I thought, sighing. I reached out and touched her arm lightly.

"You know we'll miss you. But at least you can practice at home. Maybe your husband will go on another trip, and you can come back then."

Nesrin took a deep breath. "Didi, my husband beats me . . . and my daughter. She's terrified and can't sleep knowing he is coming back."

My heart sank. I knew from experience that some Muslim men beat their wives. In my travels, I had met many good Muslim men who conducted themselves well, according to the true spirit of their faith. But not all! Walking down the streets of Istanbul, for example, I'd sometimes heard the sounds of beating and of women crying. I knew that most women in Nesrin's situation had little or no choice. They had no money of their own, no means of support, no possibility of a job. But Nesrin did.

"Nesrin, why don't you leave him? You have a job."

She shook her head and looked away. I waited as she picked up her mug and sipped.

"I can't," she finally said. "Everyone would turn their back on me. In my community, there are no divorces, no women living on their own with their children. I could lose my job. And I have nowhere to go. No one would give me a place to stay."

She had likely thought about leaving him before, spending many a sleepless night herself, tossing in bed, turning the prospect over and over in her mind, looking for a way out and finding none.

I cast about for something I could do. *You can come and stay with me,* I thought to say. But I knew that would be only the most temporary of solutions. I wouldn't be staying much longer in Lefkosa. What would happen to her after I left? I felt utterly powerless.

"I'm so sorry," I said.

"Don't be. That's just the way our society is."

We finished our tea in silence. As she got up to go, she said, "It's been such a wonderful experience coming here every week. I want to thank you for all your time, Didi."

Her voice broke. We hugged, long and hard. I felt my eyes sting. My best and most faithful student . . .

"There's got to be something I can do," I found myself saying, even though I knew there wasn't.

"There's nothing you can do. I'll try to practice at home."

We hugged again and she left. Leaning against the door, I watched her go, tears falling from my eyes. She turned and waved before going around the corner.

For days afterwards, I found myself hoping against hope that she would return, that smart and capable Nesrin would walk in the door and say, *Somebody has to stand up and do something to change things. I've decided to leave him.* In so doing, she would become the pioneer sorely needed by her society. But I wished in vain. Knowing that I couldn't fully understand the difficulties she would face if she were to take such a step, I was just an outsider looking in, a visitor from another world.

I never saw Nesrin again.

Natalie's situation was similar, even though she was an American. Tall, blond, and attractive, she lived with her Iranian husband and two young children in Tehran. I sometimes stayed in her spare bedroom when I was in the city. (In places like Tehran where we had no yoga center, I usually conducted classes and meditation in the homes of students. Natalie was one of those who came regularly to my classes in the spacious apartment of a Swiss woman who had come to Iran for a tour of diplomatic duties.)

The husband was a businessman who was often out of town and was apparently doing well: Natalie's kitchen was bigger than many of its counterparts in the States and was equipped with not only a large refrigerator, but a dishwasher and a food processor.

During evening conversations in the kitchen, she would confide that her husband disapproved of her yoga practice. "He doesn't like me to go out." she said. "He accuses me of going to group orgies when I tell him I'm going to yoga class."

One afternoon when I arrived at her home, Natalie welcomed me in but didn't seem her usual self. She had shadows under her eyes, and she looked ill. "I'm fine," she said when I asked. "Just a bit tired is all. Are you hungry?" she asked leading the way into the kitchen. She seemed not to want to talk about what was bothering her as we sat there having a cup of tea and a snack, and I didn't press her.

That evening, after she put her children to bed, Natalie joined me for a meditation lesson. We got settled, I sitting cross-legged on my folded blanket and Natalie sitting with a pillow for support. I gave her the second lesson, and we settled in to meditate. Then we heard shouting.

"Natalie! Natalie, where are you?" It was her husband, and he sounded angry. I was taken aback. When had he come home?

"Come here at once!" he shouted.

Natalie and I exchanged fearful glances. Without a word, she got up and went out. After an ominous silence, I heard more shouts, followed by slaps and thuds. Natalie's cry, "Please, don't!" was followed by more sounds of beating. I lay on the floor and put my hands over my ears.

What should I do? I wondered, quaking. Should I go there and tell him to stop? No, that would just make things worse. He would surely throw me out, after beating me up, too. If I just stayed there, I told myself, maybe he would remember I was in the house and wouldn't really hurt her. So I stayed where I was, half expecting him to come after me after finishing with Natalie.

The next morning, after a sleepless night, I came down to the kitchen, and there was Natalie sitting at the table, her eyes and mouth bruised and a large welt turning purple on her forehead. I was shocked to see her condition. What other bruises were there that I couldn't see?

"I'm sorry, Didi, but I can't do meditation anymore," she whispered.

"Natalie, are you okay? I'm so sorry! I feel like all this is my fault! I shouldn't have stayed here."

"It's nothing serious. I'm sore, that's all," she said. She took a deep breath, then said, "Didi, I didn't know how angry he was. I should have. It's not your fault."

I wondered why she stayed with him. After all, she was an American. Couldn't she just take the children, go to the States, and stay with her relatives until she got on her feet? What compelled her to stay with such a man, or made her think she had to? Was it fear of what he would do if he found out she was trying to leave? Whatever it was, it was none of my business. I hugged her carefully so as not to press any sore spots. Then, fighting back tears, I went back to my room, rolled up my sleeping bag, packed my bag, and left.

Chapter 8

Iran: Dodging the Secret Police

Not long after the incident with Natalie, things started getting worse in Iran. Cairo Sector workers had been going in and out of the country for years, mostly passing though on our way to and from India, but it had been difficult to get much going there because of the shah. People found it hard to trust us. They were interested in learning yoga and meditation, but as soon as talk turned to other matters, especially political ones, they would fall silent. (It was, of course, quite dangerous to talk about the shah; people got picked up by the police for even the mildest of criticisms and ended up disappearing.) Finally, though, the dadas managed to get enough support to open a small center in Tehran, which Dada Mohan was running.

One winter in the late seventies, I was on my way back to Istanbul along with an American dada named Ravindra and another didi. We got to Tehran early in the morning. Along with being tired, hungry, and dirty (the usual state of affairs), we were also cold. We'd just been in Calcutta, where even in January, it was warm in the daytime. In our rush to leave, we hadn't given much thought to what it might be like in Tehran and had arrived wearing sandals. Now, freezing winds were whipping around our exposed feet as we hurried along. We could hardly wait to get to the jagrti and were looking forward to having a bath, changing our clothes, and getting something hot to eat. Our plans were to rest for a few days, get money from Mohan for bus tickets, and then continue on to Istanbul.

But things didn't exactly go according to plan. When we got to the jagrti, we found it locked, with a sign posted on the wall: THIS CENTER IS CLOSED. ANYONE COMING TO IT SHOULD REPORT TO THE IRANIAN AUTHORITIES. A phone number and an address were listed.

We had no intention of following those directions, which had surely been posted by the SAVAK, the shah's brutal secret police. Instead, we went to look for the landlord, who lived in the same building. He came to his door and in whispered tones described how the authorities had shown up one day a few weeks earlier, seized Mohan (the same dada who'd been briefly arrested in Egypt for taking photos), and locked up the building.

"Do you know anything about Mohan?" I asked. "Where he's being kept or if he's all right?"

The landlord shook his head. "No, I haven't heard anything since that day." Then he looked around us towards the street. "You should leave now," he whispered. "If anyone sees me talking to you, I could get arrested."

It had started to snow, and we had to find shelter quickly because none of us had any warm clothing. The only warm things we had with us were blankets. These we wrapped around us; then we headed to the train station. "That should be a safe place to stay until we figure out what to do," Ravindra said. We got some curious looks as we made our way there. Ravindra was tall, thin, and bearded; with his sandals and blanket, he cut a Christ-like figure as we walked, surrounded by swirling snowflakes.

Once at the station, we pooled our meager resources and bought some bread.

"I have the number of a sympathizer," Ravindra said, "Dr. Mostashari. I'll try to call him." I had met Dr. Mostashari. He was an intellectual, a progressive thinker who hoped that Iran would soon be rid of the shah and would have a democratically elected government.

Ravindra was gone for what seemed a long while. I was just beginning to try to come up with someone else we could call (not Natalie, of course—and I was pretty sure the Swiss diplomat was away on vacation) when he came back with some good news. "Dr. Mostashari's invited us to stay with him. He's sending a car. But we have to be careful. He told me the shah's police have been watching him."

We waited at the station until late in the afternoon. Then under cover of darkness, we were whisked away to Dr. Mostashari's home. He and his wife welcomed us in. For once, I had a hot bath even though as a didi I was supposed to take only cold ones. I have to wash away the grime of the trip, I told myself and my spiritual superego.

When we sat down to our first hot meal in days, Dr. Mostashari told us about the situation in the country. "There's a real movement going on to get rid of the shah," he said. "Many of us are hopeful that there will be a change soon. But we have to be so careful! The police are very vigilant. I have friends who have been arrested."

Then he gave us a serious look. "You have to stay indoors. No one should see you coming or going—it's very dangerous." We were not even to look out the windows.

A few days later, Dr. Mostashari gave us money to get to Istanbul. We were so grateful for all the help he'd given us, even while putting himself and his family at great risk. "We don't know what we would have done if you hadn't been here to help us," I said right before we left.

He waved off my remark. "It's nothing," he said. "Just have a safe trip."

We got to Istanbul safely, but Mohan didn't fare as well. He ended up being held by the Iranian authorities for a long time.

When they released him after months of jail time, they took him to the Turkish border and dropped him off. Having no money, he had to hitchhike and arrived one day at the Istanbul jagrti dirty and gaunt—but alive. We were overjoyed. We hadn't heard anything the whole time and had feared the worst.

When I arrived in Tehran for the last time late in the summer of 1978, banks were burning and people were marching in the streets.[33] I dodged the fires and crowds and managed to get to the home of the Swiss diplomat. She had a fifth-floor apartment that afforded me a good view of the streets and the demonstrations. One day a crowd of school children were out marching and chanting anti-shah slogans.

"This is amazing," I said to her. "The last time I was here, most people were afraid to say anything against the shah, and now even school children are out in the streets!"

"Yes," she said. "Who would have thought it possible?"

I'd come to Tehran on my way to India, planning to get a new passport. I suspected I was blacklisted in India because they had my name from my visits with Baba. My hope was that a new passport, without old visa stamps, would get me into the country without any problems.

The day I went to the American Embassy, an angry-looking bunch of young Iranian men were there, some sitting on the steps and others milling around. I went up to a kindly looking older man who was standing off to one side, watching. I asked him what was going on.

"I'm not sure, but these men are up to no good," he said.

---

[33] Between October 1977 and September 1978, anti-shah protests grew from weekly to daily events. The protests culminated in a demonstration of some two million people in Tehran on September 7, 1978. It was among the largest demonstrations in history. In response, the shah imposed martial law, and his troops massacred more than two thousand demonstrators.

"I'm an American," I told him. "I'm thinking about going in to get a new passport."

"I wouldn't if I were you," he said. "There is a great deal of anti-American sentiment now in Iran. You'd be better off leaving."

I took his advice. Without getting a new passport, I went on to India (managing to get in by entering a border crossing where they likely had no list of blacklisted people). Little more than a year later, the American Embassy in Tehran was seized and hostages taken, maybe by some of the same angry young men I'd seen prowling around.

We never heard from Dr. Mostashari again or anything about him. I've often thought about him, though. I'm still grateful for how he helped us at the risk to his own family. What would have happened to us if he hadn't? He must have been disappointed with the way things turned out for his country. Ayatollah Khomeini and his cohorts were surely not the democratically elected leaders he'd had in mind all those years ago.

Chapter 9

I Blow My Chance at Ananda Marga Fame

(or: The Baby Comes to Haunt Me)

In the summer of 1978, the event which every Margii had been waiting and praying for finally happened: Baba got out of jail. His release made the front page of every major Indian newspaper and was also covered by papers around the globe. The headline in the *Washington Post* read, "Leader of Indian Sect Freed From Jail on Bail."[34] In its article, the *New York Times* put it this way:

> NEW DELHI, Aug. 2 — Prabhat Ranjan Sarkar, a former railway clerk who heads a controversial and mysterious Indian religious sect, was released today on bail after nearly seven years' imprisonment for the murders of several of his followers.
>
> The 58-year-old Mr. Sarkar, the leader of internationally known Ananda Marga Yoga Society, was carried out of jail in Patna, capital of the eastern

---

[34] *Washington Post*, August 4, 1978.

state of Bihar, in a chair and placed in a car, from
which he led a colorful procession of several hundred
followers. Mr. Sarkar, who is revered as the Anand
Murti, or "bliss incarnate," by sect members, reportedly
has grown weak during a fast in prison.[35]

Now that Baba was out of jail, Margiis would soon have
opportunities to see him. It wouldn't be long before crowds
would begin to descend upon Ananda Nagar, a large tract of land
owned by Ananda Marga in rural West Bengal, as well as other
places for *Dharma Maha Cakras*, or DMCs.

These were the greatest gatherings of Ananda Margiis.
Thousands would attend, including devotees from all over the
world. At DMCs, Baba would usually give several darshans,[36] the
last one, the official DMC talk which took place in the evening
of the last day, being the most important. At the conclusion of
the DMC talk, Baba would perform *Varabhaya Mudra*, a hand
position which was said to bestow blessings upon his devotees
while taking away their sufferings and fears. Margiis would
swoon, topple over, laugh, shout, or cry. Many were known to go
into deep states of samadhi.

The first DMC after Baba's release took place in Madras.
I made it there just in time, having arrived after yet another
grueling overland trip from Istanbul, just a few hours before the
DMC talk started.

After that DMC was over, I went to Calcutta, where I began
copying the senior acarya diary. I was the first Western didi to
copy the diary and was told that I would take an exam on its
contents, after which I would be eligible to become an avadhutika.
Avadhutikas (women) and avadhutas took special vows and were
given a new name by Baba. As mentioned earlier, they practiced
a more advanced kind of meditation, and in contrast to acaryas,

---

[35] *New York Times*, August 3, 1978.

[36] darshan: Sight. The guru gives a talk (while being gazed upon) in the
presence of his devotees.

wore full orange. If I passed the test on the senior acarya diary and became an avadhutika, I would be distinguished as the first Western didi to receive an orange sari and belt to replace my white ones.

After a few weeks of constant work, I finished copying the diary just in time to travel to Baba's next DMC in Patna. Baba gave a series of talks there, and I was fortunate to be able to sit near him often. I also tried to study for my upcoming senior acarya exam, but found it frustratingly difficult because I was sharing a room with others who had come to see Baba, a large group of children from one of our homes. I found it close to impossible to shut out the babble of their high voices. I had no problem meditating with noise, but studying was another thing all together.

All too soon, the day for Baba's departure arrived. He would be flying out from Patna airport, so before dawn that morning, I set out for the airport with Didi Vishaka. We walked part of the way, then hailed a rickshaw. In the early morning, all was quiet. The only sound was the creaking of the leather seat as the rickshaw wallah steadily pedaled. I looked out at fields still shrouded in fog, smelled the scent of cow dung rising from the earth, and was filled with peace. Almost no one was about, a minor miracle in a country where nearly everyone was an early riser.

Once at the airport, we went directly to the departure lounge, where a few Margiis were preparing a place for Baba to sit. Vishaka and I sat down close to where Baba would be and shared a smile. It had been well worth getting up so early! We would spend the time before Baba's arrival meditating. As I settled in, my senior acarya exam came to mind. I would be taking it the next day, and I had a lot of studying to do. The children would be leaving that afternoon, so there would be silence at last. But for now, I wasn't going to think about the test. I was just going to savor time spent with Baba.

As I meditated, I heard sounds of shuffling, of Margiis greeting one another as they pressed into the lounge. A large crowd had surely gathered. I opened my eyes to see devotees of all ages: little ones bundled up in blankets held on their mother's laps, toddlers, children with their black hair carefully oiled and combed, women in colorful saris, men in traditional kurtas and dhotis, and others in Western-style dress wearing pants and short-sleeved shirts. The oldest devotees, who'd been with Baba since the beginning, were bent over and walking with canes. A woman who recognized Vishaka came over with an infant and asked her to hold the baby as she wanted to do some meditation before Baba came. Didi happily complied, taking the infant onto her lap.

Returning to meditation, I found myself sinking into a profound state. There are times when meditation seems to just happen, when you close your eyes and plunge into deep absorption without effort. This was one of those times, and I was filled with profound serenity and a pervasive sense of bliss.

There was a flutter of activity: people stirring all around me, the electric sense of excitement that always swept through a space when Baba was arriving. I opened my eyes, and there he was, doing namaskar, looking right at me and smiling.

"How are you?" he asked.

An intense jolt of energy shot through me.

"Fine, Baba," I answered.

Baba settled down in the padded chair that had been brought for him and looked around, smiling and nodding at everyone. Groups of Margiis began to sing devotional songs. Baba closed his eyes and listened.

I resumed meditation, immediately sinking even deeper than before. Baba, I found myself thinking, I'm going to take my exam tomorrow, and if it is your will, I will become an avadhutika. I want to belong to you completely. I opened my eyes again and couldn't believe what I was seeing—because there was Baba looking at me again, beaming his sweet smile and nodding! Another shot of bliss went through me. How long this went on, I have no idea, but I do know this: it was one of the most profound experiences of closeness to the Guru I ever had.

The time came for Baba to board the plane. As some dadas escorted him onto the tarmac, people pressed against the fence hoping for one last glimpse. Baba walked up the steps to the plane, turned and folded his hands in namaskar, bringing them first to the space between his eyes, then down to his chest. The crowd called out "Baba!" as if with one voice, full of longing. I stood watching the plane taxi down the runway and take off, tears streaming down my face.

The next morning I was up unusually early. After meditating, I dove into my studying, savoring the silence; the children, along with their didi, were gone. I had a morning appointment with the dada who would give me my exam, the same one who had given the classes in Calcutta before I had become an acarya. We had agreed to meet at nine o'clock.

I was deep into the diary, absorbing information easily when the time came around. Well, nothing ever happens on time in India, I thought, and resumed studying. The next time I glanced at my watch, it was nine thirty. Dada's probably eating breakfast, I thought, but I should get over there just in case. I gathered my things together, then walked quickly over to the place where we were going to meet, where Baba had given his darshans during the DMC program.

As I approached the area, there was a vacant and forlorn look about it. A vague sense of foreboding stole into my mind. Something wasn't right. So much had been going on there just a few days ago. Along with the crowds, there had been tents and the mouth-watering aroma of chapattis and curries cooking on outdoor stoves and children calling out to one another. Now, everything was gone. I became aware of a sick feeling in my stomach, which only intensified as I looked around. I spotted one of the few Margiis who were still there packing up, and went up to him.

"Dada,"[37] I asked, "have you seen Dada Deveshananda?"

"Yes, Didi. He just left."

---

[37] Although this man was not an acarya, I called him "Dada." We used the term to address not only male acaryas but older men as well.

My heart dropped into my stomach.

"Left? What do you mean? Where did he go?"

"He went to the ferry," the man said. "He's going back to Nepal." I stood there in stunned silence trying to absorb the meaning of his words. Going back to Nepal? How could that be?

Panic started to diffuse through me. I ran to the road, found a rickshaw, and urged the driver to hurry to the ferry. We raced along, the countryside and my thoughts both rushing by in a blur. *I can't believe this is happening! It's not like I was very late, just a little late . . . But everybody's late in India!* I thought. *Did he forget that I was supposed to take my test?* We got to the ferry launch. No ferryboat was waiting. The place was deserted and Dada was gone.

I took the same rickshaw back. The adrenaline rush that had buoyed me up was gone as well, leaving me limp and hungry. And to make things worse, it was a fasting day. I had to take the train to Calcutta that very evening, and I wasn't looking forward to it. *I don't think I can face fasting today,* I thought. (Our fasting days meant no food or water for nearly thirty-six hours. We'd start after dinner the previous evening, fast throughout the day itself, and end with breakfast the following morning.) I went to the market and bought some fruit, *dahi*, and crackers; trudged to my empty room, and ate my lonely meal.

I got to Calcutta early the next morning thoroughly wrung out. And there was no getting around it: today I would have to fast. With packing, getting my ticket, and making it to the train, I hadn't even had time to eat properly. We didn't have a choice about fasting. It was one of the conduct rules. We were to fast four times a month. If I didn't want to, I had to get permission not to, and it was granted only in cases of illness. I wasn't sick, at least not physically, so I would have no choice. *I should have fasted yesterday,* I thought, berating myself as I bumped along in a motor rickshaw on my way to the didis' compound in Tiljala in Calcutta's southern suburbs. (As I was thinking this, I had my nose stuck in my bottle of Tiger Balm to ward off the stench wafting from the huge mountain of garbage we had to pass on our way to and from our Calcutta compound. One would think food would have been the last thing on my mind at that moment! As I passed it by, I caught sight of people (children, mostly) on the mountain, picking through the trash, hoping to salvage anything they could use or sell.)

Upon reaching the didis' compound, I paid the rickshaw wallah and dodged the mangy-looking dogs exploring the nearby trash pile. (In many areas of India, there was no trash collection, and people would throw their trash out the window or deposit it outside their door. Shamefully perhaps, we didis did likewise.) I lugged my bag to the large iron gate and rapped on it. When it finally opened, I nodded to the guard, dragged my bag over the threshold, and entered the building.

The aroma of chapattis and *sabje* greeted me. A few didis passed by, carrying bowls of *dahi*. Everyone had fasted yesterday and would soon be eating breakfast. Everyone but me.

Just then Ananda Kripa caught sight of me. "Malatii, have you seen Auntie yet?" She had a strange look on her face, as if she were trying to read something on mine.

"No."

"You haven't heard, then?"

"Heard what?"

"Go and see Auntie. She'll tell you."

"Auntie" was what we called Ananda Bhakti, the oldest avadhutika in the organization. Thoroughly mystified by Ananda Kripa's words, I entered Auntie's room and did namaskar. As she usually did when someone came to visit her, Auntie asked me to sit on her cot. But her usually open and affectionate demeanor was absent; not even the hint of a smile greeted me. *What on earth is going on?* I thought.

"Malatii, was that you holding the baby yesterday in the airport?" Auntie asked. "Baba was furious. He said, 'A *sannyasinii*[38] holding a baby! *Chi, chi, chi!*[39] She was sitting so close to me, she

---

[38] *sannyasinii:* Female renunciate.

[39] *Chi, Chi, Chi:* Signifies disgust or scolding.

could have touched my foot! Why was she holding the baby? Its mother was there!' "

Before I could say anything, Auntie continued. "Then Baba said, 'She must not be allowed to take the senior acarya exam. She must not be allowed to become avadhutika!' "

"Auntie, it wasn't me. It was Vishaka."

Her face registered shock. A moment of silence hung between us.

"Are you sure?" she finally said, her eyes narrowing behind her bifocals as she looked at me. "Everyone thought it was you."

"Yes, Auntie, I'm sure. Vishaka was holding the baby, and I was sitting next to her the whole time. Maybe that's why people got us confused. Who said it was me?" (For some reason, I felt guilty, as if I'd actually held the child. But this was one rap I wasn't going to take!)

"There was a dada sitting not far from you who reported that you had been holding the baby the whole time Baba was there," Auntie replied. "Well, I'm sure that we can clear this up," she continued. "Now go have your bath, take your meal, and we will go over to Baba's quarters this morning. It would be best to take care of it right away."

Auntie then shooed me out of her room, her usual manner returning. I would be taking my bath, but regretfully, I wouldn't be taking that meal![40]

A few hours later, when we went over to Baba's quarters, Auntie approached Kanakananda, Baba's new Personal Assistant (a powerful-looking man who reminded me of a boxer because his nose looked as if it had been broken in the ring), and some other senior dadas to tell them about the mix-up. I stood to one side as they conferred, the dadas glancing at me from time to time with bemused expressions on their faces.

---

[40] taking that meal: An example of the expressions Indians use while speaking English, which I also began to use. Indians often say "take your meal," "take rest," and so on. In my account I have also tried to be faithful to common grammatical mistakes Indians make when speaking English.

"They have promised to tell Baba," Auntie told me afterwards. "I am also trying to get a meeting in front of Baba. We will see."

But it was not to be. I never did take the senior acarya exam. I wasn't particularly surprised by this. After all, the dadas probably never informed Baba that I wasn't the one who had been holding the baby, and the fact that he had said, "She must not be allowed to take the senior acarya exam" would have made them think it inappropriate. Ironically, it was Vishaka who became the first Western avadhutika, despite her infraction. I couldn't believe it when I first heard the news. A little later, however, it helped me to remember what Dada Rupeshanandaji had told me all those years ago: "There is only one *liila*, and that is the Lord's *liila*." It was all just the Lord's cosmic dance. That was the only way I was able to think about it without getting really upset.

Eventually, I too became an avadhutika, although Baba had me wait several more years. I never doubted that I would; as I'd sat meditating that day in the Patna departure lounge, Baba had promised me just that. (And that senior acarya exam? It was never really implemented as a prerequisite for avadhutikaship after all.)

Looking back on it, though, it's puzzling that I never wondered why Baba had made such a fuss about a didi holding a baby. It had seemed like such nice thing to do at the time: taking the infant and giving the mother a break so she could focus on Baba. Maybe he didn't want us didis associated in any way with something as messy as taking care of a child—or with the process that had brought about its existence in the first place. Maybe he was afraid that a didi's taking a child upon her lap would bring out her maternal instincts and cause her to leave her acarya life to pursue motherhood. But that couldn't have been it. Didis took care of children all the time in Ananda Marga children's homes. It must have had something to do with Vishaka's holding the child on her lap so close to him.

Whatever the reason, Baba had made holding a baby seem like something dirty.

Chapter 10

More Experiences with the Guru

A year later, I was back in Calcutta for a meeting. As I dragged my bag into the didis' office one afternoon, reeking from yet another long and mostly overland trip from Turkey, Ananda Kripa was the first to catch sight of me.

"Hurry!" she said, "You are being called for PC!" PC, or Personal Contact, was supposed to be a special event, when you would get to be alone with the Guru and he would say something special.

I was taken aback; the thought of appearing before Baba in my present state was unthinkable. "I have to take a bath first," I said.

"As you like, but you're being called now. If you don't go, you might not get another chance." She paused and almost glared at me, a tight look on her face. "Baba wants to see you," she continued in a steely voice when I didn't answer. "He doesn't care what you look like."

Even though I knew that getting on the wrong side of Ananda Kripa wasn't going to help my chances, I felt so filthy, I decided to risk it.

"I just can't go like this, Didi. I'll go another time."

Ananda Kripa was one of the original didis, one of the first Indian women to become a whole-time worker. The first one was Ananda Bhakti; the second, Ananda Gajara (a didi of truly enormous proportions who waddled more than she walked); and the third, Ananda Kripa.

She liked to tell the story of how it had come about. She'd been a young girl of sixteen from a small village. After her Ananda Marga initiation, she had felt a strong yearning to serve Baba even though she hadn't yet met him. Early one morning while her parents were still asleep, she packed a small bundle of belongings, walked to the local railroad station, got on a train (she had never even seen one before, let alone been on one), and never looked back.

That kind of spirit was reflected in her work ethic. Despite being small and thin, Ananda Kripa could work from dawn to dusk and then some. I sometimes went with her on food collections for the needy, then assisted her in preparing the food collected, cooking *kitchuri* (a mixture of lentils and rice) in mammoth pots on open fires inside Baba's walled compound in the Lake Gardens section of Calcutta. As the *kitchuri* simmered, we'd put out lines of leaf plates (large leaves stitched together to form a more or less circular plate), one line facing the other, getting ready for what we called a "mass feeding." I don't know how people knew that food was about to be served. Maybe it was the smell of food and smoke commingling and wafting over the wall or maybe it was the sounds of bustling activity, but somehow, when it was time to eat, people would be gathered outside the gate. In they would come, sitting cross-legged in front of the plates, forming two lines. *Kitchuri* was shoveled from the big pots into smaller ones, which were then carried along by one or two didis, while another ladled some of the mixture onto each plate. The people ate with their fingers in the Indian fashion, chattering with one another, then called out or gestured to their plates, letting us know they wanted more. At the end of it all, after everything had been cleaned up and most of us were nearly dropping with exhaustion, Ananda Kripa seemed hardly the worse for wear. It was as if she had some hidden reserve of energy that never ran out.

Getting PC after I turned down my first chance did prove difficult. Ananda Kripa had a lot to do with who saw Baba when, and I suspected that she had arranged things to make her warning come true and teach me a lesson.

One morning I was sitting on the floor outside of Baba's room in a line of mostly male Indian devotees, waiting to have PC. As people went in one by one, the line got smaller, until the man in front of me finally got up to go in. My heart leapt. I was next! I was about to close my eyes for some last-minute meditation when Ananda Kripa came out, announcing that Baba had finished giving PC for the day.

"He is going to take his lunch," she said.

Mutely, I got up (along with a few Indian women who'd been sitting right behind me), went to a corner of the office, and sat down. Typical! I thought. The PC line stops right when it gets to the first woman in it! Even though it might very well have been Ananda Kripa who had arranged things to turn out that way, the incident reminded me of just how often women were treated like second-class citizens in the organization.

I drifted off into a dark reverie, thinking about all the times I'd witnessed didis being treated unfairly, recalling in particular one winter DMC at Ananda Nagar. The dadas had been set up nicely in several buildings, where they could spread out and be comfortable, but all of us had been crammed into one small building. Even the most senior of didis had been packed in with the rest of us; we slept side by side, like sardines in a can, our lodgings so cramped that sleeping bags and blankets spilled out onto the verandah. It had been cold, and the only buffer between the concrete floor and the blankets was some straw. A bit like a manger, I'd thought at the time.

Add to that the fact that there was only one latrine. I tried to avoid using it at night but remembered well the one time I couldn't. Shivering with cold, I had stepped over sleeping bodies one after another, looking for a place to place one foot, then the other. Once outside, there were still more bodies to straddle until I got to the latrine. Then, turning on my flashlight (an absolute necessity—without one, you'd likely step in excrement because the latrine was overflowing), I went in, positioned myself carefully and held my nose. I suspected that some didis avoided the latrine altogether, going out to the fields under cover of darkness to relieve themselves. If so, they wouldn't have been the only ones who went there; the thousands of other Margiis attending DMC underscored the general dearth of facilities.

Mornings, we had to drape our freshly washed saris, petticoats, and uniforms over every available bush and shrub—there was nowhere else to put them. (And it wouldn't do for any man passing by to see our underwear. We had to hide it under our other clothes.) When we returned late in the afternoon, we'd snatch our things off the bushes, hoping that everything would be there, but clothing often went missing.

It wouldn't have been so bad if the dadas had had to deal with similar conditions. As it was, remembering how comfortable they'd all been still made me furious. Why doesn't Baba do anything about these things? I thought.

A sudden rush of activity brought me out of my musings.

"Didi!" someone shouted. "Didi, come! Baba is calling us for class!"

At first, I didn't get up: I was simply too depressed. I can't go see Baba feeling like this, I thought. He'll know what I've been thinking.

"Didi, hurry up! We're going!" the voice called out.

The realization then hit me that Baba would know my state of mind whether I was in the room with him or not. This made me jump up and join the others just as they were going out the door.

About ten of us, mostly women with a few dadas mixed in, crowded outside of Baba's room. Soon we were being waved in. We did *pranam* and then sat on the floor in a circle around Baba, who was sitting in an upholstered chair wearing a white lungi and a yellow satin shirt. I noticed his comfy-looking slippers; he looked just like a father sitting around with his family. Before saying a word to anyone else, Baba turned to me and said, "Never in any arena of your life should you give scope to self-cheating or hypocrisy," while raising a finger for emphasis. I had little time to digest that powerful remark because Baba looked around at all of us and continued speaking.

"Burka," he said. "Do you know burka?" Some of us, including me, nodded.

"The burka completely covers up a woman, except for the eyes." Baba made two circles with each thumb and forefinger, brought them up to his eyes, and moved his head around.

"The burka does not allow a woman to get light or air, her health breaks down, and she suffers," Baba continued, his voice taking on more power.

"Accha!" [41] Do you think Ananda Marga would allow women to suffer like this?" Baba paused and looked at each of us. "Ananda Marga will *never* allow women to suffer like this!" In the sudden silence, the room seemed to vibrate with his words.

I felt overjoyed. After I had been in the depths of depression, Baba had spoken especially to me and to what was in my heart. Not only had he addressed the suffering of women, he had given me a personal message. I took it to mean that I mustn't tolerate hypocrisy whenever I encountered it and ought to speak out about it. (I'd already seen instances of hypocrisy amongst Ananda Marga workers, Sanjogananda being one, and I *had* spoken out.) Even more important, I thought, I mustn't be hypocritical with myself.

(It was indeed a powerful message, one I have thought about and been guided by in difficult times over the years, even since

---

[41] *Accha!*: Okay! All right!

leaving the organization. However, it has turned out to be a mixed blessing. I have always had a perfectionist streak, which may have made me misinterpret Baba's remark. Or perhaps his words just served to increase my perfectionist expectations of myself and others, resulting in intolerance for other people's failings or incompetencies, as well as my own. Baba seemed to be saying that he expected perfection, but who is perfect in this world?)

Even though I'd been blessed with a personal message, I still longed to have PC and asked Ananda Kripa to remind Baba that I hadn't yet had it. One afternoon, she told me that she had spoken to him about it. "Baba said, 'I have already told her what she needs to know'," Didi reported, then raised her eyebrows inquiringly. I said nothing, but I knew what Baba meant by those words.

Even so, I did get PC right before I was about to leave and go back to Turkey. Being low on funds, I was going to go to Bangladesh first—to Dacca, where I'd been assured by Dada Pareshananda, the Office Secretary, I could get a cheap flight to Istanbul on Aeroflot. My PC didn't seem particularly remarkable at the time. Baba asked me where I was going next.

"To Istanbul, Baba."

"Are you going directly to Istanbul?"

"Yes, Baba. I'm leaving tomorrow for Dacca. I'll get a flight to Istanbul there."

Baba repeated his question. "You are going *directly?*"

"Yes, Baba," I said again. "I have to get there for RDS." This was a meeting in which we would report on our work (review), assess its shortcomings (defects), and come up with solutions. As acting SWWS for Cairo Sector, I needed to be there.

I should have been warned by his words. Everyone spending time with Baba realized he never spoke needlessly. It would have been purely incidental for an ordinary person to have repeated such a question, but not for Baba.

The fact that Baba never said anything meaningless or untrue was something I'd experienced before—like the second time

I had visited him in jail. When I had told him that I'd been reposted and would be working in Turkey and Iran, Baba had said, "Ah, Iran! Do you know why the banking system in Iran is not a strong one?"

"No, Baba," I'd replied.

"It is against Muslim law to charge interest," he said. "Today's banking system is structured around interest. Therefore, Iran's banking system is not a success."

A few months after that visit, I spent some time in Tehran and a made a point of asking a Margii sister about the banking system.

"Do banks charge interest here?"

"Of course, Didi," she had answered. "Banks function here just like in the West."

For a while, I was mystified. How could Baba be wrong? Many months later, however, the shah was overthrown, and hard-line clerics, headed by Ayatollah Khomeini, came to power. They established Islamic law throughout the country. At that point, the banks did indeed stop charging interest. Baba had been right, merely speaking in present tense about an event that was to take place in the future.

But despite this powerful experience of what I considered to be Baba's omniscience, on this occasion I remained oblivious.

I flew to Dacca the next day as planned, went to the Aeroflot office to book my flight, and was told that there were no flights to Istanbul within my price range. I had been misinformed and had gone to Dacca for nothing. How was I going to get back to Istanbul in time for RDS? How was I going to get back at all? The only real possibility was to return to India, then travel overland, alone. It would mean days without bathing, and days and nights sitting in smoke-filled buses surrounded by men—but it could be done.

Previous overnight journeys on Turkish buses then came to mind. It seemed like everyone on board smoked constantly. The windows didn't open, so I would sit with my nose pressed to a tiny crack in the window trying to get some air. Sometimes I would light incense, thinking if I was going to breathe in smoke, it might as well smell good. Invariably, some of the men would protest and I would have to put it out.

With this to look forward to, I found a cheap hotel for the night and then took a morning flight back to Calcutta. While going through customs, I was taken aside by an official and told to wait in a small room. Another official, wearing a khaki-colored uniform complete with a thick black leather belt and a nightstick at the waist, came in and sat down in the chair opposite me, placing his elbows on the table.

"You are not being granted permission to enter India," he began. "Are you not known by the name of Acarya Malatii? Are you not an Ananda Margii?"

There was no use denying it. "I am," I said.

"Ananda Margiis are not allowed to enter India."

Now what? Ever since visiting Baba in jail, I'd been sure that sooner or later, I would be prevented from entering India. My present predicament might have resulted from those visits. More likely, though, it was the result of something more recent—the time I had renewed my visa in Patna when I'd been there attending DMC and studying for my senior acarya exam. My visa had been about to expire, so I went to the local immigration office to renew it. Nothing unusual about that—tourists did it all the time. What was unusual, though, was how I'd gone about it. While all other Margiis renewing their visas had always made every effort to hide the fact that they were members of Ananda Marga, I'd decided to go in full uniform. I'm proud of who I am, I remembered thinking. Why should I hide it?

On that occasion, when I walked into the office, the officials sitting there stared at me with shocked looks on their faces for what seemed like a long time. Finally, one of them cleared his throat and said, "Yes, madam? How may I help you?"

"I'd like to renew my visa."

He asked me to sit down.

"Excuse me, but you are an Ananda Margii, isn't it?"

I told him I was.

"Excuse me, madam. What is your good name?"

"Acarya Malatii," I said.

"Well, we don't usually extend the visas of Ananda Margiis, madam."

"I know," I said, "but I'm only asking for another month."

"Oh," he said, "are you here for the present gathering of Margiis?" He had obviously heard about the DMC taking place not far from the office.

"Yes," I told him. "And it's been wonderful! So many Margiis have come to see our guru after all the years he was in jail."

"Are there many people like you—from outside India?" He then produced a handwritten list with acarya names on it. The paper was tattered as if it had been handled over and over again. "Are these some of them?"

I looked at the list, recognized some of the names, but said I did not. He wasn't going to get any information out of me!

"Tell me . . . What is it about Anandamurti that you people are so attracted by?"

Then ensued a long discussion about Baba and the philosophy of Ananda Marga. The official must have been curious about it because he seemed quite taken by me and what I had to say.

In the end, I got the visa extension. I left the office feeling jubilant and proud of what I had accomplished. Getting a visa extension while in full uniform: had any other worker from outside India ever done such a thing?

But that was then. The situation I found myself in now was different. Unfortunately, the luck I'd had in Patna was unlikely to be duplicated here in the Calcutta airport; it was known that these officials were especially difficult to get around.

Still, I tried, telling this one that I wanted only to travel though India on my way to Turkey. "Impossible," he said. "You will have to fly out of the country. Because you came from Dacca, you will have to return there on the next flight." Then, pushing his chair back, he got up and left.

Return to Dacca? That would be going in the wrong direction. I'm not going to do it, I decided. And since they already know I'm an acarya, I might as well put on my uniform.

I found a bathroom and put everything on. I would show them I was proud of who I was and that I wasn't scared of them.

Once I emerged, another official took me to an isolated area of the lounge with a few chairs scattered about and told me to wait there. Now that I was in uniform, I noticed that I was treated with a little more respect. A while later, the same man came back and said, "Didi, are you not hungry? You should take food. I will bring you some meal tickets."

"I'm fasting," I told him (another thing I'd decided to do). "It's wrong for you to refuse to let me pass through India, so I won't take any food from you."

There would be no flight to Dacca for more than a day. Knowing I had a long wait ahead of me, I settled in for some serious meditation.

Towards evening, they told me that I had to pay for a ticket to Dacca. Even though I had heard stories of didis who'd been literally carried on or off planes by airport policemen, I was adamant about not buying a ticket. There was no way they could force me to do it; they would have to search my body to find my money, and I doubted that any Indian man would go that far. If I had to go back to Dacca, it would be with the Indian government paying my way. That would be my revenge.

Around noon the next day, the first in a series of officials, looking progressively more nervous the closer we got to the evening departure time, came up to me.

"You have to pay for your ticket," he told me.

"I don't want to go to Dacca," I said. "If you want me to go there, you'll have to pay."

The last appeal was one hour before departure. I refused again. Shortly thereafter, I was handed a ticket to Dacca, courtesy of the Indian government. I had won my small victory. As I stood there looking at my ticket, Baba's words suddenly came back to me: "Are you going to Istanbul *directly*?" How could I have been so clueless?

It took me over three weeks to get to Istanbul. From Dacca, I spent most of my remaining funds on a one-way ticket to Karachi. Once there, I called the jagrti in Istanbul and informed the dadas about my predicament. After it became clear that no one was going to send me anything, I went to the American Consulate and asked them for a loan. They would give me money, they told me, but only if I went to the United States. "But I don't want to go there," I said. "I want to go to Turkey. It costs much less to fly to Turkey than it does to the States. Why can't you give me a loan for that?" My superior powers of reasoning were lost on them, and I didn't get a cent. Eventually, the consulate contacted my parents, and they sent me some money. I was mortified that it had come to that. I felt shame that I had to take money from my parents, but I had no other way out of Pakistan.

It had been a while since my parents had heard from me. Before the consulate contacted them, maybe they had been thinking I was still in Israel. I knew they weren't happy with what I had decided to do with my life, but I sometimes imagined them telling each other that at least I was doing it in Israel. I didn't spend any time, though, imagining what they had to have been feeling once they got the news that their Jewish daughter was stranded in Pakistan, of all places, and wanted to go to Turkey. Very different from Israel! At the time, I didn't allow myself to think about any of this. I didn't want to think about my parents at all.

When I finally got to Istanbul, I had missed the RDS meeting by two weeks. Shivapriya was the first person I saw. "You won't believe this," she said in the impish way she had, "but we didis had a close call one night during RDS."

"A close call? What do you mean?" I asked, smiling. I was expecting a funny story; Shivapriya liked to joke around and make small incidents seem like major ones.

"One night, Dada Sanjogananda kept us in our meeting later than usual. When it ended, he told us we would have to stay at a sister's house. He sent us out alone, without an escort. We took a *dolmuş*.[42] I felt a bit funny getting on because we were the only passengers. After a while, the driver made some turns he shouldn't have. When we questioned him, he just smiled in a strange way and kept going. That's when we knew we were in trouble."

The smile left my face. "What did you do?"

"We thought of opening the windows and screaming to passersby, but there weren't any. The back streets were all deserted, so we decided we had to do something. We waited until he slowed down to make a turn. Then we opened the door and jumped." My face must have shown the shock I was feeling because Shivapriya hurried to say, "Don't worry, no one got hurt. He wasn't going very fast."

At first, I felt relief. Then, seconds later, anger welled up, partly at Sanjogananda, partly at my own stupidity. How could I have ever trusted such a man? He took my money so we had no jagrti for the didis to stay in! (We'd long since gotten rid of that freezer of a room Shivapriya and I had been renting.) And now he keeps them late at RDS and doesn't even bother to provide safe transportation, or a Margii brother to accompany them!

This incident achieved a certain notoriety in the organization and would come to be known as the "The Kidnapping." Believe it or not, I ended up being held responsible, despite having been thousands of miles away in Pakistan at the time. And the one who had told people at Central Office about it? Sanjogananda himself! He had managed to put the blame on my shoulders where, despite my best efforts, it stubbornly remained.

News of "The Kidnapping" even reached Baba. In 1979 he went on a tour of several sectors, including Cairo Sector. While visiting Istanbul, Baba talked about the incident while meeting with all the Cairo Sector didis who were present.

---

[42] *dolmuş:* A shared taxi or mini-bus running a pre-determined route.

"I have been told about the kidnapping," he said. "Where was your SWWS when this happened? She should not have allowed you to go unaccompanied so late at night."

Baba, it was clear, had been given a version of events similar to the one related to the Central workers. And I hadn't been there to defend myself. Once again, I wasn't where I needed to be; I was in Israel, brokenhearted at having been left behind when Baba's party had left Israel for Istanbul. I had accompanied Baba to the airport, but unlike the other workers, I hadn't gotten on the plane. Once again, lack of travel money was to blame.

The organization didn't provide financial support to its workers, so, like all workers, I had to raise money. As SWWS, I had to travel more than most workers; some of the places I went to had few Margiis and, thus, few resources. I even ended up getting to Israel late, after Baba had gotten there, because I'd had to travel overland. At the same time, Sanjogananda had managed to get a grip on most of the purse strings in places with more Margiis, such as Turkey and Israel. Despite all this, as acting SWWS of the sector, I should have gone with Baba to Istanbul. If I had just spoken up, the Central workers who were traveling with Baba would surely have forced Sanjogananda to arrange my ticket. It is one of the great regrets of my life as a didi that I did not.

It was only when I finally did get to Istanbul, a week or two after Baba had left, that I heard what Baba had said. Once again, Shivapriya was the one who told me.

"Shivapriya," I said, "why didn't any of you say anything to Baba about Sanjogananda? Why didn't you say I wasn't there? You should have told him!"

"Baba was in an irritated mood, Malatii. You know what it's like when you're sitting right in front of him. All we did was listen. No one dared say anything."

I knew that Baba, the all-knowing master, knew the real truth. He knew I had been in Pakistan while the RDS had been taking place. He had known what was going to happen; he had even warned me I wasn't going to get to Istanbul when I thought

I was! But Baba was speaking here as the organizational figure who relied upon what his workers told him. In this case, what his workers had told him was seriously flawed—and totally unjust.

I knew what Shivapriya meant about being afraid to say anything to Baba about it, though; people were often afraid to say anything lest he become angry. I knew I shouldn't be upset with Shivapriya, but that didn't keep me from feeling anger—and despair. Not only had my reputation been tarnished, but Sanjogananda had lied through his teeth and gotten away with it. I had to do something—but what?

After a few days of internal debate, I decided to go to India to state my case. It was important for the overall well-being of Ananda Marga that I go, I told myself. After all, I wasn't making the trip solely for the sake of my reputation. I was going to expose the true culprit in the incident—Sanjogananda, a dangerously ego-driven individual who was harmful to the organization. Baba's words echoed in my mind: *Never in any arena of your life should you give scope to self-cheating or hypocrisy.* If anyone was a hypocrite, Sanjogananda was!

What followed was a mad dash to Athens to raise money for my ticket. While renewing my visa to Turkey the year before, I had spent a few weeks with the Margiis in Athens. I'd been the first didi to go there, and they had been warm and welcoming. I figured they would help me raise the money. Not having enough money to take a train or bus to Athens, I decided to hitchhike.

When I told him of my plans, RAWA Dada tried to dissuade me. "Malatii, please don't do this," he pleaded. "It's much too dangerous for a woman. Just write a strong letter to Center." I saw the concern written on Dada's fine face and felt grateful for it. But I was determined.

"Thanks, Dada, but I really have to go," I said. "It's important."

RAWA Dada was proved right. Halfway to Athens, a truck driver lunged at me after making a lewd offer. As he tried to grab me, the truck slowed, and (just like those didis in Istanbul) I managed to jump out to safety. After that, I decided to get on an

Athens-bound train in a small Greek village, the name of which I no longer remember, rather than continue hitchhiking. I tried to collect money for a ticket from people at the station and got plenty of strange looks, but nothing else. So when the train pulled in, I got on without one, tried my best to look inconspicuous (at least I wasn't in uniform), and tiptoed around the train all night long to evade the conductor. Remembering that Baba, in one of his books, equated ticketless travel with stealing, I felt tremendously guilty all the while.

The Athens Margiis did their best to help, but I only managed to raise enough money for a one-way ticket. That just wouldn't do. The authorities had my name in Calcutta, so I couldn't fly there. There was a fifty-fifty chance of getting in if I flew into Bombay or Delhi; even though officials often passed the names of blacklisted Margiis from one airport to another, Indian bureaucracy was famously inefficient. But I simply couldn't risk it with a one-way ticket. If they stopped me, I would find myself in limbo: no ticket back, no ticket to anywhere. I'd had enough of that for a while! With reluctance, I made the decision to go back to Istanbul.

RAWA Dada was happy to see me.

"I think I'll send that letter to Central Office you suggested," I told him—but I never heard back from them about that letter, either.

Chapter 11

I Stop Off in Philadelphia on My Way to Fiji

By December of that year (1979), I found out that I had been reposted to Suva Sector and would be going to Fiji. This was great news. Not only would I no longer have to deal with Sanjogananda (which was wonderful in itself), but I'd be leaving the Middle East, a place where I'd had my fair share of struggles. It would be good to work in another part of the world.

I would be going to the States first. Although acaryas rarely returned to their country of origin (it was considered risky because the pull of family and old friends could prove too strong), I was going with the blessing of the organization: since I was blacklisted in India, I needed a new name. For that, I would be heading for Colorado—to Denver, the Ananda Marga Stop-N-Go for names. Word had it that you could get a new one there in a day, almost no questions asked. I'd already figured out what reason to give. My last name sounded too Russian, I was going to say, and people acted negatively towards me because of it. All that I needed was a copy of my birth certificate, which I would get in Philadelphia. Truth be told, I was looking forward to doing this. I had never liked my family name because it was so difficult for others to pronounce. Throughout my elementary school years, I had dreaded the first day of class when the teacher would call out my name and badly mispronounce it, sending all the other students into peals of laughter.

I flew into New York on a chilly evening a few weeks before Christmas. The city was ablaze with lights. On my way to the train station, crowds rushed past me, everyone bundled up and heavily laden with parcels. At one point, I stopped and peered into a decorated store window at little frosted trees loaded with ornaments and red and green lights. I watched the lights wink on and off for a moment before I went on my way, shaking my head. After six years of minimalist living, the abundance I now found myself surrounded by seemed overwhelming and decidedly decadent. Half a world away, people were living on the streets—bathing, cooking, and, yes, even dying—and here, people were lining up for the latest gadget, their lives already over-stuffed with goods, with no room left for the spirit. Thank goodness I've left all this behind! I thought, dodging one shopper after another.

At Penn Station, I bought a ticket to Philadelphia. . . . Philadelphia! The thought of returning there as a didi filled me with excitement. In just a few short hours, I would be at "the Castle," the jagrti in West Philadelphia where I had stayed right before leaving for training. Ananda Marga, having outgrown its original building on Regent Street, had bought the building from the followers of Guru Maharaji. The Castle, called that by local Margiis because of its rounded, turret-like upper floors, was spectacular. One of the upper rooms had been set aside for Baba,[43] its walls painted white and its floors covered in thick, luxurious wall-to-wall carpeting. Even though Baba had never been there, the room had a special energy, and I was looking forward to doing some meditation there.

---

[43] In many jagrtis, rooms had been set aside for Baba in the hope that he would come to the U.S. Although efforts were made to obtain a visa for him, he was never granted one.

But there was one thing I wasn't looking forward to: getting in touch with my parents. There was no way they would know I was in Philadelphia unless I told them. But even though Ananda Marga discouraged us from contacting our families, it just didn't seem right not to. I wouldn't be going to their house, though; as per the conduct rule, they would have to see me in the jagrti. It was hard to imagine my parents coming to the Castle; they belonged to such a different world. Even if they ended up coming, there was no question about how I would be dressed. I would be wearing my uniform. I was a didi, after all, and there was no way I was going to put on civilian clothes for them.

I was proud of my uniform, and the only time I would compromise on the wearing of it was when I deemed civilian dress necessary—when trying to get into India, for example. I hadn't even put on normal clothing when I had applied for Israeli citizenship a few years back. Because the Israeli "Law of Return" gives Jews the right to settle in Israel and gain citizenship, I had my parents send me a letter from the synagogue my family had attended when my brothers and I were little, verifying that I was indeed Jewish and had attended services there. I then took the letter to a hearing with the authorities in Jerusalem. Even though it would have made sense to dress like a normal person, I insisted on wearing my uniform. The only concession I made was to wear an orange scarf (which looked nothing like the one Didi Mohinii had once gotten me to wear, however!) instead of the veil. I can still remember sitting in front of the panel of three elderly Orthodox men in dark clothing who looked at me quizzically, then at each other, shaking their *payes* and beards and mumbling to each other in Hebrew. Needless to say, I didn't get Israeli citizenship, despite my letter. So if I hadn't compromised then, I wasn't about to now by wearing regular clothes for my parents.

But I was worried about their reaction. They're old, I thought as I boarded the train and took a seat. Maybe seeing me looking like a nun would be too big a shock. Maybe it would be better not to subject them to that. It was all so hard to figure out. I promised myself to think about it after evening meditation.

The seat next to me was vacant. As the train raced south in the darkness, I took off my shoes and, tucking my legs into a half-lotus, closed my eyes and tried to meditate. But it was no use. Painful images of my childhood slowly rose up like smoke, obliterating my mantra and everything else.

A summer's night when I was around seven: The family was in the car on our way home from somewhere, and my brother David and I were having a tickle fight in the back seat.

My father yelled at us to stop, but I was having too much fun.

"She's still doing it!" David shouted.

My father suddenly pulled over to the side of the road, the car careening to a stop.

"Get out," he said in a low, steely voice, "right now." I stole a glance at my mother, but she just sat there, staring straight ahead, her face like a mask.

"Get out!" he repeated, pointing towards the door with a thick, hairy finger. Slowly, I climbed out into the darkness, my heart thumping, and looked around me. I was standing in the middle of a dark road. Long and deserted and seemingly without end, it stretched out and faded into the night.

After letting me stand there for what seemed like an eternity, he told me to get back in. "Next time, I'll leave you if you don't behave," he threatened, pulling back onto the road with a lurch.

Another summer's night: I awoke to the sounds of a dog yelping in pain and my father's shouts. I jumped out of bed and looked out the window. There he was out in the back yard next to the doghouse, beating our dog with a rolled-up newspaper. Jingles often barked and howled at night, and this night it seemed my father was determined to get him to stop. Standing stock-still at the window, I felt helpless. Should I go down and try to make him stop? What if he beats me? In the end, I did nothing, getting back in bed and sticking my fingers in my ears to block out Jingles' cries, until my father dropped the newspaper with a curse and came back inside. Not long after, we found out that Jingles had a skin disease. Maybe that's why he barks so much, I thought when I heard the news. Later that summer, Jingles—the only dog we'd ever had—was put to sleep while I was away at camp, but the image of my father yelling and beating him over and over never faded from my mind.

A winter's day: I was running away from my mother, laughing. She had a belt in her hand and was chasing me up the stairs and into the bathroom. I took refuge in the tub, but she came at me with the belt and started hitting me. Although I put my hands up to shield my face, I wasn't at all afraid and found myself laughing harder than before. That seemed to make my mother even angrier, and she hit me with greater force. I kept right on laughing. Maybe I was happy because she was at least showing some emotion. Anger was better than nothing. "You'll never amount to anything!" she finally said, throwing the belt into the bathtub and turning away.

Our pet chicken: She would run around in the back yard, squawking. Every day, I would come out with some rice and she'd run towards me, her bright white feathers looking like a mini-blizzard, waiting for me to toss out the grain. Then I'd watch her peck at it until it was gone. That summer, I went to camp for a few weeks. When I came back, I was looking forward to seeing my pet; I'd been surprised by how much I'd missed her. In the car on the way home, I asked my mother how my chicken was doing. A look hard to read passed over her face and she didn't answer. "Mom?" "Oh," she finally said, "Grandmom took it to the butcher's."

I was astonished when I found myself wanting to cry.

"Thirtieth Street Station!" The conductor's voice washed over me like cold water. The train was already pulling into Philadelphia, and I was no closer to a decision about seeing my parents than when I had gotten on.

A Margii sister was waiting for me by the track. She took my bag, and we went outside to her car, then on to the Castle, which was now functioning as both a sister's jagrti and the local

Women's Welfare Office. It was much as I remembered, except a bit shabbier. It also had fewer people; the small number of women who were staying there almost seemed to rattle about in its large rooms.

"We don't know how much longer we can keep it," one told me, "This place is a white elephant. The heating bills are huge—almost a thousand dollars a month!"

I felt sadness at her words. So many of our centers were cramped places with low ceilings and little light. The Castle was one exception to that rule, and I would be sorry to see it go.

It felt really odd being back. One day, as I walked through Penn's campus and passed by the area that students called "the Green," I reflected on the totally different person I was from the girl who had attended classes, worried about her weight, smoked dope, and tried to fit in. When last I had been on the Green, there had been students strewn across its springtime lawns, swigging wine from jugs (despite everyone being clearly underage) or playing frisbee. Now, the trees were bare, and leaves were blowing around the feet of bundled-up passersby as they hurried along the wind-swept paths. I turned my thoughts away from the vulnerable and mixed-up person I had been when I had last walked here, to the one I was now: sure of my path and role in life, proud of what I had become. One bitingly cold afternoon, as a Margii sister and I set up an information table on Locust Walk and offered Ananda Marga literature and details on local yoga classes to students passing by, I marveled at just how far I had come.

But the issue of my parents wouldn't go away. I knew I had to see them but kept putting off making the arrangements. I couldn't bring myself to pick up the phone. *I shouldn't call them myself,* I would think every time I tried to get my courage up. *It would be more in keeping with the conduct rules to have someone else do it.* I couldn't acknowledge what I knew deep down: I wouldn't be able to handle the raw emotion that might be in their voices and wouldn't know how to turn down the request they would surely make that I come home.

One morning during meditation, the perfect person to make the call came to mind: Maetreyii, or Harriet Jenkins as she was known to the world at large. She was the deeply spiritual woman who, as the oldest Margii in the unit in the early days in Philadelphia, had been like a mother to me and others in their teens and early twenties. Maetreyii had met my parents before, so I figured it wouldn't be like a total stranger calling them. She was also Jewish, which would make it more comfortable for them, I thought.

Maetreyii and her husband brought them on a Sunday afternoon. I had spent the entire morning cleaning and rearranging the small sitting room where we would sit. As the time for their visit drew near, I wandered around, adjusting one chair, moving another. I fidgeted with my veil and straightened it. I couldn't sit still. And I had no idea what I would say. (Years later, Maetreyii would tell me what it had been like driving them to the Castle. "On the way over, I told them how wonderful I thought you were and all the things I had learned from you. I know they were touched, but they were scared to death. They were people who were afraid of emotion. Your mother really wanted to accept what you were doing. She was proud, but she was terrified as to what people would think.")

The doorbell rang. As I opened the door and they came in along with a rush of cold air, I was struck by how old my father looked. He seemed beaten down and shrunken in his overcoat and old-fashioned tweed hat with the feather in it. He gazed at me with sad, watery eyes. My mother was as made-up and powdered as she always had been, with the same bouffant hairdo and every hair spray-netted into place. She looked thinner than I remembered. They took turns embracing me and struggled not to let their emotions show, hiding the shock they surely must have felt at seeing me in uniform.

They had always been good at hiding things. Years later, when I discovered a secret my parents had kept from my brothers and me throughout our childhood and for many of our adult years,

I wondered if the cold atmosphere in our house had resulted from that secret. The effort to keep it locked within, the constant vigilance that any mention of it should not escape unawares when their guard was down, must have suppressed their instinct to express themselves freely to us.

My father asked if I would be staying in Philadelphia.

"No," I said. "In a few weeks, I'm going to a new place. I'll be working in Fiji."

A look of alarm passed between them. Then my mother said, "Marsha, we don't mind that you are involved with this group. But did you have to go so far away? Why couldn't you have stayed here and been involved?" I don't remember what I answered. I just remember that hearing them call me by my old name made me feel strange. And soon, I would be changing that name in Denver. What would they think if they knew?

Finally, it was all over. They hugged me again and asked me to keep in touch. Then they were gone. I could go back to being my new self, unfettered by parents and a past I would prefer to forget—that I was honor bound to forget as one who had been reborn to a life of service as a *sannyasinii*.

Chapter 12

Fiji: Working Underground

By March, I was on my way to Suva, Fiji's capital, arriving there late at night and checking into a hotel near the airport—a temporary measure as I couldn't afford to stay there more than a few days. There were no Margiis in Suva to stay with, so I would have to scramble. I had the addresses of some local Indian groups and planned to look some of them up the next day in the hope that someone would offer me a place.

Besides the dearth of Margiis, working in Fiji was going to be challenging for another reason: the deportation of some of our workers a few years earlier. This meant I would have to work underground, that I wouldn't be able to wear my uniform or introduce myself as an Ananda Marga teacher. Here I wouldn't be known as Acarya Malatii, but only as Sandra Holmes, the new name I had gotten in Denver.

I didn't regard it as underhanded or illegal to operate this way. After all, I had come to do good things, to teach people meditation and yoga and help in any other way I could. If working underground meant doing those things without giving away my true identity, so be it. Besides, I rather liked the prospect of working underground: it was kind of exciting.

I wasn't sure what to replace my uniform with but knew it would need to be something modest, something hinting at my status as a nun. I went to a tailor and had some long cotton-print skirts made, wide enough to sit down and cross my legs in for meditation; and some pastel-colored shirts of a cotton-polyester mix that wouldn't need ironing, with Nehru collars and long sleeves.

Through one Hindu group, I met an Indian woman, a middle-aged teacher who had never been married and lived alone. I guessed she sensed a kindred spirit in me because she offered me a room in her house located on the outskirts of Suva. I gratefully accepted. Our lifestyles were compatible; like me, she was a vegetarian and lived simply, dedicating her time to teaching and her Hindu practices.

The first part of my time in Fiji was unique in my Ananda Marga career in that I was completely alone: no other didis, dadas, LFTs, or higher-ups to work with or answer to. (There was an Indian dada there who was going by the underground name of Pragun, but our paths weren't to cross for quite a while.) Although I doubt I would have done much differently had there been others to work with, I did find it a bit liberating to do everything on my own and in my own way.

Now that I had a base of operations, I took a little time to explore—something I'd never taken time to do in any of my other postings. I found the island breathtakingly beautiful, with extravagant, multihued flowers, white sand beaches, and blazing sunsets over the ocean, which I took to watching while sitting in the shady waterfront park next to the YWCA.

Suva was a small town, quaint and Victorian at its center, no doubt the result of Fiji's having been a British colony for almost a century. On its streets were nearly equal numbers of native Fijians and Indians, with a smattering of Chinese and Europeans mixed in. I had known there were Indians in Fiji but was pleasantly surprised to find so many. (A large Indian population would surely bode well for my work, I thought.) I learned that the British had brought them over to work on Fiji's sugarcane plantations towards the end of the nineteenth century. Eventually, the Indians were given the choice of returning to India or remaining in Fiji. Most chose to stay; many who did so went on to become successful farmers or business people.

I soon learned about the native Fijians as well. Most lived in *koros*, or villages, the larger of which contained several *mataqalis*, or extended families. They worked on their plantations, raising bananas, cassava (tapioca root), taro, and other foods native to the islands. Some villages were quite large, numbering several hundred residents. Whenever I visited one, I found the people friendly and hospitable.

A few months after my arrival, I was invited to visit a small village of this kind by a Fijian man I'd met at a larger *koro* nearby. When I got there, one of the villagers invited me to stay for lunch. As we sat down on a coconut mat to eat, I was introduced to everyone, including a small boy who was sitting between two adults. Joeli appeared to be the darling of the village, with his sweet smile and the funny faces and gestures he made, sending everyone into gales of laughter.

But despite Joeli's smile, I found it hard to look at him. All over his body, he had weeping sores covered by flies, which the adults tried to keep away by waving fans. I felt drawn to this small boy. There had to be something I could do to help him. Towards the end of the meal, it came to me as I watched Joeli's mother preparing his bottle, pouring in black tea and adding several heaping teaspoons of sugar.

"Felise, black tea is too strong for such a small child," I said. "So much sugar isn't good for him either. Make him Fiji tea[44] instead." Later, I showed her how to pound fresh tumeric roots to extract the juice. "Just add it to some milk and have him drink that as a medicine," I said. "Tumeric is a blood purifier. Impurities of the blood often lead to skin problems like Joeli's."

---

[44] Fiji tea: Tea brewed from the young leaves of lemon trees or from lemon grass. Both were plentiful in the village.

"Anything that can help Joeli, we will try," Felise said, thanking me. Because I'd gotten the turmeric remedy from Baba's book about yogic health remedies, *Yoagika Chikitsa o' Dravyaguna (Yogic Treatments and Natural Remedies)*, I was confident the boy's condition would improve—if his relatives followed my advice.

That afternoon, I left the village to go to another part of the island. When I returned two weeks later, it was almost to a hero's welcome—for little Joeli's sores had disappeared! The villagers asked me to stay and I gladly accepted. I was happy to learn I wouldn't have to share anyone's living space: there was a small one-room building sitting vacant that would now be mine to use.

But the joy I felt at having a place of my own was short-lived. The wooden building's corrugated tin roof made it uninhabitable most of the time, so stifling in the heat of the day that it was impossible to stay inside. I didn't fare much better during the surprisingly chilly cold season nights. *How can it be so cold here?* I would wonder as I'd lie awake, shivering. *Isn't this the tropics?* Fiji, of course, is in the Southern Hemisphere, so by the time I had moved into my little house, winter had begun. Even so, I had never imagined that I would ever feel the least bit cold.

Next door was a traditional Fijian house made entirely of grasses and coconut leaves. It was wonderfully cool in the daytime heat yet warm and cozy during the chilliest of cold season nights, and I envied the family who lived there. Others in the village lived in more modern dwellings with corrugated tin roofs similar to mine, so they had the same problems. And during cyclones, such roofs posed a deadly danger: when ripped off by powerful winds, sheets of tin would become airborne and would fly around the village at great speeds, and woe to anyone who encountered one! Villagers shared stories of people being seriously maimed or even killed in this way when they'd gone outside to tie something down during a cyclone.

I soon learned that these so-called modern houses with their tin roofs were just one of several not-so-beneficial changes brought to the Fijians by the outside world. Their diet had undergone a similarly drastic transformation. Previously, the islanders had subsisted on native foods such as fish, cassava, breadfruit,[45] and coconut, but these had largely been replaced by white rice, white bread or chapattis (which the Fijians had learned to make from their Indian neighbors), sugar, and black tea. Breakfast in the village was usually rice or chapattis and black tea with sugar. Lunch was only slightly better, usually consisting of cassava, taro or breadfruit, green leaves and, very occasionally, fish; cassava or rice and tea with sugar were served at dinner. Many of the children showed signs of skin problems similar to Joeli's.

Mornings, as I watched the children eat their breakfast of rice and tea, I wondered how they could possibly function in school after such a meal. After mulling over the problem for a few days, a solution came to me, and I took a bus to the market in nearby Nadi to buy some powdered milk and oatmeal. Early the next morning, I fired up my kerosene stove and set a large pot of water to boil, adding oatmeal and milk to make porridge. Poking my head out the door, I saw one of the older girls and called out to her.

"Mili, tell all the children to come with bowls and spoons. And tell them to hurry! There's something hot for them to eat!"

"All right, Miss Sandra!" she shouted as she ran off.

It wasn't long before a crowd of curious youngsters gathered outside my house wondering what I had for them. One by one, they came in and had their bowls filled with porridge. They sat on the floor and ate. Soon, the last spoonfuls had been ladled out. The children looked up at me, remnants of porridge on their dark faces.

"Miss Sandra, that was good! Will you make it again tomorrow?"

"I'd love to. Just come again at the same time. And don't forget your bowls and spoons!"

---

[45] breadfruit: A type of starchy fruit. Villagers would pick the fruit before it ripened and would roast, boil, or bake it like a vegetable.

At breakfast time a few days later, who should come hurrying to my door in their brightly colored sulus[46] and carrying their bowls and spoons but two mothers! Despite myself, I felt annoyed. It's for the children, I thought, and if the mothers eat it, there won't be enough for them! But I said nothing, filling up their bowls and dishing out the remainder to the children who had lined up outside. Mothers and their little ones sat on the mat together eating porridge, enjoying it equally. If the mothers like it so much, I thought as I watched them, why don't they make their own?

That afternoon, I gathered the women together and explained the benefits of a porridge breakfast compared to one of rice and tea. "You see," I began, "not only is porridge delicious, but it's a very healthy food. Oatmeal with milk gives you lots of protein. White rice doesn't give you as much. And for the same money you would spend on a kilo of rice, you can buy a bag of porridge. The rice will be used up in one meal, but the porridge, when you cook it with water and milk, lasts for three or four!" I concluded.

They were all very attentive, nodding and smiling, seeming to agree that buying porridge and powdered milk made great sense. So with great anticipation, I waited to see the fruits of my demonstration breakfasts and my sales pitch. I was sure I'd soon see pots of porridge popping up all over the village—but the women all continued to cook rice or chapattis for breakfast and kept on coming to my house with their bowls asking for porridge. I wondered why. Maybe it was because rice, chapattis and tea, while not native foods, had become traditional ones for the villagers. Or maybe it was because oatmeal wasn't available at the local store and required an effort to go and buy in town. Whatever caused it, the failure of my breakfast experiment was a real blow to me. There were soon to be others.

Each day I would witness a constant stream of children and adults winding down the dirt track leading out of the village and

---

[46] *sulu:* A garment similar to a sarong.

onto the road where the local Indian grocery store was located. There they'd make their purchases; then the stream would wind its way back. One day as I watched, I found myself puzzling over the fact that even the largest families in the village would buy only the smallest quantity of food, a kilo of flour or rice, when they went to the shop. I puzzled over this. Maybe it hasn't occurred to them to buy large sacks of rice and flour, I thought.

So I asked one of the village men about it. "Buying things in bulk would save you time and money," I said.

The man, Waisale, gave me a long searching look. "You know, buying things in large quantities works for Indians," he said. "But we Fijians can't do it."

"Why not?" I asked.

"If I buy a large sack of rice, certain people would come and *kere kere* the rice, and then I would have nothing left," Waisale said. "But if I buy only a one-kilo bag of rice, everyone knows it is for my family and they won't *kere kere* it. *Kere Kere* is one reason why few Fijian people go out of their villages and plantations to get jobs on the outside," he continued, "because if they make money and buy something new, like a sofa or table, a relative or chief is sure to *kere kere* it, and off it will go."

I'd already heard of *kere kere*. I knew that when a Fijian's senior relative or some other respected person came to visit and saw something to which he took a fancy, he would point to it and say, *"Kere kere na . . ."* and name the desired object. The Fijian host was then honor-bound to give it to his or her guest. But I'd never imagined that it would go so far as to include food purchased for one's family!

A confusing mix of emotions passed through me as I understood the situation: sadness that a custom developed when the economy was based upon barter and everyone had a similar standard of living was now keeping the Fijians down, thus making them incapable of adjusting to the new ways which had come to their islands; admiration for a people generous to a fault, who would always welcome you into their homes and share with you what little they had; and frustration: no matter how hard I tried, nothing I did or suggested made any impact on the villagers or changed their lives for (what I thought was) the better.

I also visited Indian villages and was warmly welcomed to most; Fijian Indians were still strongly attached to the traditions of their ancestral land, yoga included, despite the fact that most of them had never been there. They still spoke Hindi, but their Hindi, known as "Fiji Hindi" (or as what they self-deprecatingly called "Jungly Hindi"), differed from that spoken in India. Their traditional foods had also undergone change. For example, they made chapattis from coarsely ground white flour called "sharps" instead of from whole wheat flour, which was used in India. As a result, Fijian chapattis lacked the vitamins, bran, and fiber of their Indian counterparts.

Aside from chapattis, poorer villagers could mostly afford only potatoes and eggplants. Those vegetables plus white rice and dahl made up the bulk of their diet. Their health suffered as a result, and many developed anemia and diabetes. They'd be much healthier if they made chapattis from whole wheat flour, I thought.

One day, I had what I considered a brilliant idea. I decided to carry some whole wheat flour around with me. Then I would make some chapattis and show the women how good they were.

So that's what I did. The first village I went to with my bag of flour was one where I'd been before. I promptly whipped out the bag and began preparing brown chapattis for the women to sample. (Having made stacks of them in training was really helping me out here!) As I rolled out one pancake-shaped chapatti after another and placed each one on the *tawa* (griddle) to cook, I explained that people in India ate brown chapattis and they were more nutritious.

"And they're very tasty as well," I said as I finished. "Try some."

As they did, their expressions of doubt changed to smiles.

"Sandra Didi, you are right, they *are* tasty!" they said. Several of the women even told me that they would try making them at home. I was overjoyed.

As I boarded the bus to go to another village, I had fond hopes of returning to the one in which I had just finished my demonstration, with visions dancing in my head of brown chapattis cooking on every outdoor mud and brick stove and the villagers' health improving by leaps and bounds. Soon, there would be less diabetes and anemia—all the result of the all-powerful whole wheat chapatti—and me.

When I returned a few weeks later, villagers came to greet me as I got off the bus and escorted me to the home where I'd be staying. After I finished my noon sadhana, some children carried in my lunch and placed it in front of me. As was usually the case, the enamel plate containing my meal was covered up with another. With great anticipation, almost holding my breath, I lifted the plate to find potato curry, rice, dahl—and three pale, weak-looking white chapattis, staring up at me balefully. I went to see my hostess, struggling not to let my disappointment (and yes, even anger) show. She was washing pots.

"Delicious as always," I began. "But what happened to the brown chapattis? I thought you wanted to start making them."

The thin, worn-out woman drew a deep breath. "Yes, I really wanted to . . . but, you know, my husband likes the white ones . . ." Her voice trailed off.

That was all I needed to hear. In an Indian village, the man's word—the man's whim—was law. It didn't matter if his wife found the brown variety delicious; it didn't matter if his children did; it didn't even matter if the brown variety was healthier. Nothing else mattered because he liked the white ones. And so it went, in village after village.

I didn't give up, though. Around the same time, the smell of molasses near the sugar mill in Nadi gave me another idea. The Fijians, I knew, never ate molasses. They considered it unfit for human consumption, so they fed it to their livestock. I remembered how dismayed and even outraged I'd felt when I had first learned that fact. So many of the village women suffer from anemia, and people are giving this iron-rich food to the *cows*? I was convinced there had to be a way to get the women to consume molasses. It was just what they needed.

So one morning I went to the mill with a few plastic gallon containers and convinced some of the men working there to give me molasses. I took to carrying a container around with me. Whenever I went to a village, I'd mix a spoonful into some warm milk, hand the glass to one of the exhausted-looking women, and say, "Try it. It kind of tastes like chocolate milk."

But getting the women to consume molasses proved no easier than getting them to switch from white flour to whole wheat. To them, molasses was animal feed, and animal feed it remained. So the cows stayed healthy, and the women remained anemic. Once again, I had failed to change lives and was disappointed. Would I never learn?

These incidents made me wonder if I had accomplished anything at all as a didi. When I had decided to become one, I was determined to be different from my parents, who, it had seemed to me, had a profound distrust of anyone unlike them. In contrast to them, I was going to embrace the world and all its peoples; I was going to help others and see the inherent goodness in them, no matter what their race, religion, or nationality. I was convinced that through Ananda Marga and its practices, including health practices like yoga postures and remedies found in Baba's books, I could help people live better lives and make the world a better place. When my idealism began to take hits from the real world, I began to realize that true changes in people's beliefs, traditions, and habits only take place gradually. In the meantime, the lack of tangible results to most of my efforts distressed and puzzled me.

It also made me reflect on how little I had really absorbed some of the yogic teachings. Ever since my initiation, I had contemplated the age-old philosophical truth that you own your actions, but not the fruits or results of them. Those you must be unattached to. This was one of the most useful of yogic teachings, but I found it difficult to put into practice. Time and time again, I was confronted by situations which required non-attachment to the results of my actions. Time after time, I had anticipated that my efforts would lead to change and improvement in people's lives. And time and time again, I ended up being sorely disappointed.

It never occurred to me that my very desire to change people's habits or impact their lives had more than a touch of arrogance to it.

I spent long hours on buses traveling from one Indian village to another. Since my living expenses were few and people usually shared food with me, fares were my main expense. I didn't charge for any of my classes, so I had to figure out a way to raise money. Meditation lessons in Ananda Marga were always free. Sometimes I would take money for teaching yoga postures, but I felt reluctant to charge even for that. Besides, even if I had wanted to, few in Fiji could afford to pay much of anything.

So I started little businesses, carrying pencils and erasers with me and selling them for pennies of profit. At one Indian village, I grew a patch of cilantro and sold small bunches of it. In other villages, I made coconut sweets from freshly grated coconut, sugar, and cardamom. Stirring the coconut and sugar over an open fire until the oil came out and the mixture began to harden, I would press the mixture into a pan, cut out squares, and sell them.

I even learned how to use a coconut grater, a long piece of metal with a rounded, pronged edge attached to a piece of wood. You'd place it on a chair, sit on it with the pronged edge facing outwards, take a coconut half and scrape the inside against the grater. With practice, I became good at it, though I never was able to match the speed of the Indian women. They could grate coconuts without even looking, tossing one emptied shell after another onto an ever-growing heap nearby.

It was impressive how villagers used all parts of the coconut. They made coconut milk by squeezing out the liquid from the meat. Coconut oil, used in cooking as well as for skin and hair care, was also extracted from the grated meat. In kitchens the empty shells often served as containers. Women kept their dishwashing scrubbers in them, which were themselves the fibers from husks peeled away from coconuts. The villagers, Fijian and Indian alike, produced little waste as they lived their lives.

As someone coming from a throw-away society, I was impressed and inspired by what I saw. There was something so beautiful and simple in their lives that I wished to emulate, something so close to the earth and its rhythms. I guess I never realized at the time that, for most of the villagers, it was a lifestyle imposed by poverty, tradition, or a combination of the two. I doubt if many would have called it beautiful if I had asked them. But it was beautiful to me.

The way I got into villages was usually by word of mouth. In one village, I would meet a visitor from another or someone who had a relative elsewhere. Days or weeks later, I'd arrive in the village and seek out my contact. Most of the time, I would be offered a place to stay, and then I'd organize a talk or class. Most of the villagers would turn out, squeezing into small rooms to chant or meditate or listen to my talks, translated into Hindi by someone sitting at my side.

Most Indian villagers were Hindu and followed daily rituals. Nearly every house had a *puja* placed high in one corner. These were not unlike our *pujas* in Ananda Marga, but instead of a picture of Baba, theirs had one or more pictures of a deity: Krishna, Shiva, or Kali with her necklace of skulls. Hibiscus or other colorful flowers were placed around the pictures along with bananas or coconuts; garlands of marigolds or frangipani blossoms were draped around them. Every morning and evening, members of the family would stand at the *puja* to chant and offer *arati* (an offering usually performed by waving a lighted candle on a plate in front of the deity) and fresh flowers to the Hindu gods. Some villages had small temples where Brahmin priests would perform fire ceremonies, tossing ghee into the flames and chanting Vedic hymns. Villagers also organized their own chants, getting together with a drum or two, a harmonium,[47] and some finger cymbals.

Since I wasn't in uniform and was known to them only as Sandra or Didi, what I was doing bore little difference from the traditions they knew, at least as far as the chanting and certain aspects of the philosophy went. Even so, many found inspiration in what I had to offer. I was convinced that it was driven by the power of the Guru. I often spoke of Baba (I referred to him only by that name), and most villagers were spellbound by my stories of him. Maybe, though, it had at least a little to do with the fact that a white woman from America had come all the way to their little village to teach yoga and meditation. I was something they had never before seen or experienced, a curiosity providing respite from their everyday lives whose presence no doubt sparked speculative conversations in every village I visited. *Why?* they must have asked each other. *Why is she doing all these things?* All this, though, never occurred to me at the time. I was convinced the appeal was due to Baba and Baba alone.

At most villages I stayed for a few days or more. In one or two, I remained longer. One of them was near Nadi. It wasn't a village in the true sense of the word; it had no name and consisted entirely of a number of houses, most of them strung out alongside the dirt road running through it. I had my own dwelling there. The villagers helped me renovate an empty hut made of hammered-out reddish brown iron barrels, men repairing the holes and women assisting me in putting down a new floor. This involved mixing together cow dung and mud and spreading it over the ground. When the floor dried, it was

---

[47] harmonium: A reed organ with a hand-pumped bellows. The bellows are pumped with one hand and the keyboard is played with the other.

smooth and felt good under my feet. Unlike a concrete floor, it was cool in the warm season and warm during the cold, and I was quite happy with it.

My hut wasn't big enough for classes, but a few villagers would sometimes join me for meditation in the mornings and evenings. One who did so regularly was Subhadra, a teenage girl to whom I'd given initiation as well as higher lessons. We quickly became close. Subhadra, who lived with her grandmother and extended family in one of the larger houses, was a bright girl. It was clear she felt stifled in the village and aspired to a different kind of life than the one she would have to face if she were to remain: marrying, moving to her husband's village, bearing children, and performing long hours of housework. Already, her relatives were trying to arrange a match.

From time to time, Subhadra would come to my hut in tears and say, "Didi, they're looking for a husband for me. I don't want to get married! What can I do?" "Don't worry," I'd reply, "we'll figure out something." In her, I saw a true devotee who might someday become an LFT and leave the village to work with me elsewhere; in me, she must have seen her ticket out of the village.[48]

Often coming to me with red eyes and smelling of smoke, Subhadra complained of long hours spent cooking in her outdoor kitchen. I sympathized; I had also begun cooking over a smoky fire. All the houses had outdoor kitchens built of corrugated tin or hammered-out barrels, with stoves made from bricks and cow dung. Wood or dried cow dung patties were used for fuel and smoked badly. As a result, all the women coughed, and some had breathing problems. My stove, which Subhadra had helped me make, lacked a shelter to protect it from the elements. In hot weather, I cooked only when the sun

---

[48] Subhadra eventually did leave her village. She went with me to American Samoa and worked with me there. After returning to Fiji (and probably realizing that I could do no more for her), she joined a Christian group and moved to Suva.

was not directly overhead. Thankfully, I didn't have to make my own food too often; I was usually invited to lunch or dinner somewhere in the village.

No one had running water in their homes. There was only one pipe where everyone got their water. The women washed clothes on a stone by the pipe, a task which took hours. Near the pipe was a corrugated tin bathhouse shared among several families. It was hooked up to the water source and had cold running water. It was exhilarating on hot days to pour a whole bucket of water over my head at the end of a bath. If no one else was waiting, I would wash my clothes at the same time.

As I entered into the rhythms of village life, I felt proud of myself: proud that I could cook tasty curries on my own stove, that I could get my clothes clean (just as clean as any of the women could) by pounding them with a stick, that I had learned how to make my own coconut milk and oil. The simplicity of the life appealed to me. Even the fine layer of dust that would settle over everything in the dry season, including clothing left out on the line, didn't much bother me. One time, a cow ate most of the skirt I had hung out. Subhadra and I chased it away, laughing. On another occasion, I was disturbed by a scratching sound in one of my drawers. I got up, pulled it open, and discovered a nest full of baby mice, so young that their eyes were still closed. The babies were so cute I couldn't bear to move them. Nothing really bothered me. And if anything did, I had my spiritual practices. No matter what, I could sing some kiirtan, sit down and close my eyes, and find that deep wellspring of peace that was always there within.

For Fiji, an island group out in the middle of the Pacific Ocean, cyclones were a regular feature of life. I experienced the awesome power of one of these storms when it made a direct hit to the islands. At the time, I was staying in one of the Indian villages, this one near the town of Lautoka.

As it began raining and the wind started to pick up, I went into town to get some candles, a flashlight, and other emergency supplies. Few stores were open and the streets were almost empty. When sheets of rain started whipping across the streets and the wind rose to a frightening scream, I began to regret the trip and rushed off to the bus station. Like the streets, it was nearly deserted, except for one lone bus. I ran to it nearly out of breath and clambered aboard with my purchases right before the door swung shut and the bus departed. Utterly relieved, I sat down to catch my breath, water dripping off my clothes and pooling in my seat.

Despite the increasingly powerful winds, the driver managed to inch the bus up the road. At my stop, I got off and struggled up the path to the house where I was staying, fighting against winds which made me feel as if I were about to be lifted up and blown away.

I would be weathering the storm with the wealthiest family in the village in their sturdy concrete house. The other villagers' houses would likely not fare as well. As the winds blew with greater and greater force and the eerie howl grew so loud that it was difficult to be heard without shouting, thoughts of the other villagers filled my mind. How terrified they all must be!

As evening fell, my hosts and I looked out at coconut palms lashing back and forth. Torrents of rain savagely beat the red earth, turning it into a morass of mud. Muddy water began to trickle into the house, and we jammed rags under all the doors to try to prevent its advance—to no avail.

No one got much sleep that night. Along with the constant sound of howling wind and pounding rain, we heard corrugated tin banging against walls. In the middle of the night, when I looked outside and saw sheets of it flying around the yard, I prayed no one would encounter them.

A weary dawn finally arrived. The rain had slowed to a drizzle, and the wind, though still blowing, had died down considerably. We greeted each another with wan smiles of relief. Except for some minor flooding, the house had not been damaged.

I went out to see how the other villagers had fared. Branches and debris were strewn everywhere. Whole trees had been uprooted. Fields of sugarcane lay flattened as if by some giant hand. Mud, reddish-brown and thick, covered everything. In the space of a few short hours, the colorful Fijian landscape had been reduced to a monochromatic mess.

As I picked my way slowly through the debris, taking care to avoid sharp sheets of tin partially hidden in the mud, I felt a sudden stinging pain behind my right knee. Some chicken wire had cut my leg. The wound was long but not too deep, so I mopped up the blood with my handkerchief and continued on my way.

Much to my relief and great surprise, all the homes in the village were standing, each with its roof intact. Only the outdoor kitchens and outhouses had suffered damage. Not only were the homes spared; the sugarcane crop, although flattened, had also basically survived and would right itself. But less than a mile down the road was a completely different situation. There, homes had sustained heavy damage, with roofs blown off and walls collapsed. In addition, the entire sugarcane crop in that area had been ruined, with the canes all twisted and broken. How, then, had our village escaped a similar fate?

Returning, I saw one of the village women. She waved me over and invited me into her house, where a few others were sitting and discussing their good fortune.

"Sandra Didi," said one as I sat down, "when the storm really started to blow, everyone went to Kalpana's house. Of all our houses, hers is the strongest. We sat in a circle and chanted *Baba Nam Kevalam*—and our village was spared!" I felt my hair stand on end as the full import of her words hit me. To my mind, there was one and only one explanation for this outcome: Baba had protected the village. He had performed a miracle.

Reports of damage to other villages began to filter in. When we learned about a particularly hard-hit area, I decided to go. (I would be going there not to look but to help. Whenever and wherever a disaster took place, Ananda Marga went with food and medicine. The organization even had relief teams. Relief work organized by dadas and male Margiis fell under the auspices of the Ananda Marga Universal Relief Team, or AMURT; and work organized by didis and female Margiis, under AMURTEL, or the Ananda Marga Universal Relief Team, Ladies.) But first, I needed supplies. With the help of some of the village women, I set about getting donations of dahl, flour, powdered milk, and sugar. When the buses started running out of Nadi again, we hauled our sacks of supplies onto one and set out.

I will never forget the total devastation I saw as the bus approached the area. Not only had homes and crops suffered great damage from the wind with most houses missing roofs and walls, but the entire village had been flooded. Mud covered everything, and a terrible smell of decay permeated the air. With what little clean water there was being used for drinking or cooking, none could be spared for cleaning up.

We learned of a man who had been killed by a sheet of corrugated tin. Stunned, we visited the family but had no words with which to comfort his wife and children. The supplies we had brought with us that so recently had seemed substantial were like drops in a vast ocean of need.

People responded to the disaster in differing ways. In general, I found that those who were better off and had more resources with which to recover were more prone to self-pity than others less fortunate. One woman I met, whose substantial house had sustained some damage but was still standing, lamented, "I've lost everything. I have nothing, and life is over for me." Then she put her head in her hands and cried.

Such a contrast I experienced a few weeks later when I went to an isolated riverside village for some follow-up meditation lessons. It was so remote that visitors had to be ferried back and forth in a canoe. Most of the villagers were poor, and many of their houses had been destroyed. I visited a family who had been living on top of a hill. Nothing of their former home remained. All that could be seen now were poles with strings attached to mark the dimensions of what was to be the family's new dwelling. The father's name was Arun. He and his sons had been gathering wood, corrugated tin, and other materials for the job. They had few resources with which to rebuild, but they thanked the heavens that they were still alive.

"Sandra Didi," Arun said, "God blessed us. We are all alive and unhurt!"

I saw this again and again among people who had almost nothing.

Chapter 13

I Am Purified—Again

In July of 1981, I was in Australia for RDS, a minor miracle accomplished mostly through a loan given by a Sun Myong Moon devotee I had befriended in Suva. The day before I was due to go back to Fiji, an Australian Margii returned from India with some electrifying news: Baba was calling all Margiis to come to Calcutta. To anyone who arrived by the end of the month, he was going to give something called *Dharma Samiiksha*, which was said to be even more significant than Personal Contact, a once-in-a-lifetime opportunity when he would take on the *samskaras* of the devotees so they could start over with a clean spiritual slate.

I was overjoyed. Because I was in Australia, I had at least the possibility of raising the fare. If I had been in Fiji, there would have been no chance at all. It's no accident that I'm here and not in Fiji, I thought. Baba's calling me. I'm meant to go!

A flurry of fund-raising followed. Over the next few weeks, dadas and didis did everything possible to raise ticket money. We baked banana and spice cakes and sold them door to door. We rolled sweets that local Margiis called "bliss balls" (a name which often got a laugh out of customers) and sold them at festivals.

Family Margiis donated money as well, even though many of them were trying to arrange their own fares. I managed to raise the money without too much difficulty and arrived in Calcutta by the middle of the month.

Baba's quarters in the Lake Gardens neighborhood of the city had a festive air about it. Every day, more excited devotees from all over the world would arrive and squeeze into its already overcrowded small rooms. Sometimes, when Baba gave darshan on the roof, there were traffic jams on the narrow stairwell. With people temporarily unable to move up or down, good-natured arguments would break out.

Because of the risk of being seized by the police and deported, all non-Indian Margiis had to stay at Lake Gardens from dawn to late at night. Long before dawn, we non-Indian didis (along with Indian ones lending us moral support) would get up, do our morning practices, and head over to Baba's quarters under cover of darkness. We knew that the police would never be up as early as we were. Once there, we would send Indian Margiis out to buy us food and other necessities. Late at night we would leave together in rickshaws or taxis, or in the occasional bus hired for the purpose. Once back at the didis' quarters, we'd wash our clothes, meditate, and catch a few hours of sleep before starting the routine all over again.

One afternoon, I gave some rupees to an Indian brother and asked him to buy some flowers. "Buy the nicest ones you can find," I urged. "They're for Baba." He brought them to me just before evening darshan. I scattered the petals where Baba would walk, then on the dais where he would sit. Just as I finished, people started shouting, *"Param Pita Baba Ki, Jai!"*[49]—the phrase shouted in unison preceding Baba's arrival. In he came, walking on the petals, doing namaskar. Then he sat on the dais and gave his talk. The moment he left, a mad rush for the petals ensued. I managed to get only one, but was satisfied with that, happy I had created *prasad* for others.

---

[49] *Param Pita Baba Ki, Jai:* Victory to the Supreme Father.

Each day, long lines formed outside Baba's room as people waited their turn to go in. We heard shouting and sometimes the sound of Baba's cane hitting flesh. Male devotees would come out, and some would lift up their shirts, proudly displaying the red marks and welts already rising on their skin. It was considered a blessing to get a beating from the Guru. It meant he was taking on your *samskaras* and purifying you. Didis and sisters, we were told, didn't get beaten like the men. Instead, Baba would hit women on their palms with his cane.

We heard stories of *Dharma Samiikshas* that had taken place over the past few weeks. One that was making the rounds was of a didi whom Baba had castigated for her lack of hygiene. As the story went, the didi was having her period and had some blood on her underwear. "*Chi, Chi, Chi.* So dirty!" Baba was reported to have said. I knew the didi in question; we had lived together in the Regent Street jagrti in Philadelphia before going to training. My face burned with shame. What if that had happened to me? The dream I'd had years before, when Baba told me I was dirty, was still vivid in my mind.

Sometimes didis and dadas got to go inside Baba's room and watch him give *Dharma Samiiksha*. A day or two after I arrived, I got shooed in along with the others. I stood at the rear and watched, trembling, hoping I wouldn't get called up front; despite my anticipation, I was terrified of what Baba might say about me in front of everyone. Much to my relief, an Indian didi was summoned instead. Baba gave her a stern look and started shouting at her in Bengali. What has she done to make him so angry? I wondered. My knees were knocking together as I tried to hide behind the others. More shouting followed, and the didi started to cry. She extended her hand. Baba took his cane and gave her some sharp raps on the palm.

As we filed out of Baba's room, I had a sudden intuition: that didi had been called up in front of Baba in place of me. Whatever she had done, she had been punished instead of me because I wouldn't have been able to take it.

"Didi," I asked Ananda Kripa, who was walking beside me, "what did that didi do to make Baba so angry?"

"She hadn't been following the worker code of conduct," she said. "Baba asked her, 'Why did you spend so much time with the dadas?' "

I barely had time to digest that when Ananda Kripa stopped abruptly and peered at my face. "Malatii, she said, you have pink eye. You must not come here again until it is cleared up. Baba must not catch pink eye from you!" Come to think of it, my left eye had been feeling strange all day. I looked in a mirror to find it swollen and bloodshot. In a way, I was relieved. I was shaken by the *Dharma Samiiskha* that the Bengali didi had gotten. Having pink eye meant that I wouldn't have to have mine right away.

I would be staying in the didis' quarters until the pink eye cleared up. For the first few days, my condition deteriorated; most mornings, I would wake up with my eye glued shut. The other didis not only avoided me, they wouldn't even look at me. "Malatii," Auntie said, "don't take it personally. You can get pink eye just by looking at someone who has it. The disease vibration gets carried in the air." (At the time, I didn't question this spiritual mode of explanation. We thought we knew lots of things doctors didn't.)

Unable to go to Baba's quarters, I spent the days meditating, trying to center my mind. What if Baba talks about all the drugs and sex I had in college? I kept thinking, shivering despite the oppressive heat. I found myself wondering which episodes Baba would choose to reveal.

I had plenty of time to review the gory details.

My experimentation with marijuana had started slowly in my freshman year in college, gathered steam when I was a sophomore, and rushed full speed ahead in my junior and senior years. It seemed like everyone was smoking grass and dropping acid. Spring would find students sprawled out on the Green at Penn, stoned and drinking cheap Gallo wine. Drugs loosened inhibitions, and with many students eagerly engaged in the pursuit of free love, sex with multiple partners was rampant. My freshman year, I didn't take part in any sex, but I still went to lots of parties where others did. During one that was particularly memorable, I had stumbled in disbelief, from one room to another, finding naked bodies in varying stages of intimate relations with any number of partners. In direct contrast to almost everyone else there, I kept my clothes on and left.

In my sophomore year, I took a Russian history course with the legendary and eccentric Professor Riasanovsky. During lectures, he would pace back and forth on the podium, haranguing us about nineteenth-century Russia, taking furious puffs on one cigarette after another while waving his arms about in a sweeping manner. I loved it. The course, coupled with the fact that my father had come from what had been the Russian Empire, fueled a fascination in me for all things Russian. I began studying the language, joined the campus Balalaika Orchestra, and started learning Eastern European folk dances with the University Folk Dance Club. Many of my newfound friends were also second-generation Americans of Eastern European heritage. Like them, I dreamed of visiting Russia someday.

I met Mikhail that year. He was a graduate student and, as a teaching assistant for Riasanovsky's course, led my study section. Late in the fall, we started dating. He had a mustache, a deep voice flavored with a Russian accent somewhat muted by his years in the States, and lived with his mother in the forests somewhere outside Bangor, Maine. During winter break, he sent me romantic letters written with a fountain pen in his careful script, describing the deep, dark forests "in whose spell I am bound, by whose will I know not." It was thrilling to read his letters while sitting on my mother's carefully fluffed-up cushions. Every once in a while, I'd raise my eyes and steal glances at my parents sitting just a few feet away totally oblivious to what I held in my hands.

I lost my virginity in Mikhail's tiny off-campus apartment soon after school was back in session. It was only years later that it occurred to me that my first sexual experience was really a case of date rape. We were drinking tea laced with honey when we decided I was going to sleep over. I told him I didn't want to go all the way. He seemed okay with it. He gave me a pair of his pajamas and we went to bed. Maybe it was my fault for having allowed myself to be in such a volatile situation; maybe it was naiveté and a desperate need for affection. Whatever it was, I thought he cared for me and we could express affection for each another without having sex. I was wrong. We broke up in the spring. He was, after all, only using me. I couldn't see that at the time, however. Believing myself to be in love with him, I was devastated.

My junior year, I found myself another boyfriend. Tim wasn't a hippie; at least he didn't look like one. He was clean-shaven, wore shirts with button-down collars with his jeans, and didn't wear his hair all that long, not by the standards of the day. He also wore cowboy boots and had a bit of a southern accent, being from Virginia. Looking distinctly out of place, he'd sit with me in Cy's Penn Lunch, better known as "The Dirty Drug" on the corner of Thirty-fourth and Walnut, drinking vile coffee in plastic cups, along with all the longhairs who hung out chain-smoking, planning parties, and occasionally attempting to do schoolwork.

Looks were deceiving, however. Tim smoked a lot of grass and took LSD. I found myself staying at his apartment more and more. Days passed in a haze of marijuana and hashish smoke, with us getting lost in the music of the time. There was always a record on the turntable. The Beatles were my favorite group. (I considered myself a bona fide Beatles freak. I'd been an ardent fan ever since they'd appeared on the Ed Sullivan Show. The second time they came on, I started screaming, rudely shocking my parents and brothers—not in character for a shy and studious girl who spent long hours doing her homework, but perhaps fitting for someone who wrote dark, mournful poetry kept carefully hidden in her room. I went out and bought a Beatles magazine, cut out and scotch-taped their pictures onto my mirror—and was stunned when my mother let me keep them there. *Those pictures,* I imagined my mother saying once I had become estranged as a teenager. *It was all the fault of those pictures!)* My favorite Beatles album was *Sgt. Pepper's Lonely Hearts Club Band*—as it had been from the first day I laid eyes on it during the summer of 1967, my brother David having brought it home. When he laid the vibrantly colored album on our dining room table, it seemed to radically alter the table, liberating it from the burden of all those heavy Sunday dinners our family used to partake of there.

Besides the Beatles, there were the Cream, Neil Young, the Doors, Hendrix, the Moody Blues, and the Grateful Dead, Tim's favorite. Joints were rolled and smoked, roach clips were passed around, and then the hash pipe, the ball of hash rotating merrily in the little bowl as we toked. Just me, Tim, and his two unlikely roommates: a tall, gangly lad also named Tim, who had a Western twang to his voice from Texas or maybe from Wyoming, played guitar, and also smoked a lot—so tall and thin that he looked like a rubber band bouncing when he walked around; and a short, stocky motorcycle guy with tattoos, long sideburns, and a short beard named Julio, who loved steak and beer.

I first took LSD with Tim. As we listened to the Dead, the acid took effect and I felt as if I had left a cramped and darkened room and had stepped out into an open universe, where all things were possible. I never wanted to go back to that dark place again and tried to open up to Tim and let him know how I was feeling. "Don't let me go back there," I said as we were coming down. That remark really upset Tim for some reason, and I ended up pretending I was just kidding, to cover up my feeling of being emotionally naked.

That relationship didn't last and was followed by a series of boyfriends and brief sexual encounters, some not more than one-night stands. It wasn't love, of course, it was sex, and often not very good sex at that—and it was so long in the past. Would Baba reveal it to the world?

When my pink eye finally cleared up and Ananda Kripa gave me permission to return to Lake Gardens, I must have been expected. I found myself being whisked into Baba's room along with other didis and dadas who had gathered outside his door. Once inside, I felt hands pushing me up to the front; before I knew what was happening, I was standing in front of Baba, my heart in my throat. I thought of that Indian didi again.

Baba didn't ask me my name or posting like he always did. Instead, he started talking to me as if he were resuming a conversation that had been interrupted.

"Don't you know how important it is to follow Sixteen Points?" he said sternly.

"Yes, Baba."

"Shouldn't you have followed Sixteen Points more strictly?"

"Yes, Baba," I said again.

"Why didn't you follow Sixteen Points more strictly?"

I had no answer.

"Give me your hand."

I extended my right hand out to him, palm up. With a look of intense concentration, Baba took his cane and hit my hand lightly three times. I felt a surge of energy like an electric current pass through my entire body, leaving me with a feeling of lightness and bliss.

Baba looked at me intently, then uttered, *"Matsyamudra, matsyendrasana, badhapadmasana*[50]. . . "As he said the names of the asanas he was prescribing for me, a dada and didi at his side both scribbled furiously, writing them down. Baba motioned for

---

[50] *Matsyamudra, matsyendrasana, badhapadmasana:* Fish Pose, Spinal Twist, Bound Lotus. Baba also mentioned the three postures Ananda Marga considered as the general asanas for women: *Diirgha Pranama* (Long Bowing Pose), *Bhujaungasana* (Cobra), and *Yoga Mudra*. Baba prescribed personal asanas for every Margii during his or her *Dharma Samiiksha*.

me to come close. I kneeled down. He placed his hand on my head and uttered a blessing.

Before I knew it, I found myself outside his door. The whole thing had taken only minutes, but I felt like a new person. I looked at my hand. It was a bit red, and it felt warm.

I cradled it. It was physical proof: I had been reborn—my sordid past unrevealed and wiped clean through Baba's grace as if it had never happened.

Marsha at age 7 with older
brothers David and Barry

In third grade
wearing gym uniform

Author's parents Max and Mina
in yard of her childhood home

High school graduation
Left to right: Diane (Barry's wife),
Max, the author, Mina, David

With balalaika and friends
at the University of Pennsylvania
a year or two before coming
across Ananda Marga

Didis and dadas waiting in line to vote. Original caption: Devotees of a radical Hindu sect, the Ananda Marg, wait to cast their votes near Calcutta Tuesday, May 6, 1996. The sect was under investigation after a private aircraft dropped crates of automatic weapons near their center in Purulia in the eastern state of West Bengal, allegedly for subversive activities. (AP PHOTO/BIKAS DAS)

This and previous page: Author's
passport as Hanna Hartt;
envelopes from letters sent
home from Australia;
(fake) teacher ID

With half brother Howard, looking at family photos

With Harriet Jenkins (Maetreyii)

Marsha with husband David, family, and in-laws, on her wedding day

Hiking in the Pocono Mountains

Chapter 14

The Visitation

It was late at night a year or two later, back in Fiji. As I puttered around barefooted on the cow-dung floor of my hut preparing for bed and humming a chant to myself, I felt good. We'd just concluded a talent show I had organized, and it had gone well. All the villagers had participated, some making costumes and props, others performing skits and songs.

I put up the mosquito net over my sleeping bag and glanced at my watch. I needed to get to bed fast: only six hours until I had to leave. Setting the alarm for five o'clock, I picked up my toothbrush and paste and white enamel bucket and was on my way out the door to wash up when I felt a sharp, piercing pain in my left foot.

"Yeeoouch! What's that?"

Dropping to my knees, I discovered a nail deeply embedded in my heel. I yanked at it a few times, and it soon became clear that I'd have no luck pulling it out. There was no telling how long it was.

In just a few short hours, I was supposed to be on my way to meet Didi Ananda Sudha, SWWS of Suva Sector, at the airport. I'd been preparing for and looking forward to this visit for weeks. And now I had a nail stuck in my foot!

There was no getting around it: I would have to go for help. Reluctantly, I pushed myself up and holding on to the walls, made my way out of the hut and hopped to the nearest house, Subhadra's, stopping every few moments to rest. Finally, I pulled myself up onto the porch and rapped lightly on the door. I didn't feel good about having to disturb people; it was approaching midnight and everyone would surely be asleep.

Hoping that Subhadra would be the only one to wake up, I knocked again and called out her name. I heard the door being opened. It was not Subhadra but her grandmother who looked out at me with bleary eyes, white hair tousled, sari askew, her petticoat partly visible.

"I'm sorry I had to wake you. I stepped on a nail and can't get it out," I said, lifting up my foot. She took one look and then quickly turned to go back in to rouse the rest of the household. Soon everyone was gathered around, debating how to go about removing the nail. One of Subhadra's uncles went to find a pair of pliers.

"Didi," he said, "Close your eyes."

I did as he asked. Grasping the nail firmly with the pliers, he pulled until it came out and fell onto the concrete porch with a ringing sound. There was some blood and a lot of pain, which I tried not to show. It would be unseemly, I thought, for a didi to show any.

They cleaned the wound with disinfectant and wrapped up my foot with some clean rags. Subhadra got a pair of crutches left over from someone's broken leg.

"Here, Didi, use these," she said, helping me up. Together, we crossed the yard.

"Thanks," I said when we got to my door.

"Won't you need someone to help you go to the airport?"

"Oh, I should be fine. Thanks so much for your help. Please go back to sleep." The sidewise look she gave me showed that she didn't believe me.

"Really, I'm fine! Go back to bed!"

Subhadra smiled that sweet, twinkling smile I had grown to love. "Okay, Didi, you win," she said and turned to leave.

I watched her make her way across the yard, then flopped down on my sleeping bag without taking my half bath. No time or energy for that. Now I had only five hours before I had to go to the airport. Despite what I had told Subhadra, I suspected it wouldn't be easy getting there without help. But I had been enough trouble already. I couldn't cause any more.

I woke up just before the alarm went off. Hobbling around, I managed to brush my teeth and have a wash. Then I sat for a brief meditation propped up against the wall, my left leg stretched out in front of me. It still hurt and there was some swelling. Maybe I should get a tetanus shot, I thought, but hadn't I had one not too long ago? I wasn't sure, but there would be no time to get one now, not with Didi coming.

Using the crutches, I got myself out to the road and caught a bus to the airport. I somehow managed to get off, then swung my way into the arrival lounge, bearing my bandaged foot like a war wound. I was looking forward to having Ananda Sudha meet the villagers. We were going to have a welcoming meditation that evening, and special food would be prepared.

Despite having to work underground in Fiji, despite the physical hardships and perennial lack of money, I felt proud of what I had been able to accomplish. I was living among the people as one of them and was sure they respected me for it. In this Indian village alone, I was conducting regular meditation sessions, yoga and health classes for the women, and an afternoon program for the children. I was sure that Ananda Sudha would feel right at home. It would be a relief for her, I thought; after all the years in Australia, she'd find the village familiar, so much like her native India.

I hadn't yet spent much time with Ananda Sudha. She was one of the first avadhutikas, coming after Ananda Bhakti, Ananda Gajara, and Ananda Kripa. I'd seen her a few times in India before either of us had been posted to Suva Sector. She was short by Western standards, light-complexioned, solidly built (just shy of chubby), and had recently begun to wear wire-rimmed glasses. I thought of her as very devotional; one image that stuck in my mind was of a photo I had seen of her on the cover of an Ananda Marga magazine published in Australia: doing kiirtan, her hands raised up over her head, her eyes closed, a smile playing at the corners of her mouth. I'd been struck by the look of innocent bliss suffused across her face.

Since coming to Suva Sector, I had left Fiji only once because airfare to Australia had been too difficult for me to arrange. At the RDS I'd attended before going to India for *Dharma Samiiksha*, Ananda Sudha had been both funny and imposing. When in a good mood, she had an impish way about her and had us laughing at her jokes and imitations of various personalities in Ananda Marga. Once or twice, I saw her lose her temper, but most of the time she had been comfortable to be around. I was looking forward to spending time and meditating with her. I had been alone for so long.

She waved a greeting when I saw her. "Where's the car?" she asked as we left the airport.

"Sorry, Didi, we'll have to take the bus. Very few people have cars in Fiji. There are a few people in the village with cars, but they had to go to work."

"But my bag is heavy . . . and you're in no condition to carry it!"

I didn't know what to answer, so I just lead the way to the bus, Didi muttering something behind me as she dragged her bag along.

The bus stopped at the village, letting us off in a cloud of dust. Ananda Sudha took out her handkerchief, covered her mouth, and followed me to my hut.

"Is this where you live?" she asked, wide-eyed, a shocked look crossing her face.

"Yes, Didi."

We went in. She looked slowly about her, turning as if looking into every corner for the furniture that wasn't there.

Then she said, "They wouldn't even use this for a garage in Australia."

I felt a little breathless, almost as if I'd been punched. How different is this from lots of places in India? I thought. She must have spent time in villages even poorer than this. And besides, I fumed, wasn't that what we had devoted our lives to—helping the poor?

Too flabbergasted at her attitude to respond, I turned away and indicated the area with a small rug I had prepared for her. "Here, Didi, this is your place. Let's get you set up. We'll have lunch at Subhadra's house, and this evening there will be dharmacakra there."

As dusk fell, the villagers came for meditation. People filed in, wearing their best clothes, folding their hands in the namaskar greeting when they saw Ananda Sudha. Soon the room was packed. A few villagers approached Didi with garlands made of orange marigolds and placed them over her head, then bowed, hands folded. She returned the gesture and smiled, looking pleased.

After meditation was over, Ananda Sudha gave a talk in Hindi, throwing in a few jokes. Soon everyone was laughing and my spirits began to lift. I anticipated Didi's good impressions of the evening and the villagers who had welcomed her with so much respect. Everyone left the same way they had come in, one by one, hands folded in namaskar, this time exchanging some friendly remarks with Didi.

When we returned to my hut, Ananda Sudha turned to me. "Why did you have so many men at meditation?" she demanded. Her face, just minutes ago so open and smiling, had a hard look to it. "That's not proper," she continued, "and you were sitting so close to them. And those clothes you wear! Your breasts were bouncing around right in front of them!" She made a gesture indicating massive breasts.

Another blow. This one I felt deep in my stomach. Once again, I had no idea how to respond; she was my superior and to contradict her directly would be unseemly. One thing was clear: the visit I had looked forward to for so long was quickly becoming a nightmare.

Over the following two weeks, nothing seemed to please Ananda Sudha. Often she would shout at me, sometimes so loudly I was sure the villagers could hear. She told me the work I was doing was no good. With a cruel expression, she imitated the song I had taught the children to sing while teaching them English. " 'Where is Arun? Where is Arun? Here I am! Here I am!' What kind of nonsense is that?" she said. "Rubbish! Everything you're doing here is rubbish!" In the mornings, I would rise earlier than usual, before dawn, so I could meditate and then prepare her breakfast on my outdoor stove. While Ananda Sudha slept, I prepared the chapatti dough, cut the vegetables, and built the fire, blowing on the coals to get it going. Just as I would finish all this—sweaty, smoky, eyes watering—Didi would rise and stretch contentedly. Then, having done little meditation, she would sit and wait for her food. We would also travel around to other Indian villages. At one, Didi accused me of being lazy, probably because I didn't jump up and fulfill her commands the instant they'd been uttered.

I have no positive memories of Ananda Sudha's visit. After I had seen her off at the airport, I went back to my hut and lay down on the mud floor. I stayed there for a long time. I cried. Thoughts I had never before entertained filled my mind. For the first time, I seriously thought of leaving Ananda Marga. What am I doing here? I thought. Why don't I just leave? She thinks that everything I've done here is rubbish. Maybe it is. Maybe I'm not cut out for this. For two or three days, I lay there, thinking those depressing thoughts.

In the end, I got up and continued to work. But something had changed. A wound had opened up in me that would never quite heal, no matter how much kiirtan and meditation I did. Before, it had always been enough to inspire me and keep me going—the deep peace I experienced during meditation, the joy I felt while chanting *Baba Nam Kevalam* and dancing. But now, my work started to become more of a duty and less of a joy, as if some light had gone out of it and rendered it heavy and burdensome. Cynicism took root in me. No longer would I regard the senior Indian didis and dadas as one step removed from godhood. They were just human beings, and some were even more imperfect than I.

Ananda Sudha's conduct bothered me for a long time. I felt the need to vent to someone, so the next time I went to Australia for RDS, I decided to talk to Dada Anishananda about it. He was acting SS for Suva Sector (the only non-Indian one at the time, he was SS due to the difficulties most Indian workers faced getting visas for Australia—heaven knows how Ananda Sudha had managed hers!), and it was known that he'd had similar encounters with her. As I told Anishananda my story, sitting on the rug in the meditation room at the dadas' office in Sydney, his eyes were kind, mirroring my own pain, understanding it. When I finished, he had a perplexed look on his face.

"When she got back, she told everyone what great work you were doing," he said.

I stared at him, trying to make sense of his words. "How can that be?" I replied, incredulous. "She didn't have a nice word to say to me the whole time. She yelled at me so loudly lots of people in the village could hear. She told me everything I was doing was rubbish, as she put it. 'Rubbish! This is rubbish! That is rubbish!' "

Anishananda looked mystified.

"When she got back, her face was glowing, she looked so happy," he said. "She talked about the different villages you took her to, all the people who are meditating. Oh, and the food you made her. She said, 'Every morning, Malatii made me the tastiest *sabje* and chapatti, right on her little outdoor stove.' "

I thought of those mornings, how she expected to be served like a queen, rising right as the food was ready, the chapattis nice and hot. I was silent. We looked at each other. Then Dada said, "But you know how she is."

I certainly did, and not only because of what had happened in Fiji. My talk with Anishananda had reminded me of another encounter I'd had with Ananda Sudha, one I hadn't exactly forgotten, but now saw in a very different light. A few years earlier, the didis in Australia bought land, some sixty-three acres of it, for a master unit.[51] Even though I had barely enough money at the time for basic living expenses, I'd had a hand in the purchase.

It had happened the time I had been in Australia for RDS. One evening, I was in the Melbourne jagrti preparing dinner with Ananda Sudha and another didi. I was peeling some potatoes when Ananda Sudha told us about the land. It was located about one hundred sixty kilometers north of Brisbane, near an old mining town named Gympie, and it sounded beautiful. "We can get it for a good price," she was saying. "We have to get the money together to buy it." In a flash, an idea, seemingly coming from nowhere, popped into my head. "What if I write to my parents, tell them I'm settling in Australia, and want to buy some land?" I blurted out.

My words had an almost palpable presence, vibrating in the silence that had fallen around us. I was shocked by what I'd said and immediately wished I could take it back. But any hope that Ananda Sudha would respond with indignation and say, *You'll do no such thing!* were soon dashed.

"Yes, you must do it!" she exclaimed, her eyes glowing as she contemplated the windfall coming from this totally unexpected quarter. If her hands had not been occupied with cutting vegetables, she would surely have rubbed them together with glee.

She didn't let me back out over the following days. "Did you write to your parents yet?" she asked more than once. When I

---

[51] Master units, like Ananda Nagar in India, were rural properties meant to be models of cooperative and self-sufficient living. An ideal master unit was one in which agricultural, industrial, commercial, educational, and medical facilities were established, but few matched the ideal.

responded in the negative, she got that hard look on her face, pointed her finger and said, "You must do so immediately!"

Because Ananda Sudha was my superior and was to be obeyed, I felt I had no choice. At the time, I was so wedded to the organization that I thought if I were to refuse to send the letter, it would mean disloyalty to the mission and an unwillingness to go to any lengths necessary to help establish it. It was as if I had to prove my spiritual vision and show by my actions that my birth parents were no longer my real family and that Ananda Marga was.

So, reluctantly, I wrote the letter, telling my parents I wanted to buy the land with a friend, telling myself that if I got it, the money would be put to good use. Otherwise, it would just be spent on material things, I rationalized. Now, it would help us get this land, where so many good things would happen. After some correspondence back and forth, which required still more storytelling, my parents sent about eight thousand dollars. Together with the money was a note asking for a copy of the deed for the land. At first, I ignored their request, but when they repeated it a few months later, it was becoming clear they had begun to suspect I hadn't been telling the truth.

I felt an odd mixture of emotions as I read their letters and composed my replies: pride that I'd been able to contribute to the purchase of the property; guilt, which I countered by telling myself that the money was going to better use than if they spent it on clothes or furniture or other things; then more guilt when I thought about how little money my parents had had as we'd been growing up, how they'd never spent anything on themselves, and how I was now taking their hard-earned money away from them. There was also a kind of hard-edged "serves you right" attitude. They had never shown me much love growing up, and now I was getting back at them. I made a half-hearted attempt to put together some false papers, but in the end, all I sent was one blurry photo of the land.

So yes, I thought to myself as I sat with Anishananda in the dadas' office, I certainly did know all about Ananda Sudha—and I was determined never to be manipulated or hurt by her again.

Chapter 15

The Kindness of Strangers: Surviving in American Samoa

I got over the initial shock of Ananda Sudha's visit but continued to contend with some lingering resentment. It just wasn't right, I told myself, that I'd grown overly lean and my hair was thinning because I hardly ever got to eat decent food and worked so hard while Ananda Sudha continued to live like a queen in Australia.

She doesn't have a clue what I go through on these islands, I thought as I prepared to leave Fiji for American Samoa the second time, a trip necessitated by my ever-worsening visa situation. Initially entering Fiji with a three-month tourist visa, I had renewed it over and over; when the time for another renewal would come around, I would just go to a different town and hope they wouldn't notice how many stamps I had in my passport. Eventually, though, I had to leave to avoid giving the authorities the impression that I was stringing them on forever. That's when

I would go to American Samoa. I would spend some weeks there, then return to Fiji and start the process over.

American Samoa proved to be challenging. The first time I went, I had no names or addresses. In contrast to Fiji, here I would find no resident Indian population with an interest in yoga and meditation. Food presented a particular problem. Since little could be grown in the volcanic soil of Tutuila (American Samoa's main island), traditional foods like taro, cassava, papaya, and green leafy vegetables were imported from Western Samoa. By the time I arrived, though, a lot of it came from what everyone in Samoa called the mainland. Candy, chips, and cookies, which I hadn't seen much of since leaving the States, had turned American Samoa into a junk-food paradise. It seemed like everyone had adopted this diet. Even those who had papaya trees usually fed the fruit to their pigs instead of eating it. Predictably, many of the Samoans were severely overweight and diabetes was rampant. So much for the benefits of being an American territory! I thought.

The first time, I stayed with a Samoan woman named Sepela, whom I had met while trying to sell popcorn, a business I had started to support myself. Sepela had a little five-and-ten grocery store located on the main road to the town of Pago Pago. I had asked her if she would like to sell my popcorn, and we'd gotten to talking. Like so many Samoans, Sepela was gregarious and generous, and also overweight to the tune of at least three hundred pounds. We arranged that in exchange for tutoring her three children, I would stay upstairs in a little room behind the store.

From the outset, Sepela could see I was different from all the Americans she had met: I didn't have a job, dressed strangely (although not in full uniform, I was wearing a sari), and taught yoga. She'd never heard of it.

"Yoga? What's that?" she asked. "Is it a religion?"

I hurried to assure her that it was not and went through my usual summary of the benefits of yoga and meditation.

"Meditation sounds good," Sepela said, "but I like the idea of the exercises more. Can they help me lose weight?" she asked, reaching for a Hostess Twinkie.

"They can, but only if you watch what you eat," I replied.

Once I moved in with Sepela, things went reasonably well. I started a yoga class in the Pago Pago library in the hope of finding some meditation candidates. My main objective was always to get people started on meditation, and yoga classes often stimulated interest. This time, though, most people only wanted to do postures.

One morning, Sepela's daughter came up to tell me that her mother wanted to see me. I went into the store and found Sepela sitting in her usual place behind the cash register.

"Sandra, you know I'm a Jehovah's Witness," she began. I nodded; I'd seen men in suits and copies of the *Watchtower* in the store from time to time. "I'm not sure if you should stay here anymore," she continued. "My minister says that yoga is evil, and anyone who practices it is possessed by the devil."

I'd heard the "yoga-is-evil" argument before. "Sepela," I said, "you know me. Do you really think I'm possessed by the devil?"

"Well, no," she replied, a confused look on her face, "but I have to obey my minister. He knows what he's talking about. I do want to remain friends with you, though. I know you're a good person."

I moved out a few days later. Fortunately, it was time to return to Fiji anyway.

A year or two later I was back in American Samoa because of my visa. A few days after my arrival, I decided to visit Sepela, taking the brightly colored Samoan bus (which I'd always thought resembled a toddler's colorful wooden toy bus, blown up to life-size) to her store, only to find that it was being run by another family. From the new owners, I learned that she was now living on the other side of the island and had a new store. They gave me her address. Some directions from passersby and a bus or two later, and I found myself walking into her store, which was bigger than the old one. There was Sepela sitting behind the cash register, just as she had always done.

"Sandra! How are you? I haven't seen you in such a long time!" She shoved herself off her chair to give me a hug. I asked after her children and other relatives.

Making no mention of her minister, she offered me a place to stay in the family home, which was being built next to the store. The construction site looked like a movie set. There was a roof and side walls, but the front was completely open to the elements, customers, and passersby alike. At night, when the lights were on, its resemblance to a movie set only increased. Everyone—Sepela, her children, her brothers and cousins—went about cooking, eating, and getting undressed while preparing for bed in the glare of those lights. No one seemed self-conscious in the least.

I thought I knew why. In Western Samoa, where I'd been briefly, most people lived in traditional houses that were open. Instead of walls, there were blinds woven out of coconut fronds. Many homes had electricity; in the evenings when the blinds were typically still up, family members going about their business could easily be seen by anyone passing by. Because Samoans had traditionally inhabited open houses, living in one without a front wall was no big deal for Sepela and her family. It was for me, though. Not only did I need to shield myself from people walking by when I was dressing or undressing, but also from the men I was rooming with. I hung up a sheet and did my changing act behind it.

It was at Sepela's new home that my popcorn business began to pick up, taking a big step forward with the help of a larger kerosene stove and the cheaper rate I got from Sepela for materials in bulk. The stove was located in the rear of the large room we all ate and slept in. When I wasn't busy with yoga classes, I popped corn day and night (providing endless entertainment to people passing by the house), then walked the streets and sold it as best I could. I racked up many miles thus. Children would often trail behind me shouting, "The popcorn lady! The popcorn lady! Here comes the popcorn lady!" To them (and most people on the island), I wasn't a yoga teacher, a meditation teacher, or any teacher at all. I was simply "the popcorn lady."

As I walked from store to store, I thought of Ananda Sudha. She'd probably tell me that everything I'm doing is rubbish, I figured. I'd like to see her come here and survive! I was making a supreme effort to follow the conduct rules and consider my sufferings as rewards, but it was getting harder to do. Selling popcorn just to buy toothpaste and soap wasn't exactly what I had envisioned when I made the decision to become a didi.

Despite living in such close quarters with Sepela and her family, I began to feel lonely. Even meal times didn't provide much of a respite. Not only did I not partake of the meat and seafood that everyone else was having, I also didn't eat with the family because I was following yet another conduct rule: *Avadhutika must not take food while seeing others take non-vegetarian diet.* Few vegetables were available on the island, so I relied heavily on boiled or roasted breadfruit—and leftover popcorn. I ate lots of it, cracking more than a molar or two on the half-popped kernels at the bottom of bags.

My last stay on the island was an extended one. I had been deported from Fiji. Immigration officers had finally gotten wise to me, had come to the village I'd been in and escorted me to the airport and onto a plane bound for American Samoa, and had forbidden me from returning. For reasons I can't recall, I could no longer stay with Sepela. I found a place to stay with the help of an American woman who had attended one of my yoga classes at the Pago Pago library. Toni was an artist who, like so many Americans, was in Samoa because her husband was there for business. She offered me shelter in her studio in the unfinished basement of a house. It was a large, open space with a concrete floor, filled with her paints, canvases, and easels, but with enough room for my sleeping bag. It had no shower facilities, but I wasn't being choosy. At least it had a toilet—and four walls!

One morning not long after I had moved in, Toni came to see me, her face drawn and tired-looking, as if she hadn't slept well. She did her best not to look at me.

"I'm afraid you can't stay in my studio anymore," she began. "Oh, it's still fine with me," she said, answering my unspoken question, "but the owner of the building and his wife just came back from the mainland. He's a minister, and he says that he doesn't want a yoga teacher living here. Apparently, he sensed an evil presence here last night," she said, rolling her eyes.

The "yoga-is-evil" argument yet again. I'd heard it in Cairo and Israel and from Sepela. Far and away, I had found that the people with the most warped ideas about yoga were fundamentalist Christians, no matter where they lived. I sensed that Toni's landlord was one.

"I'm going to talk to him," I told her. Toni said she didn't mind but doubted it would make a difference. "I know. I just want to talk to him, face to face."

After packing my belongings, I steeled myself for the confrontation I sensed was ahead and knocked on the minister's door. No one came. I was sure he was home, so I knocked harder. I heard someone coming, and the door swung open. Facing me was a meek-looking middle-aged woman with lank brown hair.

"Yes?" she asked, screwing up her eyes. Although I had no doubt she knew who I was, I introduced myself, telling her that I would like to speak to her husband.

"He's not here," she said. I knew that wasn't true because I'd just heard him cough.

"Please let him know I'm here. It'll only take a minute." She hesitated, then, shrugging her shoulders, went to call him with a resigned look about her.

He strode up to me and told me to get out of his house.

"Evil! That's what I felt late in the night—the presence of evil!" he shouted. With eyes blazing, face twisted, neck knotted and red, he looked a hell of a lot more like the devil than I did.

As time went on, it got harder and harder to find places to stay on the island. When I called Ananda Sudha one day, she said, "You've been there too long. It's time to leave."

Time to leave? Great! But how?

"Didi," I said, "I don't have any money. And there aren't any Margiis here to help me, either."

Any faint hope I had of her offering assistance soon vanished when she said, "You'll have to get the money somehow." When I didn't reply, she went on. "You have to go to Ananda Nagar for DMC and become an avadhutika."

My heart leapt at her words. Avadhutika! It had been five years since the "baby incident," and I still hadn't become one. It was my greatest desire to take the vows and belong completely to the Guru. By becoming an avadhutika, I would be able to rededicate my life to the mission. But popcorn certainly wasn't going to get me to India. Still, there had to be a way.

That's when I thought of Ron. He was the American businessman and Rajneesh[52] devotee I'd met through another American didi who'd briefly been in American Samoa. She had since left the organization, and I suspected that she and Ron had been more than friends even back when she was a didi. So it felt odd even considering going to see him.

To get over my initial reluctance, I told myself that although didis and dadas didn't usually take ordinary jobs, Ron might know of some classes I could teach. Or better still, he might give me a

---

[52] Rajneesh Chandra Mohan Jain (12/11/31 - 1/19/90): An Indian spiritual teacher known during the seventies and eighties as Bhagwan Shree Rajneesh. He lived for a time in Oregon, where his movement generated controversy because of his lavish lifestyle (he owned as many as ninety-three Rolls-Royces), and because he advocated free sexual expression among his devotees.

donation; he was well off enough. Ron knew Didi, so he probably understands our lifestyle and what we can and can't do, I thought.

When Ron opened the door, he seemed welcoming.

"What can I do for you?" he said, offering me a place on his couch. I sat down, my pores gratefully drinking in the air conditioning.

"I need to raise some money," I said, "and I was wondering if you knew of something I could do, some yoga classes I could teach or something."

Ron paused for a second, an odd look crossing his face. Then he leaned over me.

"Well, there's *this*," he said.

At first I didn't understand. What was he was referring to? Then I saw he was exposing himself.

I was struck dumb. After a few long seconds, I managed to haul myself off the couch and walked out of his house without a word, sure my suspicions about the other didi had been correct. He had probably assumed if she had done it, I would too. That'll teach you not to follow your gut instincts, I berated myself when I had calmed down a bit.

A week or two later, it was Toni who finally came to my rescue. "College graduates can get teaching jobs in American Samoa," she told me.

"You mean you don't have to have any special certification to teach here?" I asked.

"That's what I've heard."

I took the little money I had and bought a long floral-print Samoan dress, then went to the Department of Education to inquire. "Yes, a college graduate can teach elementary school," the clerk assured me. "All you need is a college transcript."

I met the superintendent. A solidly built, affable Samoan man who didn't appear much older than I, he seemed genuinely interested in having me join the teaching staff. "If you can get your transcript to us in time, you can start teaching when school resumes in September," he told me.

After I had cleared this idea with Ananda Sudha, I set about getting my transcript, writing to my parents and asking if they could get it for me. Meanwhile, I agonized over what I would do once I received it. The name on my transcript bore no resemblance to my passport name. How to explain that?

Maybe I can change the name on the transcript, white it out and type it over, then photocopy it, I thought. But what if they noticed? I could be stuck on this island forever!

When the transcript arrived, I examined it carefully, deciding that it couldn't be done since I'd need to find a typewriter with the same typeface. The chances of that being slim to none, I would just have to face having two names. I filled out the paperwork using my current name, attached my transcript and passport, and dropped it off. I had decided not to say anything unless they asked, but as far as I can remember, no one wanted to know why the name on my transcript and the name on my passport were totally different.

They gave me the job, and one morning early in September, I walked into my second grade classroom and began teaching. Despite my lack of formal training, things went reasonably well. I also gave a few talks about yoga to the other teachers and some expressed an interest in taking lessons.

By mid-December, though, I was sitting in the superintendent's office trying to explain why I was resigning after only three months in the classroom. "I'm really sorry," I was saying, "but I have to move on. I'm starting a community school in Australia." This wasn't a total falsehood. I had clear intentions of doing that someday.

"I thought I could trust you," the superintendent said. "But you've done the same thing other *palangis*[53] have done. They come to the island, run out of money, start teaching; and then, after making enough money to get off the island, they leave. How can you leave in the middle of the school year? Where does that leave our children?"

---

[53] *palangi:* White person.

"I'm sorry," I repeated.

The superintendent's face, once so affable, now looked as if it had been carved out of granite.

"That's the last time I'll hire a *palangi*," he said.

I really was sorry. But I couldn't possibly stay and finish out the year. I had to obey Ananda Sudha (and my own desires) and get to Ananda Nagar in time for DMC. If I hurried, I just might make it in time to become an avadhutika. Besides, I wasn't acting on my own. I had Baba behind me and his great mission to accomplish. I had to—no, I longed to—become an avadhutika, and I couldn't let a class of Samoan kids get in my way. Surely, I told myself, they can find someone to take over my class.

Deep down, though, I was having misgivings about what I was doing. I saw myself as someone who wanted to promote understanding among people from differing backgrounds. Yet I'd taken a teaching job knowing full well I would be leaving in the middle of the year, and had become an agent of worsening relations between Americans and Samoans. Deep down, there was anger and resentment at having been put in the position of having to take a job I couldn't complete in the first place. Despite all my rationalizing, I felt bad about letting down the superintendent and those kids.

Chapter 16

Australia: The Raid

I was soon to find out that I needn't have hurried to Ananda Nagar. I got there early one chilly dawn after traveling all night by train. When I walked into the didis' quarters, things looked much the same as in previous years, with didis lying side by side in sleeping bags on top of piles of straw meant to ward off the cold. Only a few were up. I caught sight of Mangala, toothbrush in hand, coming in from having a wash. She was dressed all in orange, having been made an avadhutika a few years back.

"Malatii, it's so good to see you!" she said, hugging me. "It's been a long time." She was right about that. I hadn't been in India since *Dharma Samiiksha*, three years in the past.

"It has been a while," I said, "but I finally made it. I'm hoping to become an avadhutika—at last!"

Mangala, whose name was now Ananda Mukti, looked away.

"Oh, Malatii! Baba just made some last night." My face fell. "But maybe he'll make some more," she hurried to say.

But she knew as well as I that Baba never did that. On any one occasion when Baba made avadhutas and avadhutikas, he never performed more than one ceremony. I was too late.

I tried to hide my disappointment, but it was hard to do. Despite my efforts to avoid them, I kept seeing newly created avadhutikas everywhere, from the large DMC *pandal* (tent) to the didis' quarters. All were glowing, as if lit up from within. That should have been me, I said to myself every time I saw one. I had to content myself with just attending the DMC program.

As it drew to a close, I learned that I would be going to Australia. It was happy news, and I was looking forward to working in a place with lots of Margiis. There was one drawback to the posting, though, and it was a big one: I'd likely be seeing Ananda Sudha more often. I told myself not to worry. Surely, with other didis and dadas around, she wouldn't be able to treat me the way she had in Fiji.

A few weeks later, I flew to Brisbane and was met by some Margiis at the airport, who promptly took me to Ananda Palli, the master unit located a few hours from the city. Dada Anishananda was there, and so was Ananda Bhadra (Vishaka's new name: she had become an avadhutika some years back). That evening, we had dharmacakra. During meditation, it occurred to me that I'd been a didi for ten years.

After dharmacakra was over, I told Anishananda. "Ten years!" he said. "Congratulations!" I thanked him, but inside, I wasn't feeling all that good. Ten years, and I was still wearing orange and white. Maybe Baba still thought I'd been the one holding that baby. That was why Vishaka was an avadhutika and I wasn't.

A few days later, I went to Brisbane, where I would be working, and met the local Margiis. There was no jagrti there and finding one would be my first priority. In the meantime, I would be staying with some family Margiis.

Soon after my arrival, I had my initiation into the fruit-selling business. It was just one of Ananda Marga's many homegrown businesses in Australia that workers and even family Margiis participated in. Others included the selling of jewelry at festivals and markets, homemade cakes door to door, and tahini bars and bliss balls at health food stores and festivals. For fruit selling, Margiis went to the food distribution center to buy crates of apples, peaches, and other fruits, which would then be bagged up, placed into cardboard boxes, and carried into stores in the target area of the day.

After receiving a hurried mini-lesson on the basics, some Margiis took me to a street with a number of small businesses. Outside one shop, they wished me luck and in I went, carrying my box and feeling silly. This wasn't exactly what I had envisioned doing in Australia. Sure, I'd had to sell pencils and sweets in Fiji and popcorn in American Samoa—but those had been places where I'd had to work underground or where there hadn't been any Margiis. Here, there were lots of Margiis, and I had assumed that meant my days of hawking things in the street were over. Apparently not!

Forcing myself to go up to the counter, I cleared my throat and asked the big, beefy-looking man with the florid complexion and tattooed arms standing there if he was the owner. Too bad, I thought when he replied in the affirmative; I would have to make my first pitch to an unlikely prospect.

"Would you like to buy some fruit?" I asked, putting the box down on the counter so he could have a better look.

"She'll be right, mate," he answered.

Happy he'd replied in the affirmative, I waited a minute, but he didn't indicate what he wanted.

"The peaches are nice and sweet, and so are the grapes. And the apples are crunchy."

"She'll be right, mate," he said again, this time making a little wave over my box. Then I froze, realizing I didn't know what "She'll be right" meant. Did he want some, or didn't he?

"No, I don't want any!" the man shouted, answering my unspoken question.

The situation felt eerily familiar. Hadn't I experienced something like it before? Oh yes, the vegetable guy in Turkey! I thought as I went out the door carrying my box. He'd reacted just like that man in Turkey.

The Margiis were waiting for me outside. "How did it go?" they asked. "Not too well," I said, giving them a brief account. They all had a good laugh.

It wasn't long before I found a house to rent; however, just a few weeks after I'd moved in, Ananda Sudha began pressuring me to find one to buy. I finally found a house I thought would do, but getting the money together was another matter entirely, and I told her so when we met.

"Didi, we really don't have enough for the down payment."

"I don't want to hear it," she said, the severe line between her eyebrows deepening. "Central Office wants a jagrti in Brisbane, so you must do it."

In the end, against my better judgment, we secured a high-rate loan to buy the building. Located in the residential area of Highgate Hill, a neighborhood with a smattering of immigrants, it was a detached house with two floors and a big backyard. The rooms were somewhat small, but we would have to make do.

My LFT Gitanjali and I moved in, conducted a house-entering ceremony to bless the house and clear out any negative vibrations, then set about starting a preschool. The school was located in the basement; classes and dharmacakras were held in the front room with everyone just managing to squeeze in. Despite our cramped quarters, things were going well—until the morning we got some unexpected visitors.

I heard the first knock just as I was finishing my shower. I wasn't quite sure what it was over the hiss of the water, but then came another, even louder. Who could that be at this hour? I thought, annoyed. It was early, six thirty or seven o'clock at the latest, and definitely not a time for visitors.

I turned off the water, reached for my towel and dried off hurriedly, then put on my sari blouse and petticoat. I opened the bathroom door. Gitanjali was standing there.

"Who is it?"

"Didi, there are three men waiting for you in the meditation room," she said almost in a whisper, her face pale.

Three men. Men never came to our place, a sisters' jagrti, at any time of the day, let alone so early in the morning.

"Tell them I'll be there in a minute," I whispered. Then I ducked quickly into my room. Something was telling me not to let them see me in acarya dress, so instead of putting on the rest of my uniform, I changed into pants and a shirt. Then I went to the meditation room.

There they were, three big men dressed in suits, standing around and looking incongruous, making the small room look even more cramped. Wasting no time, one flashed a piece of paper in front of me. "I have a search warrant," he said. "We're here to look for incriminating evidence."

That's when I knew who they were: Special Branch, the Australian counterpart of the FBI. We'd had lots of experience with them. Ever since three Margii brothers had been arrested, tried (framed was more like it) for bombing the Sydney Hilton[54] in 1978 and sentenced to several years in jail, they'd harassed us. Just a year earlier, they had raided the Women's Welfare Office in Melbourne in the middle of the night.

"Let me see it," I said. The man held the warrant out, holding it sideways so that I had to crank my head to take a look. I glanced at our address but had no time to read what they were searching for before he whisked the paper away from me.

"What's all this about?" I said, trying to sound calm.

"Last night, some people broke into the animal laboratory at the University of Queensland and took all the mice," one of them said. "They spray-painted animal rights slogans on the equipment. We have reason to believe that you people are behind this. We're looking for evidence."

---

[54] The three men were accused of the bombing but were charged and convicted of conspiracy to murder the leader of the National Front, a little-known right-wing group. They were sentenced to sixteen years, but following a Supreme Court inquiry, they were released after seven years, in May, 1985.

"Go right ahead. But you won't find any mice, except for maybe a few resident ones!"

Not reacting to my attempt at humor, they set about searching the house. Seizing upon a few old spray cans stored on the back porch (used to paint Christmas decorations on business windows, yet another of our fund-raising schemes), they shook them in front of my face, saying, "Look what we have here!" Next, they found some leaflets about animal rights that we'd been distributing earlier in the week. "Aha! This proves it!" one said, waving the pamphlets. He was wrong about that, though: we weren't responsible for the break-in, despite the "proof" he'd found.

They didn't stop there. Ransacking the place, they barged into every room in their dirty shoes, opening drawers, taking all kinds of things—including my address book and copies of RDS reports—and throwing it all into two large cardboard boxes they had also found on the porch. I followed them from room to room as they violated our sanctuary, trampling on the area rugs and tossing things around.

"Let's see your passport," one of the men demanded. He opened it, looked carefully through all the pages, then snapped it shut and handed it back.

"We know about some of the so-called marriages you people get to stay in the country. Have you had one of them?" I shook my head, my heart pounding.

Now I was really scared, because I *had* gotten a bogus marriage (or what we called a "BM") to an Australian Margii in order to get Australian citizenship. Unlike other didis, mine hadn't turned out well. In the middle of all the required paperwork, my "husband" had vanished, taking our dole (welfare) checks with him and leaving me in limbo. If they found out, I could be deported. Maybe they already know, I thought, my heart racing. Maybe the immigration office has already told them about me.

And that wasn't the only thing to be worried about. Another didi's dole statements were somewhere in the drawers they were searching through. I'd been signing them while she was away so we could continue receiving payments. Had they taken any of those? I had never felt comfortable doing that, but like all the other semi-legal (or worse) things I'd had to do, I felt there was no choice. We needed the money and were putting it to good use, or so I rationalized.

After what seemed like forever, the men left, carrying the boxes out with them. "We'll be back," one of them threatened.

Gitanjali and I walked in silence from room to room. I felt limp. The devastation was complete. It had taken them only three short hours to totally trash the spiritually uplifting vibrations of our tidy home. Papers littered the floor. Drawers had been pulled out and left gaping. Area rugs lay rumpled and askew. There was a dull and crude feeling to everything.

"Didi," Gitanjali said, breaking into my silence, "there's a legal service we can call. They give out free advice. They'll tell us what to do."

We called and spoke to a lawyer. She'd heard of us: most Australians had. Thanks to the Hilton bombing incident, Ananda Marga was notorious. I remembered the conversation I'd had with someone sitting next to me on a bus one day. After I mentioned Ananda Marga, I saw his eyes grow big, then watched as he excused himself and moved across the aisle.

The lawyer promised to look into the incident. "Sounds like a typical Special Branch operation," she said. "They're masters of intimidation. Most likely, they didn't have a warrant to take all the things they did. Did they give you a list of what they took?"

They hadn't and I told her so.

"That's also illegal: to seize property and not provide a list. Don't worry. We'll get it back," she assured me.

But I *was* worried—and sure that I was soon to be deported. All Special Branch had to do was check my name out with Immigration. Then they'd put me on the next plane out of the country. I couldn't just sit in Brisbane and wait for that to happen.

A retreat was about to start in northern Queensland. "That's where I'll go," I told Gitanjali later that day. "Will you be okay here alone?"

"Sure, Didi. I'm an Australian citizen. They can't do anything to me."

I wasn't quite certain of that; the three Margiis in jail were all Australian. Still, that evening I took a bus north to the city of Townsville, where the retreat was to be held.

Concerned that our phone in Brisbane was bugged, I didn't call for a week. (It wasn't paranoia on my part; at that time, many of our phones were.) When I finally did, Gitanjali had some news. "The lawyer called and said that, just like she'd thought, Special Branch didn't have a warrant for most of the things they took. It was only for stuff connected to the animal rights break-in. She demanded that they give her a list of everything. We should have all of it back in a week or two, she said."

"That's good news," I said, not telling her what I was thinking: What would prevent them from copying anything they wished? The fact that it would be illegal wouldn't matter a bit to them.

"Have they been around asking about me?" I asked.

"No, Didi, no more visits. It's been very quiet."

"Good. Now tell me: how have you been doing all by yourself? The school must be a drain on you." Gitanjali assured me that it was not and that she was more than capable of running things on her own for a while. I was grateful.

After another couple of weeks had passed uneventfully, I decided to take my chances in Brisbane. Soon after I returned, we got another visit. The same three men arrived, faces set in a collective frown, carrying the boxes. They handed them over to us and said, "We'll be back."

Despite their words, they didn't return. We had won this battle. Apparently, Special Branch never contacted Immigration about me; otherwise, I'd have been long gone. A case of one hand not knowing what the other is doing, I thought. I was safe, at least for now.

Chapter 17

A Revelation

Within a year of arriving in Australia (but before the raid took place), I was back in India, hoping to become an avadhutika at long last. A week after I got there, some other hopefuls and I were called to Baba's quarters in Lake Gardens. We all felt it: today could be the day, the one we had all been waiting for ever since we had become whole-timers. A few days earlier, we had been summoned and stood, as we did now, on the stairs waiting for Baba to call us up to his room, only to be turned away. But today, there was a sense of certainty. Soon, I was sure, I would be an avadhutika—and my life would be his.

Didis I hadn't seen for a long time were waiting with me. They included Prashanti, the cantankerous woman who'd been in training with me.

"Namaskar, Malatii," she said, hugging me. "It's been a long time."

"It certainly has," I said. "You look wonderful!" She did. She had none of the hard edges she'd had back in training, and her face was glowing.

Suddenly, Baba's Personal Assistant appeared at the top of the stairs, gesturing. "Come quick!" Needing no encouraging, we flew up the stairs and crowded together at Baba's door. One by one, we stepped out of our sandals and entered his room. Baba was sitting on his cot in his characteristic pose, one leg draped over the other, cushions at each arm. He was dressed all in white and was smiling. I approached, did *pranam*, touching my forehead to the floor, then sat and looked around. There were ten or twelve of us didis and dadas sitting in front of him.

Baba began to speak of what it meant to be an avadhuta or an avadhutika. In the tradition of great spiritual personalities throughout the ages, we would dedicate ourselves to the liberation of every being in the universe. We would not accept our own liberation until each and every being achieved that exalted state. We drank in his every word, our eyes fixed on his face.

Baba put his feet on the floor and gestured for us to come near. We rushed up to Baba's cot to touch his feet, jostling for position. I managed to get just one or two fingers on his left foot. Then Baba administered the oath. We repeated his words. It was a shining moment, brief yet somehow timeless.

Baba did namaskar, signaling that our time with him had ended. We all did the same. Then we turned and slowly filed out of the room and down the stairs. We didis headed to the tiny room we had in the back of the main meditation hall. As usual, lots of didis were crowded in there with veils off, some meditating, others eating lunch. When we came in, all the didis stopped what they were doing and gave us hugs and their congratulations.

Then came another long-anticipated moment: we were going to change our dress, removing our white saris and petticoats for the last time and replacing them with orange ones. As Ananda Kripa silently passed the new petticoats and saris around, we eagerly took them and began putting them on. We knew Ananda Kripa wasn't in a good mood. The day before, Baba had taken away her avadhutika dress as punishment for some infraction. It was only temporary, but she was wearing a white sari for the first time in who knew how long, and she wasn't happy about it. We paid her no mind as we wrapped our new saris around us.

This was our day, and I, for one, wasn't going to let her mood dampen it.

We finished putting our uniforms over our orange saris, tied our new orange belts around our waists, and rushed out of the room and into the hall. Margiis and other workers who were waiting for darshan gathered around us. "You look wonderful!" one said. "Congratulations!" said another. "What an auspicious day!"

"Didi, what's your avadhutika name?" someone asked me. I didn't know. Baba hadn't yet given me one. We were all waiting for him to come down from his room. That's when he would give all of us our new names.

We pooled our money and sent out for large clay pots of sweets. Mostly we ordered *rasgoolas*, the famous Bengali white balls made from curds and dripping with sugar syrup flavored with rose water. They were the king of all sweets. Since only the best would do, we had them purchased from K.C. Das, the premier Bengali sweet maker on Dalhousie Square. We would give them out once we had our names.

Suddenly, the whirlwind of excitement and activity that always signaled Baba's approach engulfed us, and there he was, coming down the plant-lined walkway, moving slowly and deliberately, his guard walking backwards in front of him as always.

Like bees seeking nectar, we gathered around him. He stopped and, smiling, turned to us. "Are you happy?" he asked. "Yes, Baba," we replied in unison. Then he began to give us our names, one by one. Finally, Baba turned to me. I held my breath.

"Ananda Madhuchanda," he said. "One whose rhythm is filled with the bliss of divine sweetness." I felt a wave of joy at the name. It was so beautiful! Then Baba smiled his slow and blissful smile— and the whole world lit up. The sun glinted on the plants, and radiance surrounded our little group, enveloping us in blessings.

Once Baba returned to his room, we distributed the sweets. All pandemonium broke loose, as, mobbed by children and adults alike, we carried the pots and popped the sweets into waiting mouths until the last syrupy *rasgoola* was gone. It was a sweet ending to a perfect day. At the time, I thought it to be the greatest day of my life.

It wasn't long after I returned to Australia that my euphoria was tempered a little.

"What's your avadhutika name?" Ananda Bhadra asked me.

After I told her, a look hard to read passed over her face.

"I'm not sure I should tell you this . . ."

"Tell me what?"

" 'Chander' means 'vomit' in Aussie English," she said after a long pause.

"Oh, that's just great!" I said, "So here in Australia, my name means 'sweet vomit'!"

Come to think of it, I'd gotten some odd looks after telling the Margiis my new name. Now I knew why.

Despite my new name and dress, there were still things about me that remained disappointingly the same, including my bouts of depression. In Brisbane, there was an American dada, Khajitananda, whose sunny personality and jokes would always lift my spirits when I was feeling low. One day, not long after I had returned from India, he told me about a Jehovah's Witness who had come to his neighborhood, knocking on doors and distributing the *Watchtower*.

"I wasn't in uniform the first time he came," Dada said, "but we got to talking, and I told him I was a yoga teacher. 'Yoga will lead you to the devil!' he said. So the next time he came, I showed him just how right he was. I greeted him at the door wearing my uniform. And I did this." Dada drew himself up to his full height, arranged his mouth in a fiendish smile, pulled his unruly eyebrows together, and let out a hiss. "His face went white and he took off down the block," Dada continued, "then stopped at the end of the street to look back. So I went out to the street and did the same thing. He scurried around the corner—and hasn't been back since!"

Dada tilted his head back and roared with laughter, and I joined in, feeling good, my mood transformed. There was no getting around it: I liked being around Khajitananda and was glad we were working in the same city. Becoming an avadhutika hadn't erased the misgivings I'd begun to have about the organization, but the support I got from just relaxing and being with Dada, another worker committed to the same cause, meant a great deal to me. And, truth be told, I found him attractive. That didn't particularly bother me, though. I was confident of my ability to overcome any such feelings and had no plans to act on them.

Personal relationships of any kind among workers were not encouraged in Ananda Marga. While same-sex friendships were not actively discouraged, male-female ones were; since most of us were in our twenties and thirties, we had to be vigilant about sexual attraction. No written sanctions existed against such friendships, but we all got the message to keep our distance. Our in-charges relied upon a well-placed remark or two to remind someone to keep his or her distance. Ananda Sudha often took it upon herself to keep her didis in line in this way.

During one RDS in Katoomba, a town in the Blue Mountains where the Sectorial Office was located, I was in the didis' room after the morning meeting, getting ready for noon meditation, when Ananda Sudha came in.

"Madhuchanda, you were sitting so close to Khajitananda, you were almost on his lap! Be careful," she said loudly, wagging her finger at me. The other didis turned and looked. "I don't want to see you sitting so close to him again," she said, brows knitted, the deep line appearing between her eyes.

It was true that I'd been sitting next to Khajitananda, but I hadn't been sitting overly close. Even so, I didn't challenge Ananda Sudha. To do so was to invite a blistering storm of anger that left you feeling like you'd been physically attacked. I'd had my share of her anger in Fiji and had also had a few run-ins with her since, so I just nodded and arranged my blanket for meditation.

But a day or two later, the tables would forever be turned on Ananda Sudha—in my mind, at least.

We had finished our morning meeting and were gathering for lunch when one of the Indian dadas, Rajatananda, took me aside. "Madhuchanda," he said quietly, "there is something I think you should know about Ananda Sudha."

During RDS, Rajatananda had witnessed the public humiliation of one didi after another at the hands of Ananda Sudha, since she usually didn't bother to take us to task in private. A gentle and introspective man who always did long hours of sadhana, Rajatananda had been quietly refusing to eat any food that Ananda Sudha had cooked. While everyone else had been busily digging into the spicy cauliflower and potato curries and dahls that Ananda Sudha had prepared for RDS lunches, he'd been cheerfully eating peanut butter and jelly sandwiches and salads. At the time, I thought it was because of her conduct at our meetings. *He's following the conduct rule* One must not take food touched by a mean-minded person *better than the rest of us,* I thought when I saw him in the kitchen making one of his salads.

"It is something that most Indian workers know," he continued, "but no one wanted to tell any of you because it would affect her reputation here."

"What is it, Dada?" I asked, trying to keep the excitement out of my voice.

"Well, you may not believe it, but it is true," he said. "You can ask any other older Indian worker. They will tell you the same thing." Dada cleared his throat, his face taking on a reddish hue visible even beneath his full-face beard. He looked away, then back at me as I waited.

"Didi got pregnant once with a worker," he finally said. "Baba took her dress away. Didi went into hiding, had the baby, and then returned to worker life." He fell silent. I stared at him, feeling the blood drain out of my face. I was breathless. Could it possibly be true?

The enormity of it washed over me: Ananda Sudha was always dropping innuendos about other workers, implying they had uncontrolled sexual desires, and if what Dada had just told me was true, she herself had gotten pregnant after becoming a worker and had given birth! What a hypocrite she was, I thought, criticizing me for sitting too close to Khajitananda, acting as if she possessed a pure spirituality untainted by any sexual feelings, implying that we Western didis had sex on our minds all the time.

I believed in following the worker code of conduct to the letter and couldn't imagine that anyone who had taken vows and become a whole-timer could have sex and still remain one. It wasn't as if I didn't have those desires. But I knew I would never have sex as a whole-timer. If I ever decided I had to, I would leave first, I told myself. (One of the most challenging things about being a worker was the celibacy requirement. I didn't know how others felt about it, though, since we never discussed our struggles with the sexual *vritti* or propensity. You had to wrestle with it on your own. I remembered in particular my thirtieth birthday, when, after a long meditation, I had promised Baba that I would be victorious over my sexual desires, naively hoping that the most powerful of urges were behind me and things would be easier.)

I thanked Rajatananda for taking me into his confidence, then watched him walk to the kitchen, on his way, no doubt, to making another peanut butter and jelly sandwich. His words had thrown me into such turmoil that I felt compelled to check their veracity. I went in search of Ananda Vinoda, the Indian didi in charge of the sister's LFT training center in Melbourne. I'd first met her while I was in training. She had given me my sixth and final lesson, so I felt like I had a special bond with her. Surely, she would confirm or deny the truth of what Dada had told me.

I told her what Dada had said, then watched as her face paled, then reddened.

"Is it true, Didi?"

"I won't tell you if it is or not," she said and turned away. I knew that Ananda Vinoda had also suffered abuse at the hands

215

of Ananda Sudha; we often exchanged stories when we met. But Ananda Vinoda had such loyalty to the organization, I thought, that she couldn't bring herself to confirm what I knew at that point to be true.

That's what I thought then, but now I look at it differently. Most Indian workers considered themselves superior to Western ones. Ananda Vinoda's reluctance may have had more to do with protecting Ananda Sudha's reputation and with loyalty to a fellow Indian didi than it did with loyalty to the organization as a whole. Or it could have been a lack of willingness to even think about what Ananda Sudha had done; to do so would be to acknowledge the impact sexual desires had on all our lives despite our efforts to suppress them.

And what about the behavior of Rajatananda? His refusal to take food prepared by Ananda Sudha likely had much more to do with the fact that she had gotten pregnant as a worker and his disgust at it than with how she treated the other didis during RDS. After all, most Indian dadas weren't exactly champions of women.

Even though it didn't occur to me until years later, the secret I had learned about Ananda Sudha did explain a great deal about her behavior. In retrospect, it helped illuminate her actions in dealing with the "lesbian problem" in Sydney.

Every three months around RDS time, I would often spend a week or two at the Sydney sister's jagrti, Sydney being close to Katoomba. I soon learned that the Margiis there, at least the female ones, were quite different from those in Brisbane. Many of them—strong, independent women who regularly gave money and time to the organization—were lesbians. Ananda Marga's relationship with homosexuality was an uneasy one at best, so all that the lesbians contributed posed a dilemma for the organization, affecting even the Gympie land I'd helped arrange money for. In fact, soon after it was purchased, two women, Jayadevi and Chandrika, moved there and worked hard to develop it. There was no dwelling, so they bought a beautiful house with a big wraparound porch and had it moved to the property. But from the beginning, the project was surrounded by controversy, largely because Jayadevi and Chandrika were lesbians. What made matters even worse in the eyes of the organization was that Chandrika had once been a didi. So the property ended up never being recognized as a master unit despite the good work that was to take place there over several years.

The dilemma the Sydney lesbians presented was an especially difficult one for Ananda Sudha. She loved the work they did for the organization and, it seemed to me, loved their money even more. She needed as much of it as possible when she went to Calcutta for RDS; the more she presented to the Central workers, the greater her influence and prestige. But how could she accept money from people she believed, and was convinced Baba believed, were immoral?

As workers, we were meant to follow Baba's guidelines for Ananda Marga society, so it would make sense for us to search for anything he might have said or written on the subject of homosexuality. Baba had written and spoken extensively, for example, on the two roles we had to choose from: acarya or family person. Single Margiis could spend time as LFTs and work with didis and dadas on projects, but they were expected to eventually choose one of the two. As a result, there was no formally recognized role for lifelong unmarried Margiis. Such people were looked down upon; during one DMC talk, I even heard Baba refer to bachelors as "parasites." Most of us assumed that Baba was referring to unmarried Margiis of both sexes even though he used a word normally associated with unmarried men. By this definition, a homosexual Margii would indeed be a parasite, but so would an unmarried heterosexual one. The problem was that Baba had never written or spoken publicly about homosexuality, so no one was sure what he thought about it. Despite that fact, some Indian workers, including Ananda Sudha, claimed that in meetings with them, Baba had declared homosexuality to be dirty, unnatural, and immoral.

Ananda Sudha found a way out of her dilemma. While in Australia, she acted open and accepting of the lesbians, encouraging them to give of their time and energy, and collecting their money. Every time she went to India, however, that attitude underwent a radical change. Central Office knew about the "lesbian problem" in Australia, so at every opportunity, we heard that Ananda Sudha would express moral outrage and condemn the Sydney women in front of the Central dadas.

At one point, Anishananda met with Ananda Sudha in Sydney to draw up a policy concerning gay Margiis. His purpose was to come up with something that would respect their rights while still deferring to what Baba's attitude towards homosexuality was assumed to be. Anishananda and Ananda Sudha spent hours crafting the policy. Once it was finished, Dada signed it. Didi did not. At the next RDS in India, Ananda Sudha accused Anishananda of coddling the homosexual Margiis and claimed that he had written the (unsuitably liberal) policy himself, with no input from her. Dada was devastated and eventually left the organization. Most of us in the know considered that Ananda Sudha's duplicity in this affair was one of the prime reasons for his departure.

It hadn't occurred to me at the time, but Ananda Sudha must have felt compelled to constantly prove her moral mettle, as it were. After all, it wasn't every day that an avadhutika had a baby and then returned to whole-timer life. In all the years I spent in the organization, I never heard of even a single case similar to hers. The Central dadas must have been on the lookout for further lapses on her part, and she was determined to give them no grounds to find any. Otherwise, what would become of her if they kicked her out—a middle-aged Indian woman, unmarried and uneducated? She had to stay to survive and would do whatever it took to maintain her position.

The revelation about Ananda Sudha got me thinking again about relationships in Ananda Marga. You might get close to another worker with whom you had worked, but eventually one of you would get reposted, either to another country in the same sector or another sector entirely. Once that happened, you might meet from time to time in India, but certainly not often. I realized at that point that the senior dadas and didis (if not Baba himself) might have wanted it that way. If people were kept from having close relationships, there would be less discussion of some of the darker aspects of the organization, less sharing of personal issues and struggles, and more control over minds and secrets like Ananda Sudha's.

There was, in fact, a distinct anti-psychological bias in the organization. Ananda Marga workers frowned on therapeutic practices like rebirthing or even more traditional forms of psychotherapy. The response to all problems was invariably the same. "You don't need any of that," we were encouraged to tell lay Margiis. "Just do more kiirtan and meditation and your problems will resolve themselves."

Some Indian workers made fun of what they considered to be Western Margiis' obsession with psychology while demonstrating little insight into or interest in their own mental processes. It was not uncommon for didis and dadas (especially the Indian ones, it seemed to me) who daily spent hours in meditation to act like children. Despite their memorizing the list of *astha pasha* and *sat ripu* (the eight bondages and six enemies, such as anger and envy), it was not rare for workers to explode in rage over a trifle. It seemed that there were only two realms for such workers: the spiritual and the physical, with the spiritual realm being vastly more important.

However, the social and spiritual philosophy of Anandamurti held otherwise. In his *Ananda Sutram*, Baba stated that this world is a relative truth, thereby discounting the traditionally held belief among Indian spiritual seekers that the physical world is merely an illusion and the only real world is the spiritual one. In other writings, he noted the importance of developing oneself in all spheres: physical, mental, and spiritual. While many Western

Margiis took these teachings to heart, it seemed to me that many of the Indians focused almost exclusively on their spiritual development. It was as if the ancient spiritual tradition of their culture still held them in its grasp despite Baba's teachings.

But perhaps the most important reason for the lack of close relationships among workers was this: the connection to the Guru was considered to be the true relationship, the only eternal one—and the only one that mattered. Ananda Marga was a universe in which Baba was the sun and his followers planets that revolved around him, endeavoring to attain the closest orbit possible. As a result, the devotee's energy and love was directed towards the Guru, and not much was left over for others.

Physical proximity to Baba was highly valued. In the early years, family Margiis and workers had been close to Baba both physically and spiritually, but as time went on and Ananda Marga became an international organization with centers all over the world, the relationship with the Guru became more of an internal one. Even in India, physical access to the Guru was restricted. One could get a glimpse of him or spend time listening to him give darshan, but real closeness was no longer possible.

Still, we tried. When we came to Calcutta, we had no time for each other. We did our kiirtan and meditation, went over to Baba's house for darshan, did more meditation, and then returned to Baba's house, hoping for yet another glimpse. Both of the buildings the organization had built near Baba's house in Tiljala had several floors. There was a joke that went around: "Don't get sick if you're staying on one of the upper floors," it went. "You could die before anyone would notice or come to help you!"

Despite the lack of physical closeness, the end result of a worker's relationship with the Guru was that it fueled him or her to do remarkable things in the field. It was the certainty of Baba's love and protection that had infused me with a seemingly never-ending source of inspiration and energy. It had given me the confidence to travel alone through dangerous places, to go to countries without knowing anyone and with no money to speak of, to risk my life hitchhiking in the Middle East alone as a woman. My understanding at the time was that it wasn't just me traveling by myself. He was there with me. He was working through me. He would protect me. And I soon had a wealth of experience that, to me, proved it to be so.

One particular incident from my time in Cairo Sector comes to mind. I was traveling overland from Turkey to India with a young Icelandic dada; we were on our way to a DMC with little time to get there. One evening, we arrived at an isolated border post between Pakistan and India, but by the time we'd gotten the all clear to cross, it was too late; there would be no bus until the next morning. That presented us with a dilemma: if we waited for the bus, we'd miss the DMC. We ended up convincing (with some money) a few men in a pickup truck to take us to a bus depot or something; I don't remember exactly where. We climbed into the back and off we went. Night had fallen. The men drove across a desert-like landscape that reminded me of the moon; as far as I could determine, there was no road at all. At one point, we came to a deserted building site. The strange thing was that it was brightly lit, despite being in the middle of nowhere. The truck stopped, and the men got out and scurried around picking up what they could and stashing it in the rear of the truck, right next to us. Stealing! Wide-eyed, Dada and I stared at each other. We had the same thought: what would prevent these men from killing us, taking our money, and then dumping our bodies out there? Baba, obviously![55]

I was far from the only one with such experiences. People would swap amazing Baba stories at every gathering and RDS meeting. A kind of collective mythology developed. That's not to say that the stories weren't true or the events they detailed hadn't

---

[55] However, Baba's protection did not prevent the massacre in broad daylight of seventeen dadas and didis on the streets of Calcutta in April of 1982—a day known in the organization as *Dadhcii Divas*, or Martyr's Day. It is widely believed that the Communist Party of West Bengal was behind the murders. To this day, the perpetrators have not been brought to justice.

happened. Many of them had. But was Baba responsible for all of them? Since we are all divine, surely individual initiative and hard work accounted for some of what we accomplished.

The divine force exists everywhere. In Ananda Marga, we personified and crystallized it in the form of the Guru. We came to regard the Guru as the sole repository of the divine, thus often neglecting it in ourselves and in each other.

Chapter 18

The School—the Real Thing

When I became a didi, I never imagined how much of my time would be taken up with paperwork, but it wasn't long before I found out I was responsible for writing lots of reports about the progress of my work. It wouldn't have been so bad if we'd just had a monthly report to do, but there was also a weekly and even a daily one. All were usually written by hand, with copies being sent to the regional, sectorial, and central offices.

One of the most important report items was school creation. A whole-timer was expected to start a school every month, if not every week. At RDS meetings in India, sectorial workers had to report in front of Baba on the number started since the last meeting, and no one wanted to be taken to task for lack of output.

So we started schools. We recruited a few children for some after-school activities at our centers, and those were schools. In non-English speaking countries, we would get some children together and teach them English once or twice a week. Or we would persuade new mothers to drop off their infants, and we'd do what amounted to babysitting. They were all "schools" and we started hundreds of them.

Through all of this, I had a hidden desire to start a real school. In contrast to schools on paper, which I had plenty of, I wanted one that had its own building, was in session five days a week, and was recognized by the local community and government. Some workers likely regarded this desire as a bit strange. After all, why open a real school, which could take months or even years, instead of starting ten, twenty, or thirty paper ones?

One summer in 1984 or '85, I was working in Lismore, a small town in northern New South Wales. On one particularly hot afternoon, I was in a house having lunch with four or five other women. The interior was dim, the lights having been turned off to counter the heat, and I found myself fighting off sleep as I listened with half an ear to the conversation flowing around me—until someone started talking about a vacant school building. My drowsiness vanished, and I sat bolt upright in my chair.

"What did you say . . . something about a school building?"

Katrina, our host, turned to me.

"Yes, Didi. It's just sitting empty," she said. "It's been closed for two or three years now."

"Is that the school that was started as a cooperative by some hippie parents?" asked one of the other women. "I heard that things went well for a few years, but then the parents started arguing about everything and it closed."

"Yes, that's the one."

"Where exactly is this school?" I asked.

"I'm not sure," Katrina said. "I know it's not in town. It's some kilometers out, somewhere in the bush."

It sounded too good to be true. A school building just sitting there on some land not too far away? This warranted investigating! I'd need a car and someone who knew the area to help find the property. Mandakinii, a soft-spoken yet sturdy

Margii sister in her twenties, immediately came to mind. Just days earlier, I had shared my dream of starting a school with her, and she'd responded with enthusiasm.

When I called Mandakinii later that afternoon, she reacted to the news and my request just as I'd hoped. "How exciting!" she said. "I'll pick you up at eight tomorrow morning."

The next day dawned clear and sunny but promised to be a bit hot for me in my robes. Instead of the Indian skirt and peasant blouse she usually wore, Mandakinii had on shorts, which I eyed somewhat longingly as I got in the car. Mandakinii decided to take the main road out to Byron Bay, the easternmost point of Australia. "Maybe the school is somewhere off this road," she said as we drove along. We stopped to ask the few people we saw walking or working in the area, but no one had ever heard of the place.

"Don't worry, we'll find it somehow," Mandakinii assured me. "Anyway, it's a nice day for a drive."

A farmer finally pointed the way. "If I'm not mistaken, you'll find 'er about a kilometer or two up the road, off the main road a bit," the man said, wiping the sweat off his face with a handkerchief.

Thanking him, we took off in the direction indicated and soon found a small unpaved road going off to the right. We followed it in and stopped at a closed cattle gate, got out and looked down the dirt path. There were high weeds on both sides of it.

"Let's open the gate and walk down the path a little ways," Mandakinii said. I agreed, and we swung the gate open. About fifty meters in, we found it: a small building, neglected, but clearly intact.

The front door was locked, so we walked slowly around, inspecting the building carefully and looking in all the windows. It had just one room, but as far as we could tell, it looked to be in good condition. There was a set of bathrooms and sinks located on one side, out of doors but covered.

The surroundings were idyllic: rolling countryside, a few cows grazing off in the distance, and one or two chubby white clouds floating in a perfectly blue sky. I looked over at Mandakinii. "Isn't it fantastic?" I said, opening my arms as if embracing the whole scene. She nodded, smiling, her brown eyes twinkling. We were determined to make the school our own.

After asking around, we learned that the property was still owned by the original group of parents who had formed a cooperative called "Magic Pudding." Mandakinii contacted them and soon had an agreement: She and her husband Dhruva would move into the loft above the schoolroom, a cozy little space with a wonderful view of the countryside. Living there as caretakers almost rent-free, they would work on clearing weeds and cleaning up the property with help not just from me and other Margiis in the area but, if all went according to plan, from prospective parents we were hoping to attract through a meeting in town we were already planning.

Mandakinii and I got busy putting up posters in the shops and placing an ad in the local newspaper. When the evening of the meeting came around, I couldn't decide whether I should wear my uniform.

"What do you think?" I said to Mandakinii. "I don't want to scare anyone off."

"It's up to you, Didi. Either way is okay with me."

In the end, I decided upon "civies." As I watched the crowd filing through the doors and filling up the room we'd rented, I was glad I had. There would be enough to talk about without questions about Ananda Marga taking up the whole time. As it was, it was barely mentioned.

When I wore my uniform at subsequent meetings, inevitable concerns were raised. "Is it a religion?" someone asked. "Will you teach the children Ananda Marga philosophy?" But despite the negative image Ananda Marga still had in the country, most prospective parents were so eager to have the school open that their concerns didn't stop them from getting involved. It was clear they weren't happy with the public school in Lismore and saw ours as providing a good alternative.

Far more difficult were obstacles presented by Ananda Marga itself. Since other workers were opening one school after another every month or so, my supervisors weren't happy that mine was taking so much time to get off the ground. At RDS meetings, I would report on the progress being made. Mandakinii and Dhruva had moved in and had begun to clean up the property, I told them. I also reported on the meetings we had conducted, along with the number of attendees. These updates were waved off. Instead of being impressed at my progress, my superiors only grew more frustrated with me.

"Every time you come to RDS, you say the same thing," the usually soft-spoken Sureshananda, one of the Central workers who often visited Australia, said, raising his voice. "When is it going to open?"

"Dada," I countered, "you can't open a real school overnight. It takes time."

"If you can't open it soon, leave that place and go somewhere else and do it!" he shouted, then turned his attention to the next didi, hoping for a more satisfactory report from her.

Surely a real school is worth so much more than all those fake ones, I thought, fuming. Why can't they see that? But Dada wasn't about to sit around and wait for me to create a real school. Since he and others in supervisory positions had to stand in front of Baba and give him the numbers, quantity is what counted.

Besides, I'd already proved a disappointment to my superiors in another important report item: the creation of new whole-timers. It was a matter of great pride to have "created" a whole-timer. Didis and dadas worked hard to inspire individuals to go to training and emerge months later from the chrysalis of the training center ready to take flight in orange and white robes. Occasionally, there were disputes concerning who had actually created a particular didi or dada. Sometimes two or even three of us would claim the same new worker. The matter would be hotly debated during RDS meetings.

"Well, I initiated her," one didi would say. "I gave her most of her lessons, and she worked with me as an LFT for two years. I talked to her about going to training, and she said she wanted to go." "But," another would counter, "I gave her the sixth lesson and actually sent her to the training center." Each didi would then enlist help from witnesses to prove her case.

Many recruits were very young, still in their teens, some as young as sixteen or seventeen. Some had just completed high school; others had begun college but left when called to what they saw as a higher duty. Younger Margiis were often star-struck by the semi-guru mystique that surrounded the whole-timer and were easier to recruit than older ones.

In the years right after I had finished training, I was anxious to inspire others to whole-timer life. Even back then, though, it hadn't felt right to try to convince girls with so little life experience to make a decision that would change their lives forever; once you became a whole-timer, you were expected to remain one for life. Other workers had no such qualms and gladly encouraged these youngsters to go to training. "Oh, there's no need to finish high school," one would say to a potential recruit. "Why wait until then if you know that this is what you really want to do with your life? Besides, service to Baba is more important than school!"

Recently, I had worked hard to convince an older woman to go to training. Savita, a German woman who was living in Australia, was in her early thirties and had been working as an LFT. I spent a lot of time meditating with her and regaling her with Baba stories before launching into my pitch. All to no avail. "She has too much of her own mind," I complained, venting my frustration to my peers. So despite my efforts, my WT creation figure (faithfully tallied on reports) stubbornly remained zero or "nil" as we called it. So the pressure was on. For the sake of my reputation, I had to start this school.

There was one significant detail about the school I hadn't shared with my superiors at RDS: the fact that it was going to take even longer to open because Mandakinii and Dhruva had decided to go to India. Dhruva was a long-term or what we called an "old" Margii and had been to India a number of times, but this was going to be Mandakinii's first trip. She was very much looking forward to meeting Baba.

However, their trip didn't quite turn out as expected. When Dhruva presented his passport at the Bombay airport, Indian officials took him aside and forced him to board a flight back to Australia. Like other old Margiis, his name had ended up on the blacklist. Mandakinii got through without incident, even though she'd been standing right behind Dhruva; since her passport name bore no resemblance to his, they must not have realized they were together. With no one to make train reservations and accompany her, Mandakinii was too afraid to try to get to Calcutta on her own.

"I didn't know what to do," she told me when she returned. "I was sure people would figure out I was a Margii and I'd be arrested." She ended up renting a room in a hotel, where she hid for a week. Then, having never made it to see Baba, she came back to Australia, her attitude towards Ananda Marga having undergone a radical transformation. Now she wanted nothing to do with the organization—or the school.

I sympathized. I knew what a traumatic experience it must have been for her. But what would I do without Mandakinii? She was the one who had been doing such a fantastic job taking care of most of the front work. Besides her great energy and drive, she had an open manner that drew people to her. Now, it hardly seemed likely the school would ever open. Margiis in the area were supportive of the project, but not to the extent of putting in the hard work and time it would take to realize it.

For a week or two, I carefully considered my options, but there was really only one: give up my dream and leave Lismore. As I slowly packed my things, I mulled over all the time and energy I had spent on the project. All for naught. Sureshananda had been right after all. What would he say at the next RDS? Probably, *I told you so.*

The day before I was going to leave, Mandakinii called and asked me to meet her at the park in town. I agreed, wanting to thank her for all she'd done. It would be nice to see her one last time. We'd been through so much together.

When I got to the park, a smiling Mandakinii was waiting for me. She gave me a hug, seeming like her enthusiastic old self, like she'd been before going to India. "Didi," she said all in a rush, "last night I had the most incredible dream about Baba! It was so vivid. Baba spoke to me, and by what he said, I know that he wants the school to open. I told Dhruva about my dream and he agrees. He says he'll support me in this. If I start working on the project again, would you stay?"

Would I stay? We hugged, tears coming to our eyes. The school came that close to never happening.

Once we passed that crisis, amazing things began happening to make the school a reality. The most interesting of these was a car accident and the money that eventually came from it. One evening I was on my way home after teaching a yoga class, sitting in the passenger's seat of a car being driven by one of my students. She lived near the Lismore jagrti (which I'd rented a few months after starting on the school project) and was giving me a ride; in the back was another student, a woman with her toddler. As we entered an intersection only a few blocks from our destination, I caught sight of a dark blue van to our left shooting into the intersection against the light, coming straight for us.

"Look out!" I screamed. Our driver swerved, but the van still slammed into us. Amazingly, it flipped over, as big as it was, while our car somehow remained upright. A quick check confirmed that although we were all badly shaken up, no one was injured. There was no movement from inside the van, however. Ambulances were soon on the scene, and a pair of paramedics took the driver away on a stretcher.

A day or two later, I was relating the incident to a Margii sister when she interrupted me. "Did you know that in Australia you can get a lot of money for what they call 'pain and suffering'?"

"Really?" I had experienced some pain in my neck, likely a bit of whiplash, but in true didi fashion, had intended to ignore it. "Well, come to think of it," I said, "my neck hurts."

I went to the hospital and had an extensive series of X-rays taken. Next I got a lawyer, who agreed to take my case for nothing up front. "I'm sure you'll get money for pain and suffering," she said and suggested that I go to a chiropractor. "You'll need documentation of treatment."

The only chiropractor I could find within walking distance was male. Although I knew it wasn't a good idea to see a male doctor, I made an appointment, telling myself that it was for a good cause. It was important to get the money to buy the school. Hopefully, I wouldn't need too many appointments.

At first, it felt strange being manipulated by the chiropractor; no man had touched my body in years. Bit by bit, though, I started to enjoy and look forward to my appointments. I even began having fantasies about the doctor, which caused tremendous feelings of guilt. I'm a didi! I'd think whenever they happened. I shouldn't be having these thoughts! Besides the guilt, there was also frustration and surprise at how quickly such feelings could still overtake me. It felt like a failing that despite the long hours of meditation, I was still susceptible to such base desires, as I thought of them. Towards the end of my treatment, the chiropractor developed stomach cancer and died, thus saving me from myself. A new doctor—a woman, thankfully—took over the practice.

It took more than a year, but in the end, I got the money, which, after lawyer fees were taken out, came to about twelve thousand Australian dollars. I took the bulk of it to the bank for the school down payment but secretly hung on to about two thousand dollars, just enough for a ticket to India—and some much-needed dental work.

Except for having had a tooth pulled out in India during training and another in Turkey, I hadn't been to a dentist in over ten years. Even so, I had to make sure no one knew about the money I was keeping. Otherwise, Ananda Sudha would make me give it to her. I knew she considered going to dentists a waste of precious financial resources. "I never go to dentists. It's a waste of money. Why spend money on your teeth? Just let them rot, or get them pulled out," I remembered her saying once. So I opened a secret bank account, fighting against feelings of guilt, which weren't as strong as they would have been a few years earlier, before Fiji and Ananda Sudha's visit.

Around this time, another rather amazing thing happened, reconfirming for everyone involved that Baba really was behind the school. I was on tour in northern New South Wales and was visiting a newly initiated sister named Emma in one of the ubiquitous small towns to be found there, when our conversation turned to the school.

"How are you going to buy it?" she asked.

"We have enough money for a down payment. We'll get a bank loan for the rest."

"But bank loans aren't a good idea. They charge so much interest, you'll end up paying almost double for the property by the end."

"I know," I said, "but we have no alternative. We don't have any other way of getting the money."

That's when Emma made her offer. She had money, she said, and wanted to give us an interest-free loan. So that's what happened. Emma supplied the rest of the money for the purchase of the school, no questions asked.

Now that we owned the property, we turned our attention to the school building, which needed an addition for another classroom. We spent days trying to figure out how to raise the money until Dhruva said he would donate all his Christmas stenciling profits to the school building fund.

Christmas stenciling was another innovative way we raised money in Australia. After RDS meetings, we'd trace the masters of Christmas trees and Santas on to large pieces of thick cardboard, hurting our hands as we cut the stencils out with exacto knives. Then we'd show photos of previously completed jobs to prospective clients. Getting the job was the easiest part. Doing it was another thing entirely: It required long hours of lugging spray paints, rolls of masking tape, and over-sized stencils around in the hot summer streets (Australia being in the Southern Hemisphere). I would tape the scene chosen by the customer upon the designated shop window and select colors; then, area by area, I'd spray the scene on, covering up parts of the window I didn't want the paint to get on with smaller pieces of cardboard and more tape. It was hard and dirty work, and the heat didn't help matters. It always seemed to get hotter as the job progressed, and the snowy scenes I was creating did little to cool me off as cars and buses barreled past, spewing fumes. So I was grateful to Dhruva when he offered to donate his profits. I knew how hard he would be working!

Each Margii in the business had his or her own territory, so Dhruva checked with everyone else who was doing stenciling in the area, then canvassed those places that were left. Most days he went out, working not only in Lismore but in Mullimbimby, Byron Bay, and other nearby towns; doing job after job and not stopping until we had just enough money to go ahead with the new classroom.

A friend of Dhruva's in the construction business drew up the plans for the addition, and a volunteer crew carried them out. The project attracted some strange types, as Ananda Marga often did. One was a hippie with long hair who went around bare-chested claiming that drinking one's own urine had great health benefits. Even with the strange types helping out, a great deal of work got done, as day after day, sounds of sawing and hammering filled the air.

During the final push to get everything done, a new didi arrived in Lismore. Her name was Vandana, and she was from Japan. Short and thin, she had an open, smooth face, large black eyes with thick lashes, and an engaging smile made somewhat impish by some crooked teeth. She plunged right into the work

233

and helped us solve the problem we had with giant lantana plants. The plant was considered a pernicious weed in Australia, spreading quickly as it did over large areas, morphing into a complex of huge plants with deep and intractable roots. Large areas of the school property were covered by it. Day after day, armed with machetes and pruners, Vandana and I would go out and fight lantana, Vandana wielding her machete like a samurai warrior. Thorny stems would scratch us as we cut them to the ground, and getting all the roots out proved next to impossible, but we finally emerged from the battlefield victorious.

As the days passed and the first day of school grew near, everyone redoubled their efforts, working at a feverish pace and putting in long days. We finished working on the building the day before the school opened, staying up all night with the last of the painting, getting the furniture set up, and making sure everything was in place.

At nine o'clock the next morning, fifteen children arrived, carrying brand-new book bags and looking smart in their red and black uniforms, their scrubbed faces shining. Mandakinii, Vandana, and I congratulated one another. We had done it! Vistara[56] Primary had opened! After turning over the students to our newly hired teacher, we went home, collapsed onto our sleeping bags, and were asleep within minutes.

Over the next few months, Ananda Marga bigwigs visited the school, looked around, and liked what they saw. Even Ananda Sudha seemed impressed—but not for long.

"Now that the school is up and running," she said during one visit, "you should be able to give a lot of money to the organization."

"What do you mean, Didi?"

"Well, the school surely brings in a good amount of money. You should give some to me."

I couldn't believe what I was hearing. "Didi, I can't take any money from the school," I said.

---

[56] *vistara:* Expansion.

"Why not? Why did you bother opening it if the organization doesn't get anything?"

"Didi," I said in as level a tone as I was able, "the school receives government funding. We have to keep proper records of the money we receive. We can't take any out and give it to Ananda Marga. Everything has to be accounted for."

Ananda Sudha stared at me. "What use is such a school?" she finally said, turning away.

Nowadays, I sometimes think about Vistara's beginnings and how close it came to never opening. Indeed, if it hadn't been for two people who believed in the project despite all the odds— Mandakinii and me—it never would have happened. As it is, Vistara is still going strong and celebrated its twentieth anniversary some years back. It remains one of the most immensely satisfying accomplishments of my life.

Chapter 19

On the Move Again

In the middle of all the school-starting preparations, I would occasionally go to other places for meetings or organizational duties. On one such trip to Brisbane, I was in the jagrti kitchen preparing some dinner with a didi named Sujata when she asked me an odd question.

"Madhuchanda, are you close to your father?"

I stopped peeling potatoes and just stood there, taken aback. We didn't talk much about our families in Ananda Marga.

"Why do you ask?"

"Well," she said, "there's been some news . . . but I wasn't sure how to tell you."

"What news?"

She hesitated a moment, then reached into her pocket and handed me a telegram. It was from my brother Barry. DAD HAS PASSED AWAY it read. CALL HOME IMMEDIATELY. I looked at the date. Several days had already gone by. Only dimly aware of some emotions warring deep down, I cleared my throat.

"You don't have to worry about me," I said. "My father and I were never close." I said nothing more, and we resumed making dinner.

At the time, it didn't occur to me to ask why someone else would have opened the telegram, sent to Brisbane and addressed to me, or feel angry about it. It was known that our higher-ups opened mail from workers' families and friends; most of the time, it never reached the person in question and ended up being destroyed.

A few days later, I went back to Lismore and immersed myself in work to keep from thinking about the news, pushing away the memory of a vision I'd had not so long ago: during meditation, I had seen a coffin and had known it was my father's. That was why I hadn't been surprised by the news; I had been expecting it for some time. He was well over eighty, I told myself. Everyone has to die sometime. I tried not to think of other things that had happened during meditation. More than once, I had heard my mother calling out my name, her voice filled with longing.

Finally, I made myself phone home. A woman answered. The voice was not that of my mother but of someone young and efficient sounding, and it threw me into a state of confusion. Had I called the wrong number?

"This is Marsha, Mrs. Goluboff's daughter," I said. Sudden anger welled up from somewhere. "Who is this? Where's my mother?" I demanded.

"I'm Kelly, your mother's nurse," the woman answered.

A nurse! I knew that my mother hadn't been well, but there was no way she would agree to having a stranger in the house unless her condition was serious.

"Would you like to speak to your mother?"

"Yes, please."

It took her a while to get to the phone. I was calling from a pay phone and was starting to get worried that I would run out of coins when I heard her voice.

"Marsha, how are you?" she asked. Her voice was weak, almost unrecognizable.

"Fine, Mom. How are you?"

"Well . . . I'm not so good. How is your husband?"

My husband! In one of my letters, I had told her about my "marriage" as if it had been a real one. Now, here she was, very ill and us not having spoken in years, asking about my husband—just one more indication, I suppose, of how desperate she was that I be living a reasonably normal life.

"He's fine," I lied.

"Are you coming home? Please come home."

"I'll try, Mom."

Too soon, the brief conversation was over and the agonizing began. There was more than one problem with the possibility of going home. First and foremost was my visa situation. Ever since my bogus marriage hadn't worked out, I had been without a valid visa and had no idea what would happen if I tried to leave the country. Then there was the usual lack of money. But the biggest obstacle of all would be getting the organization's permission to visit my family in the first place. Such visits were strongly discouraged. And my higher-ups would realize that I might not be able to get back into Australia once I was ready to return. I entertained the possibility of going without permission for a minute or two, then dismissed it. After all, there could be serious repercussions.

I ended up doing nothing. Years later, I was told that my mother had tried to hang on after my phone call, hoping I would come home, but passed away not long afterwards. "Grandmom was dying, lying in that bed under the window," my niece Sascha would tell me. "She kept asking for you. I felt really angry at you. I still do."

Two years later, I began making arrangements to go to India. Since the Special Branch raid, I hadn't had any problems but still hadn't dealt with the issue of my lack of legal standing in the country. My status hadn't changed since I had decided I couldn't go home to see my dying mother, but I was willing to confront the situation when it meant seeing Baba. The question remained, though: Once I was ready to leave Australia, how would I do it? Immigration officials might check my passport upon departure, see that I had been in the country illegally, and arrest me. I would have to leave Australia sometime, however, and now seemed the time. I was eager to go to India: I hadn't seen Baba for so long, not since becoming an avadhutika.

After days of internal debate, I made up my mind to go to the Brisbane immigration office. I would tell them I had gotten married, but my husband had left me without completing the paperwork necessary for me to obtain citizenship (all of which was technically true). Once that had happened, I would go on to say, I didn't know what to do, so had done nothing. "I know I'm in the country illegally," I would tell them, "but now I just want to leave."

Early one spring morning, I fortified myself with a good breakfast, went to the office, presented my passport, and told the officer on duty my story. He looked carefully through my passport, and then summoned two other officers who did the same thing. I soon found myself in a stark interviewing room with a prisonlike feel to its white walls and steel cubicles. When the officers seated themselves facing me with features set, I knew I was in trouble.

"We've been looking for you," one of them began. "We know about your case. You've been staying illegally in Australia for over four years. This is very serious."

Thus began a grilling that would take several hours. They asked me where I had been staying and what I'd been doing. They had me fill out forms. I answered their questions and filled out the forms the best I could—all without mentioning Ananda Marga.

I told them again that I wanted to leave. "That's why I'm here," I said.

"We could arrest you, you know," one of them said.

Thinking it best not to say anything more, I held my breath and only nodded, imagining that soon I'd be experiencing firsthand what those jailed Margii brothers had. My heart thumped dully at the prospect.

"You should consider yourself lucky that we won't," the officer said. "Book yourself a flight and present your ticket to us. You must report to this office every week until you leave and give us an update on your activities." I nodded again.

"And," he continued, "you are forbidden to travel outside of Brisbane until your departure. Make sure that you stay put—or else!"

I still didn't say anything, afraid that if I spoke, they'd change their minds and arrest me. So I nodded yet another time, trying to keep my face composed.

Inside, though, I was in turmoil. Skirting the law wasn't giving me the thrill that it used to. In earlier years, it had all been kind of exciting, and I had been more than willing to do whatever it took. But after I had been forced to take a flight to Dacca from Calcutta and escorted to a plane in Fiji and warned never to return, what was happening now was anything but exciting. There had to be a better way to do the organization's work!

A few weeks later, they let me board a flight to India without any of the last-minute glitches I'd been half expecting.

After I spent a few weeks seeing Baba in Calcutta, the organization sent me to New York. My higher-ups must have felt that any risk in my going to the States was now minimal since both my parents were deceased. My mission there, as far as they were concerned, was to change my name yet again so I could return to Australia, and to look into the possibility of getting at some of the money my parents had left me in their will.

I flew in one frigid morning early in January and found my way to the Women's Welfare Office in the Bronx. As with most Ananda Marga offices, the didis' headquarters also served as living space. With all New York Sector didis coming to stay every few months for RDS and with others often passing through on their way elsewhere, the three-bedroom (and one-bathroom) apartment was severely overcrowded most of the time. Add to that the train tracks nearby and the shaking of the apartment walls every thirty minutes or so when a train rumbled past, and you didn't have great accommodations. The first time I felt the walls shake, I was startled. "Don't worry," one didi said, seeing the look on my face. "You'll get used to it."

I spent a few weeks at the office making plans to carry out what the organization had sent me to do. Even though I would go through with the name change, I had no intention of returning to Australia. I'd had enough of Ananda Sudha and was hoping for a new posting. I also had mixed feelings about trying to get at my inheritance. Over the years, I had seen far too much squandering of scant resources by the Central Office big shots. In Ananda Nagar, for example, you couldn't avoid seeing stark reminders of gross mismanagement: the master unit was littered with half-completed buildings, structures which had been started with funds siphoned off from other sectors and then abandoned, their jagged walls looking ghoulish. There was also a voice deep inside that urged caution: I just might need that money myself one day, and that day might not be so far off.

Chapter 20

Philadelphia: I Learn a Family Secret

One morning a few weeks after arriving in New York, I was on my way south to Philadelphia to visit my brothers. As I looked out the window at trees speeding past, their skeletal limbs reaching into a pale sky, I detected more than a little nervousness in myself at the prospect of seeing Barry and David after so many years. At the same time, I was looking forward to it and was hopeful they'd be happy to see me.

I would be visiting Barry first and had prepared myself carefully for an overnight stay at his house. I had bought a small bag and all the basics I would need, including a pair of flannel pajamas. (They were the first pair I'd bought in years. None of us didis ever used them. We just slept in sari blouses and petticoats.) The one thing I wasn't happy about was the box of chocolates I had with me. The day before, I'd been seized with a mixture of panic and regret because I didn't have anything to give Barry and his wife. I hurried to a supermarket and wandered up and down the aisles, finally deciding upon some chocolates, all the while berating myself for not having brought Barry and Diane something exotic from Australia or India (as if I had known then that I'd be visiting them!). The chocolates, boring as they were, would have to do.

I arrived at Thirtieth Street Station and boarded a train out to the suburbs. Barry would be meeting me at Jenkintown Station. On the way, the train pulled into Fern Rock. Things looked different from what I remembered, but not markedly so. As a young girl, I had often come to Fern Rock on the fifty-five bus with my mother; then we would get on the subway to go downtown together. A sad and confusing mix of emotions washed over me as I sat looking out the window, lost in my memories.

As the train stopped at Elkins Park Station, I wondered if my junior high school, located less than a quarter mile down the road, was still there. I looked out at the nearby shops, catching a glimpse of where the Villager clothing store used to be (my parents couldn't afford Villager clothes, but I used to go there to window shop, longing after the cardigan sweaters and plaid skirts that all the popular girls were wearing) and a store I remembered being a bakery.

An image of the girl I'd been then—growing chubby and dressed in imitation Villager clothes or my cousin's hand-me-downs—flitted across my mind. I'd been skinny as a child, and the weight I had started to gain as my body changed had filled me with alarm. I remembered how I would take little pieces of the giant Hershey chocolate bars my parents kept in a dining-room cabinet when I thought no one was looking. One evening my father came down the stairs and saw me. I looked up at him, frozen; he looked down at me, disgust showing on his face as he said, "What are you doing, you fat pig?"

Other images soon followed: There I was as a college freshman, taking the train every day on my way to Penn my first semester. There I was again as a junior, coming back from campus (scared that I was pregnant) to visit a friend still living at home. It was all so far in the past, yet the parade of images left me with an odd feeling of having lost something.

Barry was waiting when I got off the train at Jenkintown Station. We hugged each other guardedly, then got into his red truck and went to a nearby restaurant for lunch. He was as thin as ever and going gray. His thick mustache and abundant salt-and-pepper hair made him look distinguished, and the khakis, turtleneck, and sweater he was wearing gave him an air of laid-back prosperity. I added eight years to my age to calculate his, coming up with a number that surprised me. How could Barry be forty-seven already?

Our conversation over lunch was strained and frequently lapsed into silence. I asked Barry about his teaching job. He'd been at Penn State teaching math since his mid-twenties.

"Oh, it's fine," he said, but offered no details. He brought me up to date on his daughter Sascha. I hadn't seen her since she was an infant. "She's in college, studying cultural anthropology," he said, his voice warming as he talked. He was clearly proud of her.

"Diane's the headmaster at a Quaker middle school in Germantown," Barry said in answer to my question about his wife. He didn't ask me anything about what I'd been doing with my life, and I offered nothing on the subject. Ananda Marga—and the years I had spent away from the family—hung between us like a heavy curtain.

We went to their house afterwards, a place I had never been. Diane greeted me at the door. A somewhat heavyset woman, she had curly reddish hair, a nice change from the straight brown I remembered her as having, and was wearing a long dress and dangly earrings.

Barry showed me around the house. It was similar to what I had imagined, with throw rugs on the wood floors and weavings and native art decorating the walls. I spotted a collection of photos on the piano and went over to look. They were mostly of Sascha: as a young girl, as an adolescent, as a high school senior on her prom night wearing a gown. She was tall like her father and had long dark hair.

"Marsha, recognize this?" Barry asked. I thought I did. A strange feeling of regret stirred in me as I looked at the golden samovar, polished to a high shine. "It's the one from our house," he said, "the one that used to belong to Grandmom and Grandpop."

Barry led me upstairs to Sascha's room and then to the master bedroom, showing off the furniture and cupboards he'd built. I hadn't known that Barry did such work and admired it; everything was well made, with an eye for detail. He pointed out the special piece he'd crafted for Diane's substantial jewelry collection. As I admired her earrings, I remembered how I used to enjoy wearing my own. I'd had my ears pierced while in high school but hadn't worn any jewelry in over fifteen years.

We went downstairs and sat in the living room. Diane served tea and cookies. After a while, I gave them the box of chocolates. Diane and Barry looked it and then at each other in a puzzled manner. "Thanks," Barry finally said. Diane took the box and carried it out to the kitchen, holding it gingerly. What does she think is in there? I found myself wondering.

Barry and I began to talk about the will. "Mom and Dad left you twenty thousand dollars," Barry said. "We decided to take out a twenty-year bond. That way, it'll make some money for you. You know the will stipulates that you have to be cult-free for five years before you can get the money, right?" I nodded. A copy of the will had been sent to me in Australia.

Diane returned to the room, and the conversation wandered on to other topics. Then without warning, Barry said, "Do you know that we have an older half brother?" I stared at him, my eyes opening wide in shock.

"An older half brother? You're kidding, right?" I said, half stumbling over my words.

Barry shook his head. "I wish I were. A few years before Dad died, he told me he had to talk to me. I went over to see him. 'I have something to tell you,' he said. 'You're not my oldest son.' That's how he said it. Just like that. I said, 'What do you mean,

I'm not your oldest son?' That's when Dad told me he'd been married before and had a son before meeting Mom."

Barry fell silent. I struggled to find words with which to reply.

"But why didn't we know anything about it?" I finally asked.

Barry leaned forward with his elbows on his knees, clasping his hands together. "Dad and Mom must have decided it would be better if we didn't know. You know how things were back then. I guess Mom's family thought it was terrible she was marrying a divorced man. Maybe they wanted to pretend that Dad's previous marriage had never happened."

That had to be it, I thought. Back in the thirties, it would have been considered improper for a girl from a good Jewish family to do that.

"Dad was afraid we'd find out when he died," Barry went on, "afraid that his other son would see the obituary and show up at his funeral. That's why he told me."

My heart went out to Barry. How shocked he must have been! "Did you ever meet him?" I asked.

"Once. He's about twelve years older than me. He's a butcher."

"What's his name?"

"Howard. Howard Goldberg."

"His last name's . . . *Goldberg?*"

Barry nodded. "It's strange. Apparently, Dad changed his name to his first wife's last name during the Depression, hoping to be taken into his father-in-law's business. I guess he changed it back when that didn't happen. At any rate, Howard must have been born when Dad still had his wife's name."

Incredible! The idea of my father changing his name to that of his wife just didn't fit with my memories of him. Obviously, it had been just as disorienting to Barry as it now was to me. How well had we ever really known our father?

"This is all hard to believe," I said.

"I know," Barry said. "I'm still getting used to it."

It was getting late. Barry glanced at his watch, cleared his throat, and said, "Where are you going to spend the night?"

Spend the night? I thought it was clear I was going to stay with them.

"I . . . I thought I could stay here."

A look of alarm passed between Barry and Diane.

"Excuse us for a moment," Barry said.

They both stood up and left the room, leaving me aghast that they might not let me stay. After all, I wasn't a stranger; I was Barry's sister.

I remembered the last time I'd stayed with them, just a few months after Sascha had been born, during the summer when I'd had the bad trip and ended up in Penn's psych ward. After I had gotten out, Barry and Diane invited me over to spend a weekend. At dusk one evening, I watched as they held little Sascha in front of the large picture window of the ground-floor apartment where they were living at the time, singing a going-to-bed song: *Good night flowers, good night bees, good night birdies, good night trees. Sascha's going to sleep . . .*

My reverie was shattered by the sounds of their footsteps returning. I looked up to find Barry standing in front of me.

"I'm sorry, but you can't stay here," he said. "We haven't seen you in years and really don't know who you are anymore. I'll take you to the train."

I felt a pain in the pit of my stomach. Nodding woodenly, I collected my overnight bag and followed Barry to the door. I said goodbye to Diane. The door closed firmly behind me, and I followed Barry to the truck and got in. We drove silently to the station. All too soon, I was standing alone in the cold, waiting for the train—with no idea where I was going to spend the night.

I got off the train at Thirtieth Street Station. I had arranged to meet David the next morning at his vintage clothing store and briefly considered calling and asking him if I could stay at his apartment. I quickly rejected the idea, though. It wouldn't be appropriate to stay with a single man, even if he was my brother. (*Avadhutika shall not remain in a lonely place with any male,* went the conduct rule.) Even if I did call, I told myself, he probably wouldn't have enough room in his apartment. So there was no getting around it: I would have to spend the night at the station. (I can't remember why I didn't call Maetryeii, the woman who had contacted my parents for me the last time I'd been in Philadelphia. I might not have been able to find her number in the phone book, or it might have been too late.)

I walked into the cavernous waiting room and took a seat near the doors. I'll just pretend to be waiting for someone, I thought. At least I don't look homeless! For among the steadily dwindling number of people sitting there, nearly all who were left were likely homeless—the unshaven man in a grimy parka sitting to my right, the bag lady with five plastic bags stuffed full of clothes and other belongings to my left.

I looked up to find a station guard standing in front of me. "Excuse me, are you waiting for someone?" he asked. "No one is permitted to spend the night here."

"I'm waiting for my brother to come pick me up," I said, glancing at my watch. "I can't imagine what's keeping him."

The guard hesitated. He looked me over and then must have decided to give me the benefit of the doubt. "All right," he said, "but you can't stay here much longer." As I watched him walk away, I figured out my next move. Once he left the area, I would find another place to sit, someplace less visible.

The hopeful anticipation I'd felt that morning setting out from New York had been replaced by a keen sense of despair. I felt drained, and what was worse, the hemorrhoids I'd developed in recent years had started aching. The waiting room was chilly, and the hard wooden seats weren't going to help matters. It was going to be a long night, and a cold one, too.

Keeping out of view of the guards, I moved from one part of the drafty station to another. I got little sleep. At one point in the middle of the night, I buttoned my jacket up to my chin, put my hands in my pockets, and hunkered down on the chair. I could see my breath. The flannel pajamas in my bag came to mind, and I wished I had them on and were in a nice bed with a warm comforter. Every few minutes, I had to shift my body to relieve the stress on my bottom. It didn't do any good: the pain was getting worse.

I thought about the secret Barry had told me, and realized how typical it was of our family. We had never talked about problems or issues, as if not talking about them would mean they didn't exist. Nor did we talk about feelings. We had learned early on that they weren't important and were to be kept to oneself.

I felt sadness at having a half brother somewhere out there whom I had never met because of some silly ideas they'd had back then about what children should or shouldn't know. I figured it had been our mother who hadn't wanted us to know about our half brother. Like Barry had said, her family had likely thought it inappropriate for her to marry a divorced man with a child. Although it must have been very painful for him not to say anything, my father had gone along with it all. Throughout my childhood, he had seemed angry so often. Maybe that was why.

(At the time, I didn't think about how my half brother must have been affected by all of this. Years later, when I met him, Howard told me that he remembered the day my father had left him. He had been only five at the time. "I was sitting on his lap. He told my mother he was leaving, and they started arguing and shouting. Then he got up and threw me off his lap, and I almost hit the mantelpiece." My father rarely visited or called him after that. When he was just eighteen, Howard got married and then had a son, Myron, who was born just a year or two after my brother David. One day, Howard brought Myron to my father's hardware store so he could meet his grandfather. Just then, my father caught sight of Barry and David coming in. "Don't say anything," he said to Howard. "They don't know anything about you." Then he told Howard to leave. When my father passed away, Howard wasn't informed and missed the funeral. When he eventually found out and called my mother to ask why he hadn't been notified, she said, "You were never a son to him. You didn't need to know. You didn't need to come.")

The windows slowly turned gray as dawn approached. As light began to filter in, falling upon the sleeping forms of those with whom I'd passed the night, I felt a strange sense of kinship. We had all managed to avoid being thrown out into the frigid night and had thus won a small victory. I did a few minutes of meditation and visited the bathroom. After checking my bag, I went out into the cold morning sunlight, the harsh air filling my lungs.

I took a bus to South Street and wandered down the street looking for David's store. It was still early; few people were out and most shops weren't open yet. I walked by a Thai restaurant, a fruit store, and a Haagen-Dazs ice cream store before seeing the sign: RETRO. David knew I was coming, but that didn't make the prospect of seeing him any easier. I had last seen Barry when I'd been in Philadelphia in 1980, but I hadn't laid eyes on David for fifteen years.

I took a deep breath and went in. David was at the counter to the left of the entrance, wearing jeans and a black leather jacket. His curly hair was cut short. Although still thick, it was no longer the black color I remembered, but sprinkled throughout with gray. I felt something akin to an electric shock as I stood there looking at him: he looked so much like our father.

David caught sight of me. "Marsha, you're here!" he said as he came out from behind the counter. "How are you? Did you have a good trip down?" he asked, looking down at me with the same warm, twinkling eyes that I remembered. His eyes, at least, were not like our father's.

"It was okay. You look so much like Dad," I blurted out.

"Do I?" he laughed. "You look kind of like Mom."

"Really?" The thought that I might resemble my mother made me feel strange.

David showed me around the store. I admired the slinky vintage dresses from the thirties and forties and asked him about them. "I get a lot of my stuff from New York," he said. "That's where the good clothing is."

Later, we went out to the Thai restaurant for lunch, and David told me how he had gotten into the business. After graduating from Temple University, he had been teaching high school English for a few years when he starting collecting clothing on the side. He'd liked it so much that he left his teaching job and opened the store.

"I remember some letters Mom sent me in Israel saying that you were living at home and collecting rags," I said.

He laughed. "Well, it must have seemed like that to her."

I asked him if he'd ever seen our half brother. "Once," he said, and changed the subject. I remember thinking it strange that David didn't have more to say about what I considered to be a shocking revelation.

Afterwards, he showed me his apartment above the store. It was nicely furnished with a good-sized living room and a small dining room. I didn't see a bedroom, though—and had no idea where one might be, given the layout. I'd been right not to call David from the station; his apartment was clearly too small for a guest. (Little did I know that there was a floor above with two bedrooms.)

We sat down in the living room. David poured himself a small glass of wine. "No thanks," I said when he offered. He didn't ask me anything about what I had been doing in Australia, and I didn't bring up the subject. The visit dragged on for a while longer. Just as it had with Barry, Ananda Marga hung between us, and we soon ran out of things to talk about.

Later that afternoon, David dropped me off in Center City. I was going to see my aunt's attorney about the will. There was no way I would be able to get the money, and I knew it. Even so, I had to go through the motions in order to say I had tried when the didis and dadas asked me about it, as I knew they would.

"Where are you going to stay tonight?" David asked.

"I'll think of something."

"You have my number. Give me a call if you need to."

I told him I would and waved goodbye as he took off down the street.

When I got to his office, the lawyer was in. He was very old with long white hair, and the carefully tailored blue suit he wore couldn't hide his frailty. My aunt must have told him all about me; regarding me with keen interest, he told me the terms of the will, which I already knew. I asked him what the proof would be that I'd been cult-free for five years. As I knew he would, he said it was up to the executors of the will, my aunt and my brothers, to decide what that proof would be.

After leaving the office, I walked to the bus stop on my way back to the station to retrieve my bag and figure out what to do next. I had to walk in a kind of rolling gait because my hemorrhoids were getting worse. It was getting dark by the time I claimed my bag. I counted the money I had left and figured I could spend fifty dollars on a hotel room.

I found a Yellow Pages at the pay phones, got out some change, and began calling downtown hotels, inquiring at several and seriously depleting my supply of coins. My confidence began to wane as I realized how expensive they all were. Fifty dollars would have gotten me a stay in a four-star hotel in India, but here it would get me nothing. The thought of another cold and sleepless night on wooden benches spurred me on, and I kept trying. On my last call, just before my change ran out, a receptionist said they had a room in my price range. A wave of relief swept over me as I wrote down the address. I was going to have a hot shower and get a good night's sleep in a comfy bed. Maybe I would even watch some TV. Anticipating these creature comforts after such a rough couple of days outweighed any guilt I might have been feeling at the prospect of enjoying them.

I soon found myself in a section of the city where the sidewalks were cracked and the buildings were badly in need of paint and repair. In stark contrast to the bustle of nearby streets, here there were fewer pedestrians, and they looked nearly as run down as the buildings. I spotted the hotel, went in, looked around the faded lobby with its worn carpets and seedy-looking characters, and felt my heart sink. You get what you pay for, I thought. I went up to the receptionist, handed over my fifty dollars, and got my key.

The room featured a lumpy mattress that sagged and a grimy window view of an alley. At least it had a TV. After trying in vain to meditate (the rug looked filthy, so I didn't want to sit on it, and the bed drooped too much), I ate some cheese and an apple purchased at the station, and fiddled with the TV. I switched from one channel to another but couldn't get it to work. Fuzzy dots were the best I could do. I thought of the lobby—and the heavily made-up woman with the brittle black hair and the dissipated fellow who had been with her—and realized that the people frequenting this hotel were likely not interested in watching TV or getting a good night's sleep.

I lay down on the bed, more depressed than ever. My hemorrhoids felt as if they were on fire. I grabbed my legs and pulled them to my chest. That was the position which best relieved the pain, but it wasn't doing much good now. It was going to be another sleepless night. But at least I wouldn't be cold and wouldn't have to keep moving to stay one step ahead of a guard. My back aching from the sag in the mattress and longing for my sleeping bag, I felt despair but pushed it back down, trying to be grateful for the small blessings I did have.

I dozed off just before dawn. A few hours later, I awoke with a start and groped for my watch. It was nearly time to call Barry. We were going to meet up and go to the cemetery where my parents were buried.

I took the train back to Jenkintown. Much like the other day, Barry was waiting for me at the station. "David's going to meet us there," he said. We were mostly silent on the drive out to the cemetery. He didn't ask how I had spent the last two nights, and I wasn't about to say anything.

We got there and parked. With the sun glinting on the polished marble of the tombstones, it felt almost warm as we stood there. But this was a sterile place, nothing like the green, park-like setting I'd somehow expected. The few trees in the cemetery were skeletal, with withered and tattered leaves clinging here and there to naked boughs. Tufts of straw-like grass were scattered among graves laid out in rows stretching as far as the eye could see. A marble city of the dead, I thought.

David was nowhere to be seen. Muttering something, Barry looked at his watch and shook his head. "Might as well go there," he said, leading the way.

A few minutes later, I found myself at the gravesite. There was one well-cut granite tombstone for the two of them, with a menorah and a Jewish star and the name GOLUBOFF on it. They had died within five months of each other. There had been one funeral, then another. And I hadn't been here for either of them.

Barry and I stood quietly for a few minutes with heads bowed. I waited for emotions to sweep over me and found myself surprised when none did. Then, as we walked towards my grandparents' graves, we saw David running towards us.

"You're late," Barry said.

"You never called me back and told me what time," David retorted.

"I told you we would be here at ten thirty."

"It doesn't matter," I said. "We're all here now."

Silently, David and I followed Barry to Grandmom and Grandpop's gravesites. They were down the row a little from our parents. I stood there for a while, as I had at my parents' graveside, and once again waited for feelings to overtake me. Instead, I found myself meditating on the mystery of life, on all the events that had transpired to bring me into the world and had lead to my standing here on this cold winter day.

Moments later, we walked back to the parking lot, and I said goodbye to Barry. I would be going back to the city with David. "I can't believe Barry!" David wasted no time in saying once we were alone. "This morning, he told me that as soon as he heard from you, he'd call and tell me what time we were meeting. He never did. I think it was on purpose."

I didn't know what to reply. The fact that my brothers didn't get along was sad and mirrored the whole feeling of my visit.

David dropped me off on Walnut Street. "Are you sure you'll be okay?" he asked, leaning out his window. "Sure. My train's at five." We waved to each other, and I watched him drive away.

I got on a bus, went to Thirtieth Street Station, and walked into the waiting room. With all the cheerful bustle of passengers and luggage, it looked far different from the other night, as if I'd never been stranded there. But my hemorrhoids told me otherwise. It had happened, all right. So had last night's lumpy and saggy mattress. It had all happened.

I realized a few years later that I'd been half hoping that my brothers would go out of their way to welcome me home, help me find a job if I'd wanted to stay, and who knows what else. Had that happened, I might have left Ananda Marga at that point. As it was, the reception I got only served to thrust me back into the midst of the only family I had known for the past fifteen years.

I felt battered and bruised. My last day in Philadelphia had gone no better than the first two. I would be glad to get back to New York—and my Ananda Marga family.

Chapter 21

New York: I Get Some Time to Think

Later that evening, I was sitting in the didis' office, tending my wounds over steaming cups of chamomile tea as the didis listened to my tale. When I described how I had ended up spending the night at Thirtieth Street Station, their faces registered shock.

"That's unbelievable! Your own brother!" one didi said. "What did he think you would do if you'd stayed in his house?"

On the train ride back, I had contemplated just that. Maybe they thought I would steal something—or worse. I imagined their exchange in the kitchen. Diane: *Barry, she's in a cult! There's no telling what she might do.* Barry (silent for a while, the struggle showing on his face): *You're right. We really don't know who she is anymore.*

I took another sip of tea, luxuriating as the sweet fluid warmed me.

"They said they hadn't seen me in so many years, I was like a stranger to them," I said. "I can understand how they would feel that way. It was naive of me to think I could stay there just because I'm his sister."

"Still . . ." her voice trailed off. The other didis shook their heads.

We drank the rest of our tea in silence and then got ready for bed. I found a place among the other sleeping bags already laid out and put mine down. It was good to be home, good to be back in my sleeping bag. Even the familiar rattle of the apartment every time a train went by was comforting in a way.

A week or two later, a Margii sister, Irene, whose spiritual name was Rashmi, invited me to stay with her in her two-bedroom fourth-floor apartment in the Bronx. I happily accepted and moved into the spare room she had been using for meditation. We began doing kiirtan and sadhana together. Whenever we meditated, Rashmi's elderly cat would sit on her lap, purring. When Rashmi was out at work, the cat would climb onto my lap whenever I meditated, and we soon became fast friends.

I stayed with Rashmi for three months. It was a good time for both of us. Rashmi worked long hours, and I would have a hot meal ready for her when she got home—hearty soups, vegetable and tofu stir-fries seasoned with ginger and tamari, plus brown rice and salads. She appreciated it.

"Before you came here, I'd get home and be too tired to make anything for dinner," she told me one time. "Sometimes I would eat just a bag of potato chips."

"Potato chips!" I said. "Not while I'm around."

"You're my food angel," Rashmi replied, smiling.

For the first time since joining Ananda Marga, I found myself with time to sit and reflect. In the mornings, I read the paper; in the afternoons, I took walks in the nearby park and did a lot of thinking. Some of it was disquieting. Things I had tried to bury and kill off were seeing the light of day for the first time.

I was thirty-nine years old and the constant traveling was wearing me down. The painful hemorrhoids I'd developed had only worsened with the inevitable changes of diet and routine necessary on the road. And I became aware of a longing that, while not new, had up to now been successfully ignored: I wanted to be a mother. While I had struggled with sexual desires for years, this was new. In my twenties and early thirties, I had regarded infants and toddlers (and their excretions and runny noses) with distaste. I'd felt pity for the mothers whose children I had cared for in our toddler's groups and preschools. I could say goodbye to them after a few hours, but their mothers were stuck with them. The whole process of pregnancy and childbirth had seemed crude and animal-like to me. A pregnant woman, ponderous and heavy, was one firmly rooted to the earth. Not me, though! I was on a spiritual journey and would not be diverted from my goal by such messy and mundane concerns. But now, a powerful longing for connection and family life began to spar with the path I had chosen.

One day in particular stands out in my memory. It was a cold, blustery day and I was walking through the park. My hands were in my pockets, and I was staring at the ground before me, hardly noticing the crack vials and shards of glass scattered about, focused as I was on the struggle within. What if I were to leave Ananda Marga? It wouldn't be too late to marry and have a child. But what about the vows I had taken? Didn't they mean I had to remain a didi for life? And even if I decided to leave, where would I go? Who could I stay with? The spiritual superego then spoke up: *You think you can leave? Neither of your brothers showed the slightest interest in you. They didn't even bother to ask you a single question about your life! That's because they're not your real family—Ananda Marga is!*

I conceded victory to the spiritual superego and turned my thoughts to the mission. I told myself that once I got back to work, everything would be all right. I'd get posted to a new sector, go to new places, meet new people. Meditating later in the apartment, I forced my mind to focus on my mantra.

Weeks passed. Spring approached, and with it, the time for my departure. I would be going to India and then, ostensibly, on to

Australia. I had already made the brief pilgrimage to Denver to change my name. It had gone as well as the first time and had been just as easy. Now my name was Hanna Hartt. I was proud of the new name I'd come up with. Hanna was a Hebrew name meaning "Grace of God," and the unusual spelling of my new surname was quite creative, I thought. Next, I would have to get a new passport and tourist visas to India and Australia; even though I had no intention of going to Australia, I had to act like I was because I was still posted there. I also needed a new sleeping bag. But as usual, I had no money. Once again, Rashmi came to the rescue by having me do some work for her. I put together enough money for a sleeping bag, ticket, and other needs.

One of those needs was some traveler's checks for "show money," an indispensable tool for Ananda Marga workers. Back then, many countries required visitors to show sufficient funds to support a stay before granting a visa. Traveler's checks were perfect for the purpose, except for one obvious flaw: once they were used, there were none left to show. That was no obstacle for us; we never used traveler's checks for their usual purpose anyway. Cash was much more useful as it could often be traded on the black market for much more than could be gotten in a bank for the same sum in traveler's checks.

Creating show money was simple. After buying the checks and waiting a few days, we would report them lost or stolen and have them replaced with new ones. We would then cash in the new checks, keeping the original ones to show upon entering a country or applying for a visa. It wasn't really stealing, we rationalized, since we ended up with only the amount of money we originally put in. The only drawback was that the temptation to use the checks could be intense, especially being as short of funds as we often were.

On my last visit to the States, I had gotten some show money, and it had served me well: I'd presented the same checks again and again in Fiji, Australia, and other countries, until they had long lost their crispness and had become limp and faded.

Something had happened to those checks. Had I lost them? Or had I actually cashed them in under extreme duress? There had been plenty of situations when I could have. At the time, I couldn't remember if I had or not. All I knew was that they were no longer in my possession, and now was the perfect opportunity to get a new set.

I took the subway to Manhattan. A big bank would be best, I thought, more impersonal. Entering one, I stood in line for a teller and went through the procedure to get the checks. As I signed my name to the paperwork, I was surprised to find my hand shaking a little. When I got back to the apartment, I promptly stashed the checks deep in my bag under some books, thus "losing" them.

A few days later, when I called to report the checks lost, I thought I detected something guarded in the voice of the woman who answered the phone. "Are you sure you lost them?" she asked. "Could they have been stolen?" I was taken aback by her tone. Was it disbelief I was hearing?

"Yes. I mean, no, I don't think they were stolen," I said. "They must have dropped out of my bag when I opened it on the street."

"Is it possible that you could have misplaced them around the house?"

"Well, it's possible. But I've looked everywhere."

"Take a few days and look some more," she said. "It wouldn't be good if you had new checks issued and you found the old ones, you know."

"Thank you," I said. "I'll do that." I hung up the phone, my heart pounding. Could it be that she knows? I told myself there was no way she could know I hadn't lost the checks.

Don't lose your nerve. You really need that show money, said the stern, no-nonsense voice I was well acquainted with. But there was another voice, quieter, but still insisting to be heard: Maybe they suspect something. Maybe they'll investigate before they issue new ones. And when they find out about Ananda

Marga . . . *What nonsense!* the stern voice retorted. *It's not like you're in Australia. Here, hardly anyone has even heard of Ananda Marga.*

But I wasn't so sure of myself anymore. I was trying to remain committed to the mission but was growing tired of many of its methods. Would Baba still protect me while doing such things? I was no longer certain.

I called and told them I had found the checks. I had to admit, it felt good using my own sense of ethics. In a few weeks, though, I would be doing "business" for New York and Suva Sectors, carrying video equipment into India and selling it illegally. In that matter, I would have no say.

Chapter 22

The Business Trip

Two weeks later, I was on an Air India flight bound for Delhi, watching the stewardess, her hair drawn up into a bun and a black bindi between her eyes, doling out white dinner trays to one passenger after another like packs of oversized cards. Darn! No time for a half bath, I thought as she got closer. I was going to eat, though, half bath or no: it was important to keep up my strength.

The stewardess reached my row and handed me my dinner. I had ordered vegetarian food, but as this was an Air India flight, it was likely there would be onions and garlic in it. I opened the foil cautiously. Steam escaped along with spicy aromas. My mouth watered; it had been quite some time since I'd eaten, but I had to be sure there was nothing forbidden. The potato and cauliflower curry looked and smelled suspicious, but the chickpeas and tomatoes seemed all right, so I took a forkful.

A few bites later, my stomach began to churn as the task that lay ahead came to mind. My hunger suddenly all but gone, I forced myself to eat a bit more. Then I took out my passport and inspected the pages. Did I spray them enough? I wondered. It has to be okay. They said it would be.

The day before in New York, after returning from my shopping, didis experienced in the art had coated all the blank pages of my passport with a clear plastic spray in preparation for my trip. "You hold it out like this; then you spray with even strokes," one had said while demonstrating. "Make sure you cover the whole page. Then wait for it to dry and do it again." I meticulously followed her instructions, but there was a problem: I would be boarding my flight in only a few hours and didn't have time to wait for the pages to dry properly between coats. When I finished my rushed job, the didis took a look. They flipped through the passport and said it would do. "Now you'll be able to remove any writing with this," one of them said, handing me a small bottle.

On the first business trip I had undertaken, which had been to Bombay, my passport hadn't been sprayed, so I had gone through the Nothing to Declare aisle in customs hoping my luggage would not be searched. Fortunately, it hadn't been. But I knew that I shouldn't press my luck. This time, I would declare the equipment.

Once again I went over what would happen. The customs official would write what I declared in the passport to be sure that I would take the equipment out of the country with me. Then, when I left India and went through customs, they'd check my passport to see if I had anything written in it. If all went well, there wouldn't be.

I wouldn't have any equipment to carry back with me, of course. After landing in Delhi, I'd deliver it to our Delhi contact, Anil, and exchange it for money. Ananda Marga had a flourishing trade in smuggled video and electronic equipment. Because there were high duties charged on such goods, we netted a good profit on everything we brought in. After getting the money, I'd get right to work on my passport. The damaging evidence would be removed long before I would leave the country.

As I looked around the cabin at the walls of the aircraft with their pretty paisley pattern and the windows shaped like those in some temple dedicated to Ganesh or Shiva, my thoughts turned to the first time I'd been asked to do something I considered not quite right. It had been shortly after I had arrived in Australia, after being reunited with Ananda Bhadra. She was going to help me get settled in. I would be traveling often by bus, she told me, going back and forth between Brisbane and Sydney.

One afternoon in the Brisbane bus station, Ananda Bhadra handed me a ticket to Sydney. It was issued in another didi's name.

"She's going elsewhere and doesn't need it," Ananda Bhadra said, seeing my inquiring look. "It's still good. You can use it instead. They usually don't check names."

"But that's wrong," I insisted. "I can't use someone else's ticket. Besides, what if they check?"

Ananda Bhadra smiled at me indulgently as if I were a small child. Then she sighed.

"Malatii," she said, "you know that we have very little money. We're doing good work, important work for the mission. We're not buying you another ticket when we have a perfectly good one you can use."

(Later, I would find the same thinking applied to Eurorail passes: one worker would buy one and everyone would use it. The train conductors rarely asked for identification. And that was nothing compared to how we used airplane tickets. One didi with an artistic bent was expert at removing the name of the original ticket holder and supplying the name of the didi or dada who would be using the ticket. Somehow, the workers managed to get on the plane even though their names were not on the airline's manifest. This was, of course, long before the days of computer-generated tickets.)

The stewardess came back to collect the food trays. Handing my meal back largely uneaten, I thought about the rumors I'd heard about some workers and what they'd been involved in to raise money. Some dadas in Europe, the rumors went, had been mixed up in pornography. One dada posted in the States was rumored to have approved someone to deal drugs. Some Margiis found out about it, the story went, and he ended up apologizing at a retreat.

Those might have been just rumors, but one incident I had direct knowledge of certainly wasn't. A didi who had been working in South America was taken aside in an airport one day after a dog had sniffed out drugs in her backpack. She hadn't had a clue that a dada had stuffed the frame of the backpack with an illicit white powder. She'd been arrested, she told me, and had ended up spending a long time in jail.

The beep that precedes on-board announcements interrupted my dark musings. The seat belt light came on as the pilot's voice came over the PA system, making the usual announcements about the time and temperature in English and then in Hindi. A surge of adrenaline passed through me as I realized we were about to land. My hands began to shake.

I told myself there was no need to worry. This wasn't going to be as risky as last time when I'd actually smuggled the equipment in. This should be easy, I thought. Except if they noticed the coating or found my Ananda Marga things buried at the bottom of my bag: my uniform, a picture of Baba, and a *pratiik*.

I looked around at the ordinary passengers, many of them Indians likely returning from tourist jaunts to New York and other American cities or from visiting relatives living abroad. There were also some Americans on board. No doubt, they were looking forward to taking in the Red Fort or the Taj Mahal. Did I look like them, just another American tourist anticipating two weeks of sightseeing in exotic India? As the plane landed and then taxied to a stop, I retrieved my large carry-on from the overhead bin and found myself wishing ardently that I were like them—just an ordinary tourist with ordinary concerns, like where to change dollars for rupees and how to find a taxi and not be overcharged. Catching myself, I shook my head, and the stern inner voice spoke up. *You would never choose to trade places with any of those tourists*, it said. *You're a didi on an important mission, and if you have to smuggle stuff into India to raise money for the mission, that's what you'll do!*

I filed off the plane and went to customs, almost holding my breath. Once I had declared the video equipment, an official took my passport, turned to a page, and penned in a description. He made no indication of having noticed anything unusual about my passport. And other than a half-hearted rummage through its top layer, he didn't search my bag. My uniform, picture of Baba, and other Ananda Marga things remained safely undisturbed at the bottom. I breathed a sigh of relief.

I needed to get to a hotel. My usual mode of transportation in India, by motor rickshaw, wouldn't do this time: the bumpy and jostling ride could put the equipment at risk. A taxi would cost a lot more, but at least I'd be spared the usual dose of fumes from the open rickshaw's motor. I went out into the sweltering night and was immediately surrounded by taxi and motor rickshaw drivers looking for passengers and by men looking to carry my luggage.

"Madam! Madam! Come here! Good price!" they called out. I motioned to a taxi driver and got in.

"Where to, madam?" the turbaned driver asked. I made sure that he had a fare chart. Since the meters were old, you had to pay more for your trip than what the meter ended up on. Drivers without fare charts were to be avoided because they would charge exorbitant fees. I waited to make sure the driver had reset his meter (another trick), then gave him the name and address of a moderately priced hotel. Because of the equipment I had with me, I wouldn't be staying in a cheap one near the train station in Paharganj like I usually did when in Delhi.

The taxi driver pulled onto the main road and began to take what I knew would be a roundabout way to my destination. Nothing unusual about that; it was the standard procedure taxi drivers took with tourists who didn't know any better.

"Sir," I said, "you're going the wrong way."

The man turned to face me. "Excuse me?" he questioned, one eyebrow raised quizzically as if I'd insulted him.

"It's much faster this way," I said and gave him directions.

"Oh, yes, so sorry, you are correct, madam," he said as he quickly reversed course, almost running over a cow in the process.

We pulled up in front of the hotel. As the driver placed my bag on the curb, I looked at the fare on the meter, consulted the fare chart, and added a ten-rupee tip to the total.

"Madam! You are owing me ten rupees more. Madam! Madam!" His shouts trailed behind me as I entered the hotel, then faded as he must have realized I wasn't going to be fooled.

I was anxious to unload the equipment quickly and called Anil right after I checked in. As phone service in major Indian cities had improved significantly in recent years, the call went through on my first attempt, and we agreed upon a time to meet.

Late the next morning, I took a taxi to the address Anil had given me. I was dropped off in a small street just off a busy one. I found the number and knocked. The man who opened the door was heavyset and unkempt, his long hair balding on top. He squinted at the bright sunlight from the gloom of the entranceway.

"Anil?"

"Yes?"

I didn't bother with any preliminaries. "I've brought the stuff," I said.

"Of course. Come in, Didi."

I followed him into a dimly lit room. "Sit down here," he said, indicating the one chair that didn't have anything on it. The rest of every available inch of space on the table and chairs was full of electronic equipment and parts. It looked like he had a bustling business going. Obviously, we weren't the only ones supplying him!

Anil offered a price that more or less matched what I'd been told the equipment would fetch. "That's fine," I said.

I handed it over; he gave me a pile of rupees, which I quickly pocketed.

Relieved that everything was out of my hands, I returned to the hotel. All I had to do now was remove the incriminating evidence in my passport. Making sure my door was locked, I got out the small bottle of paint thinner (or whatever it was the didis had given me) and some cotton balls and bent to my task, rubbing gingerly at the words the customs official had written. But removing all traces of the ink proved more difficult than I had expected, and it soon became clear the page hadn't been sprayed enough. As I rubbed, another problem soon developed: the paper was wearing thin. I held the page up to the light—and could see right through it. There's no way this won't be noticed on my way out, I thought. Now what? I asked myself, even though I already knew: I would have to get another passport.

That was nothing new; I'd gotten several over the years for a variety of reasons. Even so, I was annoyed. I liked this passport. It was computerized and slick looking, and I'd even gone to the trouble of getting a good photo taken. Now I would have to get rid of it, report it lost, and get one issued here. It wouldn't be nearly as nice. And who knew how long getting a new one would take? Judging from my experience during training, it wouldn't be quick. What a bother!

I decided it would look suspicious to report my passport lost just a few days after entering the country. Instead, I would go to Calcutta. I'd deliver my ill-begotten funds to Ananda Sudha (fully expecting to get a new posting in return) and would spend some time around Baba. Then, when I was ready to leave India, I would return to Delhi and go about getting a new passport.

On the train to Calcutta, I got to thinking about our values in Ananda Marga. It seemed that we had them all wrong. For example, no one in the organization questioned the ways we went about making money, but everyone would get on your case for eating a mushroom or two or not fasting—Baba included. All of us had heard stories of workers being taken to task by Baba. "You took water on *ekadashi!*"[57] Baba would roar at some woebegone dada. "Why? Why did you do this thing?" Or he would reveal

---

[57] *ekadashi:* The eleventh day after the new moon. Workers were to fast on this day and also on the new and full moon days.

a dietary infraction. "You took *tamasic*[58] food while on tour! You ate onions!" and the dada in question would hang his head in shame. Yet none of us had ever heard of a time when Baba had yelled at some worker for being involved in smuggling or something worse. *You smuggled video equipment into the country! I had often wished he would say to someone. Chi, Chi, Chi! This is not the way to make money for the mission!* And then we would all stop doing it.

As it was, in the world of Ananda Marga, eating forbidden foods was a greater infraction than smuggling. In fact, in our world, smuggling was no infraction at all. So maybe that was why I didn't feel as guilty about the smuggling as I did about the one time I had eaten *tamasic* food quite by accident.

I remembered it happening one summer evening in Sydney. Didis and dadas had gone to one of the Filipino Margiis' homes for meditation and a meal. A new sectorial secretary had recently come to Australia, and this was to be a special event to welcome him.

Most Filipino Margiis, while of a devotional bent, had little interest in the organizational side of Ananda Marga, rarely attending official dharmacakras and mostly meditating by themselves. They were, however, renowned for their hospitality— and their cooking. We were all looking forward to a feast.

On the night in question, the late summer evening was fading as our new SS Dada finished his after-meditation talk. During meditation, we had been tantalized by aromas coming from the kitchen, and now it was time to eat. Armed with our plates and utensils, we crowded around the tables sumptuously laid out. A plethora of hot and cold offerings was waiting for us, still being added to as one dish after another arrived from the kitchen, each borne proudly by one of the cooks. Piping hot spring rolls.

---

[58] *tamasic:* Static (food). Onions, along with garlic, were off-limits to Margiis because they created heat in the body and were considered to stimulate the sexual *vritti* or propensity. Mushrooms were also considered *tamasic* because, being fungi, they had no *prana* or life force in them.

Vegetable dishes made with coconut cream. Dumplings. Seitan dishes. Even a veggie pizza had been thrown into the mix. One thing was sure: tonight, no one would be following the *four items only at a meal* rule.

We piled our plates high and sat down on the rug, near silence reigning as we took our first bites. I finished a spring roll and started in on the pizza. It was delicious. I was about to take another bite when I paused to take a closer look. Could those be mushrooms mixed in with the green peppers and broccoli? I wondered. It sure looked like them. But that's impossible, I thought. All Margiis know that mushrooms are *tamasic!*

I took another look. My eyes were telling me that those were indeed mushrooms, but my brain was saying, "No way!" Maybe they're special Filipino vegetables that look like mushrooms, I thought. Still, I decided to play it safe and leave the pizza to one side for the moment, concentrating on the vegetable coconut cream dish instead. It, too, was delicious. No sign of mushrooms here, I thought gratefully.

Didi Tripuri, who was sitting next to me, leaned over and whispered, "Those are mushrooms on the pizza." Tripuri, herself a Filipino, dispelled any lingering hope that the mushrooms were an exotic Filipino vegetable.

"But how could they be?" I whispered back. "The cooks are Margiis! They know we don't eat mushrooms!"

Tripuri shrugged. "They're mushrooms all right!" she said in a louder voice. "I'm not eating my pizza."

I looked around the room. Ratulananda, the Office Secretary, had heard Tripuri and was now examining his own half-eaten slice. As a blush started to suffuse across his pale face, hiding his freckles, Ratulananda laid his slice down and looked around to see if others had noticed and, most importantly, whether our new SS Dada had. My eyes followed his. No, apparently not, for the SS was just finishing off one slice and was reaching for another.

Should I do something or say something? I wondered, looking around at everyone eating pizza. I soon decided not to make a scene. Most of the workers had already eaten it, and the damage had already been done. My appetite was gone. Mushrooms! I had eaten mushrooms, something I hadn't had for years, and I wasn't happy about it. Who knows, maybe there had even been garlic or onions in something as well!

After dinner ended, we filed out into the street. A smiling SS Dada, looking well fed and satisfied, was saying his goodbyes to the Filipino Margiis. I walked over to Ratulananda as he was about to get into his car and said, "Dada, you know there were mushrooms on the pizza and that SS Dada ate it, don't you?"

"I know," he replied, "but I don't think that Dada does, and I'm not going to tell him!"

Knowing that Ratulananda had been the one to accept the Filipino Margiis' invitation and that SS Dada would surely blame him, I made a gesture indicating that my lips were sealed. *What kind of Margiis would put mushrooms in our food?* SS Dada would say if he knew. *Why did you accept an invitation from such people?* Some kind of punishment would then be meted out to Ratulananda, and he certainly didn't want to find out what it would be.

Our new sectorial secretary probably never found out that he had eaten mushrooms on a pizza prepared by Margiis. Maybe he had poor meditation for a day or two afterwards, which he might have attributed to stuffing himself that evening. Maybe. Or maybe not. As for me, I felt horribly guilty for eating those mushrooms. Don't be upset, said the more reasonable inner voice. It wasn't your fault. But the strict taskmaster inner voice lectured, *You should have looked more closely at the pizza before taking a bite.* I conceded to the strict taskmaster, dismissing the reasonable inner voice, which questioned why I should examine food prepared by Margiis who supposedly knew what foods were forbidden.

So I took *myrobalam*, a dried fruit indicated by the Guru as an antidote for mushrooms and other *tamasic* foods, and fasted for a day. Maybe I wasn't subtle enough, my sadhana not high enough for me to notice, or maybe the *myrobalam* had had its desired effect. Whatever it was, my meditation didn't seem to suffer. (After smuggling in the equipment, my meditation didn't suffer any bad effects, either—and I didn't even have to take *myrobalam!*)

Chapter 23

I Get Transferred to Berlin Sector

I arrived in Calcutta, turned over the business money to Ananda Sudha, and got the posting to another sector I'd been hoping for. Ananda Sudha got together with Ananda Preyasi, Sectorial Women's Welfare Secretary of Berlin Sector, and they arranged a didi swap. I would be going to Copenhagen, and the didi who'd been posted there would be going to Australia. The swap meant I had been demoted and would no longer be a sectorial worker, but that didn't bother me in the least. All that mattered was to get as far away from Ananda Sudha as possible. My new in-charge was no picnic either, or so I'd heard, but I wasn't particularly worried. No one, I was convinced, could be as bad as Ananda Sudha.

Meanwhile, I was determined to use the time I had left in Calcutta to focus on Baba. One morning I was sitting on a bench with other didis outside his house, hoping to get in to see him. I was passing the time by studying the clay pots lining the outside walls. They were filled with an astonishing variety of plants, most of which had been smuggled into India by Margiis all over the world. I was trying to discern if any of them could have been the ones I'd brought with me from Australia some years back when a hopeful voice with a decidedly American accent cut into my musings.

"Do you think Baba will call us for RDS this time?"

I looked to my left at the didi sitting next to me, just one in a line on the long bench. She looked young, hardly out of her teens. Her uniform was new and her sari was the kind of white that lasted through two or three washings at best. From the looks of her, this had to be her first RDS.

"Well, you never know," I began slowly. Looking at her eager face—lit up as if with some internal light bulb, devotion shining forth at eight hundred watts—I didn't want to discourage her. I'd been a didi for more than fifteen years, and I could count on one or two hands the number of times I'd been called to go upstairs to be with Baba. But I didn't want to hold up that kind of bleak landscape to such a sunny face.

"We have been called up on occasion, but it doesn't happen all that much. The dadas go up much more," I said. To say the least: they went up to the meeting room at least once a day during RDS.

I looked down the bench at the other didis. Some sat with eyes closed, trying to meditate. Others used their reports as fans, moving the humid Calcutta air around their heads with dogged determination. Despite their best efforts, sweat had claimed more and more of the material on their caps beneath their veils as the morning had worn on. Others fidgeted, fiddling with their veils, tucking wisps of hair that peeked out beneath the tight-fitting cap, or pulling back on a too-tight veil that had crept too far forward. We were desolate, marooned on this bench—so close to Baba and yet so far.

"Why doesn't Baba call us more?" the young didi asked. Others stopped their fanning and looked our way.

"Dadas need to see Baba more. We're more spiritually developed than they are," one Indian avadhutika asserted.

"I think Baba's testing us," said another. "He's testing our devotion."

Suddenly, exhilarated shouts rang out. As if out of nowhere, a river of orange streamed in the gate and gathered at the door. Dadas, all of them, on their way to see Baba. Baba's PA, Kanakananda, signaled to them, and the stream of orange went in the door and flowed up the concrete stairs. We didis held our collective breath. Could today be the day? Kanakananda glanced at us and smiled.

"Namaskar, Didis. How are you?" he said, then climbed the stairs and disappeared.

Silence, sudden and complete, surrounded us.

"It's not fair," said the young didi, her face clouding over. "We should see Baba just as much as the dadas do. Why doesn't he call us more?" she asked again, looking at me.

We all felt that it wasn't fair, of course. All of us, though, had come to accept one of the several explanations developed over the years by didis sitting forlorn on the bench. You had to. Otherwise, how could you maintain your sense of dignity and self-esteem? How could you stay?

My thoughts turned to the first time I had sat and waited and the anger (no, the rage!) I'd felt upon realizing I would not get to go upstairs to meet with Baba simply because I was a woman. Baba had often spoken about women, their situation in society, and their rights. His words were strong, even radical, by Indian society's standards. But I'd learned that what Baba said publicly about women and what he said privately to certain followers were worlds apart.

I thought back to the time Auntie, Ananda Bhakti, related to a group of us how Baba had once sent word to come and see him in the middle of the night.

"I was puzzled," Auntie said. "It was a strange hour to be summoned to Baba's quarters, but I told the messenger that I would come as quickly as possible. I dressed and rushed over." Auntie paused and looked at us. All of us had our eyes riveted on her, taking in every word.

"When I arrived," Auntie continued, "I was immediately waved into Baba's room. Baba was sitting there, looking very serious. He didn't smile at me. He said, 'You know, Ananda Bhaktiji, there are only two categories of women: goddesses and *rakshasiis.*[59] Always remember this thing.' I knew that what Baba told me was very important. Otherwise, why didn't he wait until daytime to tell me?"

We all got the message. There was to be no in between for women. We were to be either goddesses or demons, and we didis, of course, were expected to be goddesses.

I also remembered Auntie going on to say, "Baba explained that for men, there were three categories. They could be gods, demons—or just plain ordinary."

Auntie did not question Baba's words: as the first avadhutika, her devotion to the Guru was unwavering. At the time, I also didn't wonder about Baba's words. I believed that whatever he said was the truth, whether or not we could understand it.

As could be expected among young people meant to be celibate, there was the occasional case of a didi and dada becoming sexually involved. Whenever one of these affairs would come to light, it seemed that the woman was always blamed. She was the one who had lead the man into temptation, who (as a fallen goddess having become a demon) had taken the innocent, ordinary man along with her.

No one would dare question Baba or suggest that despite his words and spiritual status, he was in this regard a product of his environment. Baba had grown up in a society where women were second-class citizens. Perhaps, just perhaps, despite his words to the contrary, we remained so to him.

I came out of my dark reverie to find the young didi still gazing intently at me, waiting for an answer to her question.

"I think it has something to do with Indian culture," I said. "It's not considered proper for women to do the same things as men. By Indian standards, it would be considered improper for Baba to have the didis in his room as often as he has the dadas."

---

[59] *rakshasiis:* Female demons.

The didi looked unconvinced, and who could blame her? My words carried no ring of conviction.

We went back to waiting, meditating, and fanning ourselves. Who knows? I thought. Today might be our lucky day, and we might be called upstairs, too. Those few times we had been were very special to me, despite the fact that Baba's room had been close and stifling in the Calcutta heat with all of us packed in there.

I would gladly put up with that to get the chance to be in Baba's room again, I thought. But being crowded in was so much more uncomfortable for us didis because of our uniforms. That day when Baba had spoken to us about the burka and how it caused women to suffer, hadn't it occurred to any of us sitting there that our own uniform was not far removed from the burka? Deep down, there had been a tiny voice that had posed this unsettling question, but it had been largely smothered by my faith in the Guru and his concern for our welfare. Now the voice couldn't be ignored. I knew and had experienced too much.

Our bodies were completely covered, head to foot, and the only real difference as far as coverage went between our dress and the burka was that our faces were not. We wore (over underwear) a sari blouse, a petticoat, a sari, a jacket (which covered us from shoulders down to knees), a belt, a tight-fitting cap on our head, and the veil, worn over the cap. In the hot, humid climate of Calcutta and other such places, sweat had become a permanent part of our lives. Add the fact that our uniforms were often made out of polyester; chosen because it dried quickly and didn't crease as easily as cotton, but was much hotter; and you had one hell of a sweaty didi! Couldn't such a stifling uniform lead to poor health—just as Baba had said the burka did? If any of us thought so, no one dared say so or dream of asking Baba about it.

Why had Ananda Bhakti, who had designed it at Baba's behest years earlier, come up with such an impractical and oppressive uniform in the first place? By her own account, she had never intended it to be so. I remembered being with Auntie as she drew some sketches to show us the designs she had proposed to Baba. One had consisted of a simple sari along with a small headscarf. Baba had rejected all her designs until she presented him with the one we didis were still wearing now. Some said it had been Baba's intent to protect didis from men. Whatever had been his intention, Baba could have changed the design of the uniform whenever he wished, but he hadn't seen fit to do so. I recalled Baba's reply to Mohinii's question about altering her uniform for working in Israel. He just wouldn't have it. At the time, I'd been happy that Baba had put Mohinii in her place. But after years of wearing the uniform, I now found myself in agreement with Mohinii. The novelty had long worn off, and far from being an honor to wear, it had become oppressive.

The dadas' uniform, while not exactly lightweight either, didn't have as many layers as ours did, and dadas often went without their turbans even in public. The only time we went without our veils was when we were out of sight in our own rooms and offices, or when we wore civil dress while traveling or applying for visas. There was strong pressure for us to keep our heads covered at all times while in the presence of a male. If a dada came to a didi's office to consult with her about something, for example, she wouldn't put on her veil—but she'd likely drape her sari over her hair before going out to see him.

A flash of orange and the babble of excited voices broke into my brooding. The dadas were pouring out the door after coming down the stairs from Baba's room. The meeting was over. Radiant and filled with the Guru's love, they passed by, hardly noticing us, and went out the gate. We got up and without a word, filed out behind them. Tomorrow was another day.

What I still find confusing, looking back on the whole thing now, is how Baba's status as a spiritual master related to his treatment of women. As a great master, Baba *knew* things, so he must have known about the glaring inequalities within his own organization. Why, then, didn't he do anything about them? Was culture and conditioning really that strong, even for him?

Those are the questions I asked myself over and over while in the organization—and, in fact, ever since.

And I also find myself asking another: would Baba have taken any action had any of us had the courage to tell him what was going on? Maybe that was just what he was waiting for: us didis to stand up for ourselves. As far as I know, no one ever did; like those didis in Istanbul who didn't dare tell Baba the truth about the kidnapping incident, most of us were too scared of him to say anything. Would Baba have changed anything if we had? Would he have altered the uniform to something less burkalike if we'd asked him, if we'd pointed out that time when he talked about how the burka caused women's health to suffer, that the didis' uniform was identical in coverage save for the face? Maybe we were at least a little to blame for not trying.

A few weeks after getting my new posting, Ananda Preyasi and I left Calcutta for Delhi, where we would be staying for a few days with Margii friends of Didi's. When we got to the apartment building, located off a street and inside a courtyard, Ananda Preyasi was given a room in the family apartment, but I, along with three other didis who had also shown up, was settled in an unoccupied upstairs apartment also belonging to the Margiis. This was a rarity in India and we took full advantage, spreading out and relaxing in the nearly empty rooms and keeping to our own schedule instead of being constantly underfoot in the crowded apartment below.

One morning a day or two later, we had gotten up early as usual, had finished our meditation, and luxuriating in the privacy, had started in on our yoga postures. One didi from the Philippines was so relaxed lying on her mat that she had dozed off, hands crossed over her tightly fitting sari blouse, the edge of her white petticoat stirring, lifted by the ceiling fan whispering above.

Sounds somewhat muted by distance drifted in the unscreened louvered windows: the chants of a vegetable seller

(*"Brinjal! Phulgobi! Brinjal! Phulgobi!"*[60]), the bell of a rickshaw wallah ringing out in the morning air. Closer sounds—housewives calling out to family members in the apartments below and the clatter of pots mingling with the sharp scent of kerosene stoves and the aroma of chapattis cooking with ghee—indicated that cooking was well underway.

A fly buzzed. The ceiling fan turned lazily overhead. It was already quite warm. It was May, and in Delhi temperatures could soar well into the thirties and even reach forty degrees Celsius (104 degrees Fahrenheit).

I was doing the cobra pose when there was a sudden, sharp knock on the door. We all raised our heads and looked at each other, puzzled. Who could that be? Another, sharper rap on the door, and the Filipino didi awoke with a start, confusion spreading across her features. A third insistent rap, and then a voice called out, "Po*lish!* Po*lish!*"

We shot hurried looks at each other, the alarm on the other didis' faces mirroring my own. "Oh, my God! It's the *police!*" someone said in a hissing whisper. A shocked silence greeted her words, then frantic activity as we looked everywhere for an escape, for there were didis among us, the Filipino included, who didn't have valid visas. We raced into the back room, with those in question trying to crawl beneath the bed. All the while the insistent and now quite annoyed voice continued to call out imperiously, "Po*lish!* Po*lish!*"

Since I had a valid visa, I volunteered to open the door even though I knew that a visa was no defense against deportation. And I had something else to worry about: what if they asked for my passport, found the note about the video equipment, and asked to see it? I could end up in jail!

With that worry occupying my mind, I went to the door and opened it. Instead of the baton-welding, angry-faced policeman in khaki uniform I had anticipated, there stood a laborer wearing an undershirt gray from countless washings and a blue and

---

[60] *Brinjal! Phulgobi!*: Eggplant! Cauliflower!

white checkered dhoti. He had a pail of paint at his feet and was brandishing a large brush. "Po*lish!* Po*lish!*" he shouted. "I have to po*lish!*"

It seemed the apartment was unoccupied because it was due for some painting and renovating—a little detail that our hosts had failed to share with us.

Meanwhile, we didis occupied our time with shopping for things to take back to our respective fields: silver jewelry; bundles of peacock feathers; paintings of Krishna, Shiva, and Kali on black cloth; and plenty of skirts, blouses, saris, and woolen shawls from Kashmir. I hoped the goods I had selected would fetch good prices once I got to Berlin Sector.

I also arranged to get a new passport without too much difficulty, and soon it was time to leave. I was getting ready for my after-midnight flight to Copenhagen and had just managed to pack up all my goods (no small feat), when Ananda Preyasi informed me that she had "some things" for me to take back to Europe for her. She then hauled out some bags, one of them the biggest green-with-black-trim Indian cloth bag I had ever seen. It was the size of a coffin and was bulging with peacock feathers and books.

"Didi," I said slowly, choosing my words carefully, "there's no way I'll be able to get all of these things onto the plane."

"Oh, nonsense!" she replied. "Just ask them politely. I'm sure you'll find a way." This diminutive didi, hardly five feet tall and weighing less than one hundred pounds, had a deceptively sweet and innocent manner, but as my superior she was not to be challenged.

Besides, as Ananda Preyasi knew, limits on luggage weight didn't stop us. Our folklore was full of tales of Margiis carrying two, three, even four times the legal limit. The Guru's grace along with sweet-talking and clever carry-on luggage tricks accounted for these successes, we thought.

Because a taxi would be hard to find at that hour, Santosh, one of our hosts, agreed to take me to the airport in his minivan. On the way, I spotted people in doorways, sleeping on their pieces of cardboard. My problems paled in comparison to theirs, I reminded myself. Even so, my stomach was doing flip-flops as I contemplated my options, or lack of them. Because I wasn't feeling sweet, I wasn't feeling lucky, and I doubted that God was going to intervene on my behalf this time. Even Baba couldn't get all this luggage on the plane! I reasoned desperately.

All too soon, the minivan pulled up to the airport. "If you can wait a little bit, you can take some of the things back," I said to Santosh as he unloaded my bags. He paused to consider my request. "All right. But try not to take too much time. I have to go to work in the morning, you know."

While Santosh hung back in the milling crowd, I presented my ticket to the man at the counter. "How many bags, madam?" he asked. He didn't look at all like a soft touch who would be moved by my tearful entreaties. Instead, he was officious-looking with a perfectly trimmed moustache, his white uniform surprisingly crisp for the hour and the humidity. "Three," I replied in a small voice, the three not including my large carry-on, which I was going to put on a luggage caddy.

He indicated that I should put my bags on the scale. I struggled with the green monster, finally managing to hoist it onto the scale, which revealed that it plus my other two bags made me nearly three times the limit allowed. The man looked at me wearily and told me what I already knew: my luggage was seriously overweight, and I would have to take measures to reduce it.

I suddenly lit upon what I considered to be a brilliant idea. "Sir, I'm rather light, so couldn't I be allowed some extra kilos for my luggage?"

The man stared at me. "I'm sorry, madam," he said. "You'll have to substantially reduce the weight of your luggage. I suggest that you take your bags and make your decision, then return to the counter. . . . Next!"

One by one, I dragged my bags over to one corner of the departure lounge. Trying to be inconspicuous, I opened up the monster and began digging beneath the peacock feathers to reach the books. A wave of sudden panic swept over me. Oh, my God! The books! They identified me as a member of Ananda Marga, and if I got caught, I'd be deported and blacklisted once again. I felt eyes upon me, staring from every corner of the departure lounge; despite the late hour, the room was full of people. Frantically, I rearranged my luggage so I would have a spare bag, threw most of the books into it (hurrying so that no one could read their titles), and then rushed over to Santosh, who took the bag and headed out the door. He would take it back to my pint-sized chief. She would be angry with me, but I wouldn't have to face her wrath until I saw her again, which, thankfully, wouldn't be any time soon.

I hauled my bags, now reduced by one, over to the counter again. This time the man informed me that even though I was still a bit over the limit, he would allow me to go. Relief swept over me, only to be replaced by my next concern: getting my carry-on bag, which was larger than many people's checked luggage, onto the plane. I trundled it over to security and steeled myself for the next round. Much to my relief, I encountered no further problems. I shouldn't have expected any. After all, I was doing Baba's work!

In Copenhagen, I would be managing the preschool my predecessor had started and would be living in the same place as the school. That was nothing unusual for us; I had done just that in Brisbane. But in Brisbane, there had been an entire house. In Copenhagen, I soon learned that there was only a ground-floor apartment; the little side room I would use for meditating and sleeping was so crowded with school supplies there was barely enough room for me to lay my sleeping bag down. I didn't have much chance to get acclimated to my new posting because school was back in session not long after I got there. Mostly children of embassy staffers attended from countries like France, Egypt, and Belgium. Learning English was the main draw.

I wasn't the only worker in Copenhagen. The world headquarters of PROUT was also located there, with the well-known and respected Dada Tapasananda supervising its numerous projects and male LFTs. I had never met Tapasananda and was looking forward to doing so, having heard so much about him. One Sunday, when I went to the PROUT office for the first time to attend dharmacakra, Dada called me into his study and waved me into a chair for a talk. I remember being struck by his resemblance to an orange-clad Santa Claus; not only was he short and roly-poly, but his medium-length beard and hair were shot full of silver and he had a loud, echoing laugh. After talking for a while, we went down to the dharmacakra hall, a large room with high ceilings and several generously sized windows. As we went in, I was almost dazzled by the light streaming in—a scene in stark contrast to the dark, cramped apartment where I was holed up. This was a grand house, one which had likely been a real mansion at one time.

Besides the LFTs working with Tapasananda, the most important Margiis in Copenhagen were Lalana and Viiresh, a Swedish-American couple with three children and another on the way. They were warm and welcoming and gave generously of their time and money. Lalana even helped me with medicines for my hemorrhoids, showing up at the school one day with some homeopathic treatments.

After going to dharmacakra at the PROUT office a few times and noticing the small number of family Margiis attending, I asked Viiresh and Lalana about it.

"Didi," Lalana replied, "Dada's not very welcoming to family Margiis. He insists on holding dharmacakra at seven o'clock, which is too late for most family Margiis. The kids end up eating and getting to bed too late for school the next morning."

"Have you ever said anything to Dada about it?" I asked. Lalana and Viiresh looked at each other but didn't say anything.

"I'm sure he wouldn't mind holding it a little earlier," I said. "I'll talk to him about it."

But I found that Tapasananda wasn't open to the idea.

"Oh nonsense, Didi," he said, waving my concerns away. "They always complain about something." Dharmacakra remained at the same time.

Other tensions soon came to light. PROUT owned and ran a bakery, located just a few blocks from the school. The LFTs did everything. They were the bakers, bookkeepers, and store clerks. Some had to get up very early in the morning to get to the bakery (which, though close to me, was quite far from the PROUT office) and fire up the ovens. Working there was especially challenging during the Scandinavian winter, when the LFTs would hardly see the light of day—getting to the bakery well before sunrise, putting in long hours, and returning to the PROUT office in the darkness of late afternoon. They had little time off and, I heard, weren't treated well. It was known that Dada had a temper and was often dissatisfied with one thing or another.

One Sunday was particularly memorable. Dharmacakra having just concluded, I was still in the meditation room, finishing my lessons. I was in the middle of my *pranayama* when I heard a loud exchange taking place in the hall. First I heard Lalana's voice, then Tapasananda's. I couldn't quite make out what they were discussing, but their voices rose and the exchange quickly escalated to a shouting match. I decided to finish my lesson before going out to see what it was all about.

Moments later, I emerged to find Tapasananda standing in the hall, alone in the sudden silence.

"She just left," he told me. His face was red. "How dare she! How dare she raise her voice to me!" Dada said, his voice trembling. Then he stopped and peered at me. "Where were you while all this was happening?"

"I was in the meditation hall finishing my *pranayama*," I said apologetically.

Tapasananda, though clearly not happy, seemed to accept my explanation. I could see that he needed to talk. He motioned me into the meditation room, and we sat down on the floor opposite one other.

"You see, most people think Lalana and Viiresh are model Margiis," he began. "Well, they aren't! Lalana is a trouble maker." Dada then launched into a rambling tirade about Lalana's shortcomings and character defects. "She has even given her children cookies with eggs in them on occasion!" he concluded.

I listened, nodding my head from time to time until he calmed down. I didn't want to take sides, but the Lalana he was describing didn't sound at all like the woman I knew.

He made it clear that he expected an apology. "I'll talk to her," I promised.

Lalana would have none of it. "Why should I apologize? I did nothing wrong! I've tried to talk to Dada so many times. He never listens. Maybe now that I've raised my voice, he'll pay attention."

Neither side would budge.

"Lalana is banned from dharmacakra until she apologizes," Dada announced.

"Fine," said Lalana when I told her.

I found myself caught in the middle. Privately, I sympathized with Lalana. Tapasananda was throwing his power around and was showing the same kind of unreasonable anger I'd witnessed in Ananda Sudha. On the other hand, I wished that Lalana would just apologize so things would get back to normal.

But things only got worse. A few weeks after the confrontation in the hall, I was called to the PROUT office and was shown into Tapasananda's study. He wasn't the only dada sitting there; Gaganananda was there, too. I hardly recognized the dada who had been my trainer in Benares; he looked so different. No longer thin and sickly, he had clearly regained his health, and I was surprised by how powerful looking he was. I was happy to see him. "Dada," I said, smiling and doing namaskar. "It's so nice to see you!"

He didn't smile back. "You are here for a serious matter," he said. "Sit down."

I was being accused of being in a conspiracy with Lalana. "A conspiracy?" I asked, not believing what I had heard.

"Yes, a conspiracy!" Gaganananda said, raising his voice. "Otherwise, how do you explain the fact that you did not come out of the meditation room when you heard Lalana shouting at Dada?"

"It was right after dharmacakra and I was finishing my sadhana," I said. "I was right in the middle of my *pranayama*. When I finished, I came out, but Lalana had already left." I looked at Tapasananda. "Dada, I already told you that, remember?" But Tapasananda didn't meet my eyes and continued to sit in a stony silence.

"You will have to apologize in writing, or else your avadhutikaship will be seized," Gaganananda said, "and you will not be permitted to wear avadhutika dress." I sat in stunned silence. "You have one week to write the apology," he continued. "If it is not received in time, by the beginning of RDS, your avadhutikaship will be seized right away. You may go now," he said, turning away.

Tapasananda meant to have his apology. If he couldn't get it from Lalana, he would get it from me. So he was bringing out the heavy guns, enlisting the help of a powerful Central worker, which Gaganananda now was, to get it.

Tapasananda was the Global PROUT Secretary, but he certainly wasn't acting like the vanguard of a new society or the harbinger of the dictatorship of the sadvipra. It's a dictatorship, all right, I thought, a dictatorship of the male ego! And against it, I didn't stand a chance.

Chapter 24

Making Do Without Health Care

A few weeks later, after arriving in Germany for RDS, I went into the room where not only Tapasananda and Gaganananda were waiting, but several other Indian dadas as well. As I sat down on the rug, all of them looked at me disapprovingly, shaking their turbaned heads. Then the inquisition began. After hearing a rehash of my transgressions from Gaganananda, which were accompanied by outraged mutterings and tsk-tsks from the assemblage, I handed my letter of apology to Tapasananda, murmuring something about being sorry, about how I should have come out of the dharmacakra room as soon as I'd heard shouting and dealt with Lalana right then and there. The dadas sat there with their arms crossed, looking satisfied. "We've put this uppity didi in her place," their faces said. They got their apology. I got to keep my avadhutika dress.

From then on, my relations with Tapasananda back in Copenhagen were coldly formal, and I had as little to do with him as possible. But I wouldn't be there long: a lump in my left breast would see to that.

288

I discovered it one day while bathing. It felt enormous. Terrified, I called Lalana right away. "I don't know what to do," I said. Lalana knew what I meant: like most Ananda Marga workers, I had no health insurance.

Lalana called around and got the name of a breast specialist. "Don't worry about what it costs," she said. "I'll help pay for it." I was grateful. What would I have done without her? A few days later, I went to the doctor and had an examination. "You should have an operation right away," he said when he finished. "Don't even wait to have a mammogram. Get that lump removed immediately."

I left the office in a daze. Breast surgery in Denmark would be free for a Danish citizen but would likely cost me thousands of dollars. Lalana's offer to help extended to the visit with the specialist, not to surgery! What would I do now?

I called the didis' office in Mainz, Germany, and spoke with Ananda Preyasi. "Oh, I wouldn't worry about it so much if I were you," she said. "Chances are it's nothing serious. Ananda Udita has lots of lumps in her breasts, but she's fine." That wasn't what I wanted to hear. I didn't want much from Ananda Preyasi; just a little bit of sympathy or a tiny show of concern would have been enough. But I didn't get even that.

I decided to get a second opinion. Kaoverii, a Margii sister who was living in the didis' office, suggested that I go to Germany. "I know a doctor who would probably see you for free," she said, "a woman." That sounded good to me; I had been extremely uncomfortable having my breast examined by a man.

Ananda Preyasi arranged for another didi to come to Copenhagen while I was away. I didn't want to tell the preschool teacher or any of the parents the real reason I was leaving. It would be unseemly for anyone to express sympathy or worry or make a fuss over an avadhutika, I thought. "I have something to take care of in Germany," I told everyone. "I'll be back soon, in a few weeks."

* * *

The German doctor did see me for free, and she was kind. "Yes, I feel it," she said as she examined my breast. "It is quite large, but it might be benign. I'm not a breast specialist, though. You should go and have a mammogram done."

"You don't think I should have it operated on right away? That's what the specialist in Copenhagen told me."

She looked taken aback. "I don't agree," she said firmly. "I definitely would not recommend surgery without a mammogram being done first. Then you should take the films to a breast specialist." She wrote down the name of one and gave it to me.

After I had the mammogram, I made an appointment with the specialist. He took one look at my films and waved his hand dismissively.

"You have nothing to worry about," he said in his clipped English. "There is nothing wrong, no sign of cancer. You are fine."

"But the doctor in Copenhagen said I have a large lump that needs to be taken out right away."

"You have nothing to worry about," he repeated and waved me out of his office.

This is unbelievable! I thought. Who should I believe?

"You know, there's free health care in England," Ananda Supriya said when I called her later that day. "You can pretend you're me and use my health card and get another opinion."

I was fond of Didi Supriya. We'd know each other a long time, ever since the mid-seventies, when I was finishing my training in Calcutta, and she was just beginning hers. We were about the same age, and whenever we got together for RDS, we would sing Beatles songs and joke around together. She'd been posted to London for several years now and had started a successful school. Supriya had never developed a British accent, though. She still had the slow Southern drawl that I never tired of listening to.

"There's always room for you," Supriya continued. "Come as soon as you can." Like me, Supriya lived on her school premises, but her school had to be a lot larger than mine if she had room for me, I thought.

So I went to London. A few days after I arrived, Supriya handed me her health card and said, "Just make sure you memorize my date of birth. You'll need it to fill in forms." I looked closely at the card.

"Don't worry," Supriya said. "There's no way they'll suspect anything."

I took a bus. After getting off, I walked the few blocks remaining to the clinic. It was a blustery day, dark with clouds. I pulled my jacket closer to me, shivering, all the while rehearsing the details of my new identity: name, date of birth, address . . . name, date of birth, address . . . A hell of a way to get health care—pretending to be someone else! I thought. What if I mess up and they find out? Get the birth date wrong or something? If that happened, chances were it wouldn't be me who would bear the brunt of the consequences. Maybe they would take Didi's health card away or make her leave England—or even arrest her. That thought made me shiver even more.

The clinic was crowded with people in their dark and bulky winter coats. I went up to the registration desk and signed in, then sat down to wait. When they called Supriya's name, I took the forms they handed me back to my seat, looked them over—and saw that I would have to write in Supriya's mother's name. My heart started to pound. I didn't know her mother's name! The idea that first came to mind, using my own mother's name, I quickly dismissed. There was no getting around it: I would have to call Supriya. Thanking Baba that I'd thought to bring her number with me, I made my way to a pay phone and placed the call, looking around to be sure that no one was watching. When Supriya answered, I held the receiver to my lips and whispered, "Supriya, what's your mother's name?" "What?" she said. "I can't hear you." "Your mother's name!" I hissed. "I need it to fill in the forms." After getting the information, I hung up and looked around again to see if anyone was watching, but people seemed far too busy with their own conversations to have been paying any attention to mine. I went back to my seat, filled in the name and other required information, turned in the paperwork, and waited some more.

They ended up doing another mammogram. If I didn't already have cancer, I told myself, maybe I could get it from having another mammogram so soon after the first. I certainly couldn't have given them my other photos to look at because those had my real name on them. "Everything looks fine," the breast specialist told me, "but we'll do a biopsy just to make sure."

About a week later, I got the report: a clean bill of health. I was surprised to find that along with relief, there was also anger. If that stupid doctor in Copenhagen hadn't told me I had to have an operation, I thought, I wouldn't have had to go through all of this! There was also just the tiniest bit of regret. "If I do have cancer," I had told Supriya when I'd first gotten to London, "maybe Ananda Preyasi will let me work in Russia." Supriya knew about my fascination with Russia. Ever since I had studied Russian in college, I had longed to go there.

Instead, I returned to Copenhagen. A bill for five hundred kroner was waiting for me from the "the butcher" as I'd come to call him. That was one bill I wasn't going to pay. If I had listened to him, I might not have a breast now, I thought. Deliberately, I took the money I had put aside, including the money Lalana had given me, and spent it on other needs more pressing. I never did pay that bill.

Chapter 25

We Are Orphaned

It was October, 1990, and I was in Germany attending an RDS meeting at the dadas' office in Mainz when someone knocked on the door and quietly called Ananda Preyasi out of the room. Sureshananda had already been called out a few minutes earlier. The rest of us had thought nothing of it and continued the discussion we'd been having about Eastern Europe. We were taking stock of what had been accomplished so far and the new possibilities that lay ahead.

That spring, I had left Copenhagen for good, having been sent to Poland. Then a few months later, I finally got the chance to go to Russia. I went to St. Petersburg with Ananda Mainjula, an American didi who had been there before. With the advent of perestroika, Russia was opening up and was proving to be an exciting place to work. I was sharing some of my impressions with the other workers while we waited for Didi and Dada to return and resume the meeting.

A few minutes later, I went out to use the bathroom and caught sight of them standing in the hallway, talking with lowered voices, stricken looks on their faces. I returned to the room but could no longer focus on anything that was being said. I just kept thinking of that look on Didi's face. What could be wrong? Could it have something to do with Baba? He had suffered during those years spent in jail, and his long fast had taken a toll on his health. Baba hadn't been well recently. Something was wrong with his heart, we'd been told, and specialists had been called in to examine him.

The door opened and Ananda Preyasi and Sureshananda stepped back into the room. Something menacing seemed to enter with them. Instead of sitting down and resuming the meeting, they remained standing.

"We've just gotten word from India," Ananda Preyasi said. "They said that Baba has left his body." A shocked, thundering silence greeted her words. Then a few didis started to cry.

"Maybe it's not true," Didi continued, her voice breaking. "How could he leave us so suddenly, without saying anything?" Then she, too, began to cry.

Karuna, an Australian didi known for her beautiful singing, picked up a guitar and started to play kiirtan, a slow and beautifully haunting tune that I'd never heard before and wouldn't soon forget. Some of us, including me, got up and began to dance, going round and round in a circle, our hands held above our heads as if appealing to the heavens. Others sat in stunned meditation. Still others bowed their heads and wept.

Later that day, we were told that Baba's body would be kept on ice so his devotees would get the chance to see him before he would be cremated. "Everyone who can, should go to India immediately," Ananda Preyasi said.

The next day, we all went to the Indian Embassy to apply for visas. I had come to RDS planning to ask Didi for permission to go to DMC. Now, unless all this wasn't true, there would never again be a DMC. Such a thing was unthinkable. It just couldn't possibly be true.

"Baba has probably gone into a trance," one didi said. "He'll wake up again, I just know it."

"I think he's lying in a deep state, taking the world's bad karma upon himself," theorized another.

"He wouldn't leave without saying goodbye and leaving instructions," a third didi said.

We all had ideas of how Baba would leave his body. We had heard accounts of how great masters had prepared their disciples for their deaths by designating a successor and indicating the exact time and place of their departure. We had expected the same of Baba. Many of us had imagined a gathering where Baba would take leave of his body with thousands of disciples in attendance. No one had been prepared for a leave-taking so sudden and unexpected.

I reached India a few days later. As I rushed into the didis' quarters in Tiljala, a didi passed me on her way out. "If you want to see Baba," she said breathlessly, "you'll have to hurry! The cremation is going to start soon." I was crestfallen. All those hours on the plane I'd hoped against hope I would be told upon my arrival that Baba had revived and sat up. I had imagined him laughing at all the workers gathered around him. *You didn't really think I would leave you this way, did you?* he would say. Then he would ask for food. But Baba hadn't woken up.

I ran upstairs to the Berlin Sector room and changed into my uniform. Tying my belt around my waist on my way out, I raced along the corridor, down the stairs, and out the door.

I entered the gate of Baba's quarters as I'd done so many times in the past. All those times, there had been the joyful anticipation of seeing Baba and hearing his voice. It was unthinkable that it would not be so this time. As I approached the house, I saw several didis I knew. We exchanged solemn namaskars. Then I was waved into Baba's room.

I went in and did *pranam*. Baba was lying on a cot, his eyes closed, his utterly still form surrounded by flowers. Some older Indian Margiis sat in the corners, weeping. Others were walking slowly around the cot. Joining them, I numbly walked around it once, twice; then doing a final *pranam* by its side, I prayed desperately: Baba, please wake up. You can't do this to us! You can't go this way! Getting to my feet, I took one long last look at Baba's unchanged face and walked woodenly out of the room. Why wouldn't he wake up?

Outside, a steady stream of people was flowing out to the field where the cremation would be. I joined the stream, allowing it to carry and deposit me at one edge of the area, where I looked around for a place to stand. The funeral pyre was surrounded by Margiis standing a respectful distance back. Closest to it were the Central Office dadas. Some were supervising the workers finishing the process of getting the wood in place. Others were waving in men pushing carts heaped high with flower garlands of many colors whose heady fragrances saturated the air. Further back in the crowd, among the turbans and heads covered by saris of every imaginable hue and pattern, I spotted a patch of orange—a group of didis, their veiled heads bent. As I moved slowly through the crowd to reach them, I saw Ananda Bhadra and Ananda Supriya. We silently exchanged namaskars and hugged.

Suddenly, I became aware of a low but steadily increasing roar coming from the masses surrounding me. People had begun to call out Baba's name. I looked over to the area where the loudest cries were coming from and saw dadas carrying the flower-bedecked funeral bier carefully towards the now-completed pyre. I could see Baba's motionless form, his eyes closed, hands folded across his chest, his perfectly ironed shirt shining in the light. Flowers obscured the rest of his body. The wailing swelled as those farther away also realized that Baba was being brought to be cremated. As they laid Baba's body on the pyre, I prayed he would wake up. As they lit the fire, I continued to pray. My mind would not accept what my eyes knew to be true: Baba was gone.

The smoke from the cremation fire rose slowly and drifted like incense over the heads of Baba's devotees, gathered together like one last garland of offering. As the fire slowly consumed his body, a flock of birds flew in perfect formation across a sky brilliant blue one moment, then clouding up as if in pain the next. Again and again the birds flew across the pyre, as if accompanying Baba's soul heavenward. A few drops of rain fell from the skies as tears fell from the eyes of the thousands gathered there.

Baba's soul had taken flight.

He had left us. We were orphaned.

The tremendous sorrow we felt at Baba's passing cannot be put in words. It was as if a great hole had been ripped out from our hearts. In all of us, there was the feeling of a great void, an emptiness that had opened up. "I don't want to go on living without Baba," Ananda Mukti said to me a few days later. I knew how she felt. We all felt that way.

Even though it felt strange to be in Tiljala without Baba, those of us who were able to stayed there for several weeks. We tried to get some comfort in being together and doing hours of meditation and kiirtan. We shared Baba stories and tried to make sense of his departure and spent a lot of time listening to the senior dadas. "You will feel Baba's presence when you do his work," one after another told us.

Finally, we all went back to work. I went to Poland at the end of January. So far, it had been a cold winter, and the little creek I always passed over on my way to stay with a Margii sister had frozen solid. People young and old alike were skating, most of them just gliding over the ice in their everyday shoes. The cold felt fitting. I was frozen inside, just like the creek.

Chapter 26

Russia: The KGB Caper

On my first trip to Russia, a few months before that fateful RDS meeting, Ananda Mainjula and I had arrived in St. Petersburg in mid-summer. We went to stay with Karushka, a woman Ananda Mainjula had initiated during a previous visit. Dark and slender and endowed with a wonderful sense of humor, Karushka lived with her adult daughter in a small flat in one of the box-like gray apartment buildings found all over Russia. She was a dance teacher but had recently begun working at other jobs to pay the bills and put food on the table. The dire financial situation in Russia at the time did little to dampen her spirits, though. The dream of getting a visa to a Western European country so that she could earn some real money teaching dance was what sustained her. She was hoping we would help her.

Mainjula could speak only a few words of Russian, and Karushka spoke about the same amount of English, so I gladly stepped into the role of translator. Early one evening, Karushka and I were in the kitchen concocting a soup out of the latest produce Mainjula and I had managed to procure in the market place. We had already set the cubed potatoes and chopped cabbage to boil and were about to cut up the tomatoes and chop the dill when a loud crash came from the bathroom, where Mainjula had gone only moments earlier. Karushka and I looked at each other in alarm.

"Didi! Didi, you . . . okay?" Karushka called out. There was no response. Karushka wiped her hands and was about to leave the kitchen when Mainjula came in, sheepish and red faced, to confess that somehow she'd managed to make the toilet fall backwards. Karushka burst out laughing and, when she could get her breath back, shook her head and said, *"Russki tooalyet! Russki tooalyet!"* thereby absolving Didi of all blame. We didn't let on, but the toilet's collapse must have had something to do with our habit of crouching on toilets for sanitary reasons instead of sitting on them.

Along with perestroika and the exhilaration of people suddenly free to do things they would never have dreamed possible a few short years or even months before, hyperinflation had arrived. In Russia, people had never been wealthy, but they'd had what they needed: an apartment (small but paid for), a free healthcare system, and a guaranteed job. Almost overnight, all of that was gone.

You could go shopping in the morning and find that the price of a kilo of tomatoes had doubled since the day before. Goods became scarce and people were reduced to standing in long lines for bread and other basics. I remember waiting for hours to buy bread. When I finally got in the door, most of the bread was gone and only a few sorry loaves, the smashed or defective ones, remained on the shelves.

One day I went to the supermarket looking for some produce. All that was available at counters labeled *Frukti i Ovashi* (Fruits and Vegetables) was toilet paper. No one around me acted as if it were the least bit strange that toilet paper was on shelves meant for fruits and vegetables. Instead, each shopper took several rolls to stock up, knowing that in a day or two, toilet paper would surely join the list of goods nowhere to be found. Another day, I witnessed a near riot when a shipment of butter was rumored to be on sale. A line appeared outside the store almost instantaneously with people pushing and jockeying for position. The manager had to come out to try to calm everyone down, shouting, "You'll all get some, I promise!"

Ananda Mainjula and I went to Russia again the following year. One morning in mid-June, we were sitting in the tiny kitchen of a newly initiated sister, Anna, having tea with bread and butter with her and some of her friends. "We are lucky to have butter," Anna was saying in her halting English. "It wasn't in market last week. Yesterday, I had waiting in line for one hour and got next to last piece. I will not tell you how was cost!" Even though it had been difficult for Anna to get the butter, she preferred sharing it with us instead of saving it for herself. Most of the people I'd met in Russia had been similarly generous with what little they had.

The conversation moved on to other topics, including a new-age festival that was soon to take place in the countryside not far from Moscow. Anna and her friends were going. Sergei, who of the four spoke the best but far from perfect English, asked us if we'd like to go with them, pointing out that it would be a great opportunity for us to teach meditation to lots of people. "You really should come," he continued with growing enthusiasm, "especially because this is first time festival will be held openly, out of doors. They made it in secret before."

"Sergei," I said, "we would love to, but our visas are only for St. Petersburg." At that time, when you applied for a visa to Russia, you didn't get one to the whole country, but only to one city—and you were supposed to stay there.

"This is not problem. You can go to any city you want."

"They told us at the Russian Embassy in Helsinki that we have to stay in St. Petersburg, Sergei,"Ananda Mainjula said.

"Trust me. Every people does it all the time!" he assured us.

So we went, reaching the festival site a few days later in midafternoon. It was a beautiful spot where gentle, rolling hills were surrounded by forest. The rather substantial tent city that had sprung up in a large field already had the bustling feel of a carnival. Everyone was smiling, and there was an almost tangible sense of excitement and enthusiasm in the air.

As Mainjula and I finished setting up our tent, word had already gotten out that some yoga teachers had arrived, and a crowd soon gathered. They all wanted to learn meditation, so we organized translators. (I could have gotten by without one if I'd had to, but the finer points of meditation were really beyond my Russian.) We took our new students up the gentle hills away from the tents, where there was a breeze. There were so many to initiate that it was dusk by the time we had finished and returned to our tent.

Early the next morning, we were having breakfast when a young woman approached. I recognized her as someone I had initiated the day before. "Good morning, Didi," she said, her hands folded respectfully. "I'm Lydia, remember?" I replied in the affirmative and she went on. "I want to tell you something. There's going to be a firewalk later this morning, at ten o'clock," she said, her voice rising with excitement. "I thought you would want to go. After all, it should be easy for you. You are yoga teachers!"

Her attitude was a typical one. She wasn't the first to look at us as if we were mini-gurus, complete with all the spiritual powers they'd read about in *Autobiography of a Yogi*. The ability to walk on fire was a new one, however. Mainjula and I exchanged glances. We knew we should go to preserve our reputations, even though Lydia's idea of what qualified one to be a spiritual teacher was juvenile at best. Besides, we were curious about firewalking, having never witnessed it.

"Of course, Lydia, we'll be there." I said.

"It's down at the field past the creek. I'll see you then!"

When the time came, we were a few minutes late. As we approached the site, we saw people lying on the ground with arms at sides and eyes closed. I scanned the crowd but didn't see

Lydia. Joining the group, we lay down, then closed our eyes and listened to the hypnotic voice leading the visualization exercise, first in Russian, then in English. "Feel yourself growing lighter and lighter. You are spirit. Fire has no power over you. You will float over the coals! You are light! You are light!"

When the voice stopped, people opened their eyes, stretched, and sat up. One by one, they began walking over the bed of live coals arranged in a large circle. Everyone stepped forward, confident and serene. No one hurried or showed any signs of being in pain. I had heard that people who firewalk put Vaseline on their feet. I looked around, but no jars were visible anywhere.

I stood up. No self-respecting yoga teacher could put it off any longer. Approaching the coals gingerly, I took a deep breath and walked as quickly and lightly as possible over them. I am light! I am light! I will float over the coals! I repeated to myself. I felt some burning in my toes, but managing to keep my face composed, I finished the firewalk and sat down.

Later, out of public view, I checked my feet; the left one was burned, but not too seriously, and the right one was untouched. Then Mainjula showed me her feet, both unburned. "I guess you're the real yogi!" I said.

The next morning I didn't feel well. My foot didn't hurt, at least not much, but a veil of melancholy had settled over me while I had slept, and I couldn't bring myself to leave the tent.

"Aren't you coming?" Ananda Mainjula asked when she finished her meditation. "It's time for breakfast."

"You go. I'll be along a little later."

As the morning wore on, it grew hot in the tent, almost unbearably so, but still I remained. A familiar weariness was upon me: I was tired of living up to the role of spiritual teacher, of having to fulfill everyone's expectations, of being the one to always help others while so often inside, there seemed nothing left to draw upon to keep me going. When I'd had these feelings before, I had always managed to pick myself up and continue, but it was getting harder and harder to do, especially with Baba gone.

I thought about the time in Australia when I'd been trying to get the school up and running, and it had looked like it might not happen. At the time, I'd had little luck getting other Margiis involved, even though I had tried.

"You seem so needy," one sister had said to me after one of my pitches, looking at me intently, "like there's this big empty hole inside of you."

I'd felt a jolt of something akin to panic pass through me.

"I don't know what you're talking about," I remembered replying. "I'm just trying to help people and do Baba's work." Then I turned away, dismissing her and her words, all the while feeling hurt and misunderstood.

She'd been right, of course. I don't know who I am anymore, I thought. Maybe I never did.

Finally, toward sunset, I forced myself to leave the tent and resume my role as if nothing had happened. I simply didn't know what else to do.

"I feel better," I said to those who had noticed my absence and asked about it. "I was just tired."

The last day of the festival, we were packing up our tent when Anna came to tell us about a folk dance festival taking place nearby. She asked us if we wanted to go and told us we'd be staying in a hotel.

The hotel is what clinched it. The prospect of a shower within the next few hours proved irresistible. I felt a twinge of worry about staying away from St. Petersburg for several more days but dismissed it. What could possibly happen?

When we got to the hotel, I was surprised by its substantial size. It had a look of grandeur gone to seed, with its faded white exterior, worn green carpets, and its peeling floral wallpaper. Water spots were visible on the walls and ceiling, but the staircase still had its elegant sweep.

We had to show our passports to the couple sitting at the check-in desk. The stout middle-aged woman with a colorful babushka tied under her chin and the beefy, carelessly dressed man smoking a cigarette didn't say a word. They just stared at us, their eyes narrowing. We didn't think much of it at the time, assuming that we were the first foreigners they'd ever seen.

Ananda Mainjula and I trudged up the stairs with our bags to what was to be our shared room and flopped down on the beds. They were lumpy and the mattresses sagged, but it didn't matter: as always, we'd be sleeping on the floor in our sleeping bags.

I went in the bathroom to check things out and noticed the sink's porcelain was cracked and stained a suspicious rusty color. I turned on one faucet. All that came out was a trickle of reddish brown water. I was just about to try the other when a sharp rap on the door interrupted me. Something in that knock was alarming. Could it be that our hosts had changed their minds about having foreigners stay in their hotel? I left the bathroom as more insistent knocks rang out—only these sounded more like kicks.

As Mainjula began to open the door, it was pushed aside by a heavyset man wearing an olive brown uniform. "Where are passports?" he demanded brusquely in heavily accented English. "Give me passports!" There was something official looking about him, so we decided we'd better comply. Going over to our respective beds, each with a suitcase opened in anticipation of being unpacked for the first time in days, we rooted around for our passports, all the while giving each other "What now?" looks. I didn't know about Mainjula, but to me this scene seemed eerily familiar. Suddenly, I felt myself transported back in time to Cairo and the officials who'd demanded my passport along with Narendra's. The same thing was happening again!

After snatching the passports out of our hands, the man deposited them into a pocket without giving them even the briefest of glances. Without a word, he left, slamming the door behind him.

Almost immediately, as if he'd been watching the whole thing from his room, Sergei came in with Anna and Vladimir trailing behind. Looking downcast, he informed us that it was the KGB who'd just paid us a visit. It seemed our friendly hosts had contacted them, and they'd been quick to respond.

The KGB! My heart started to race. Images, menacing and dark, flitted across my mind. Like everyone else, I'd heard stories of the KGB, dire accounts of people taken away and never seen again. And I also had fresh accounts to dwell upon: since I'd come to Russia, people had shared with me chilling stories about relatives exiled to Siberia.

"What does it mean?" I said, trying to control the trembling in my voice. "What will they do to us?"

"We do not know," Anna admitted.

Sergei cleared his throat. "KGB man told me passports would be taken to office and shown to supervisors," he said. "They are taking them because your visas are for only St. Petersburg, so you are illegal here."

Mainjula and I exchanged glances. Was she thinking, as was I, of Sergei's confident assurances that it would be no problem to travel outside St. Petersburg because everyone does it? And, I thought, does everyone get a visit from the KGB? I shot Sergei a reproachful glance, and he hung his head. Sergei knew what he had gotten us into. There was no need to say anything.

Days passed. We sat in our hotel room contemplating the worst, imagining ourselves on a slow train to a Siberian labor camp. I sat on the lumpy bed and recalled the descriptions of the gulag in *One Day in the Life of Ivan Denisovich* and pictured myself there: snow and bone-chilling cold, grueling work, hunger, the slow weakening . . . and death.

Four days after our passports were seized, we were called to the KGB headquarters for an interview. Our Russian friends were going to take us. Sergei would be acting as our advocate because he spoke the best English. Although young and with no official credentials, our hopes rested on him. He would convince the KGB that we were innocent tourists and had meant no harm, that we had learned our lesson and would never repeat our mistake, and that we would depart immediately for St. Petersburg. Would

305

he share the fact that he himself had urged us to leave the city? We doubted it. "He wants to avoid Siberian winters just as much as we do," I said to Ananda Mainjula.

We dressed carefully for the interview, putting on our civilian clothes, thanking Baba that we had some decent-looking things with us. As we got ready, we distracted ourselves with details of our dress to forget how truly frightened we were. Then we left, closing the door behind us. As we went down the once-grand stairway, I wondered if we would be back.

Outside, we got into a beat-up Lada and were driven to our destination. No one spoke. As the car wheezed its way through the streets, I looked out the window. Quite possibly, these were our last moments of freedom.

When we arrived, I got out of the car and cast one last longing look at the perfect soft blue of the summer sky, gazing at the few puffy white clouds as if to sear them upon my memory. There was just the hint of a breeze. I stood there for a moment, allowing it to blow through my hair; then, turning from this scene of perfection, I went inside.

The contrast couldn't have been starker. We were made to wait in the hallway, which was narrow, dingy, and ill lit, with ancient posters of red hammer and sickles, and notices with brown edges peeling on somber walls bereft of any colors save tans and dark browns. We had time to contemplate our surroundings. Bad as they were, I was convinced that far worse was yet to come. The KGB officers kept us waiting for what seemed an interminable length of time.

They finally called us into the office. "We could arrest you, you know, *should* arrest you," one officer said. We nodded. I thought about the officials in Australia making the same threats. That had turned out well. Maybe this would, too.

After berating us for several endless minutes, they gave us our passports and let us go, but not before warning of the dire consequences if there were to be a next time. There wouldn't be, Sergei assured them.

We left for St. Petersburg that very night. If I had been allowed alcohol, I'd have downed a few shots of vodka right then and there. As it was, we spent hours in meditation, contemplating just how close we'd come to disappearing off the face of the earth. It wasn't lost on us that if this had happened just a few years earlier, we might very well have found ourselves on a slow train to Siberia. Perestroika had likely saved us, and Baba, too. The fact that Baba was deceased made no difference to us; we believed his grace was always there.

Chapter 27

Nearly the Last Straw

I didn't get much time to reflect on my narrow escape from Russia because I had to go to a summer retreat in Poland. The dadas had recently bought some land near the town of Jelenia Gora in the southwestern part of the country. They were anxious to show it off and had been advertising what they were calling a "Neo-Humanist Ecology Festival" in Ananda Marga publications all over Europe.

I wasn't looking forward to it. I had already visited the property in the fall of the previous year when a smaller gathering had been held for local Margiis. Based on that experience, I harbored secret doubts about the wisdom of holding a large retreat there. While the countryside was picturesque with mountains visible in the distance, the building on the property was decidedly not. It was a damp and drafty old farmhouse that would need a great deal of work to be made livable. The sole bathroom, its tiles broken and dark with mold and dirt, was as tiny as a closet and had no hot water.

Bathing at the fall retreat had been a struggle for me. Getting into the bathroom to begin with hadn't been an easy task with the twenty or so people using it. Once in, the cold water and lack of maneuvering room did nothing to improve the experience. I wondered why it bothered me; after all, I had seen and dealt with much worse in my travels across India and the Middle East. In earlier years, managing to bathe in a filthy latrine during a two- or three-day train journey—all the while keeping my clothes from touching the floor while taking them off and then putting them back on—had been a real matter of pride and even a kind of rush.

Now, though, it was all getting kind of old. For one thing, along with the hemorrhoids, I had also begun to suffer from chronic constipation. Many of our centers had only one bathroom; when the urge to go hit, it was often occupied. Once I got in there, often the moment had passed, or the thought of others waiting their turn was enough to cause me to tense up. The constant traveling and lugging of heavy bags was also starting to wear. I was waking up to the fact that I was surrounded almost entirely by younger people, many of them little more than half my age. This is really for the young, I often found myself thinking. They can handle this lifestyle. I was slowly coming to the realization that I no longer could.

At the fall gathering, I had noticed another dwelling, smaller and even more ramshackle, across the road and down a ways from the main house. The plan was for didis and sisters to stay there during the upcoming retreat, and I'd been told the dadas had been scrambling to get it in some kind of suitable shape in time.

When I arrived for the retreat, I saw little evidence they had succeeded. We didis crowded into a single hot and dusty room, laid our sleeping bags out in rows, and slept sardine style. The sole bathroom for all the women was located in an open area of the house with no door. That meant when you went to the bathroom or attempted to bathe, anyone could walk in on you. My constipation worsened.

One morning, I awoke feeling low and couldn't bring myself to get up. I lay on my sleeping bag as all the other didis finished their practices and put on their uniforms preparing to go out. No one said anything to me. Soon I was all alone.

It grew hotter in the room as the day wore on. I told myself that I should get up, but I couldn't make myself do it. The familiar feeling of being at the bottom of a pit overwhelmed me. Just the thought of the effort it would take to climb its walls to get up was exhausting. So there I lay.

The didis came back before lunch, left again, and returned early in the evening to do their asanas before evening dharmacakra. They stepped over me as if I were a log or something inert. No one asked what was wrong, if I was sick or upset.

When they left for evening meditation without saying a word, I decided to get out of there. All day I'd been mulling over a plan of escape; when the entire day had passed and not one of my so-called sisters had shown even the slightest bit of care or compassion, I made my mind up to do it.

Ananda Margiis talk so much about serving humanity, I thought. We rush around from place to place, from one project to another, but we don't even know how to take care of each other. We don't even think that caring for each other is important. I thought about those sick women on the upper floors of the didis' office in Tiljala and the jokes about how you could die up there and no one would notice. Didis and dadas generally didn't even take care of themselves with the constant travel, poor diet, and lack of sleep.

When you're young, of course, you think you'll be healthy and live forever. "Health benefits for workers? What a waste of money! Baba will take care of me." That had been my attitude for years. So far, I'd never been seriously ill, despite the scare I'd had with the lump in my breast. But what would happen when I got older? I couldn't count on my luck to continue indefinitely, could I?

Maybe the didis hadn't shown me any concern because of the conduct rules—or maybe because of the lack of one. After all, there was no conduct rule instructing workers to care for one another. And the conduct rule about accepting sufferings as rewards made you believe that the best workers were those who suffered for the mission without complaint. Maybe they think I'm not following that conduct rule, so they don't want to have anything to do with me, I thought. But whatever the cause, I'd had it. I was ready to leave the retreat—and maybe even Ananda Marga itself.

Before dawn the next morning, I got up, packed my few things, stepped over the still forms of slumbering didis, went down the stairs as quietly as possible, and left the building. Looking up at the sky, I could see just the faintest glimmer of the approaching dawn. It was pleasantly cool, but I knew the freshness in the air would be short-lived. I began walking quickly down the dirt path, filling in my sketchy plans as I walked the mile or two out to the road, where I would catch a bus to the station in Centrum. I hoped I wouldn't have to wait too long for one. Next would be a bus to Jelenia Gora and then a train to Frankfurt. But this time I wouldn't be going on to Mainz, where the didis' office was. Obviously, I couldn't stay there. So where would I stay, and with whom? That's when Vinita, a German sister who used to be a didi, came to mind. I had her address in Frankfurt. Surely, she would be sympathetic to my plight and would let me stay at her place.

Reaching the road, I put my bag down and sat on it. It was a Sunday and buses were likely to be few and far between. I felt exposed, concerned that some dada or didi coming or going would see me. One hour passed, then another. The sun was climbing higher into the sky and it was getting hot. The few vehicles that passed by raised clouds of dust, which settled on my clothes. After what seemed an interminable wait, a bus came. Thanking God that no one had seen me, I got on.

It was a fasting day, and I already had a raging thirst. If I were to drink, that would be it—I'd be breaking my fast. I decided not to fast. It would be too much, what with traveling and the heat, I told myself.

Once at the bus station, I counted my meager collection of złotys and bought a bottle of water and the few snacks that were available on a Sunday. I consumed the watery ice cream somberly. It didn't taste very good and gave me no comfort. The voice of the spiritual superego spoke up: *That's what happens when you choose the life of the senses,* it admonished me.

That's what all those didis and dadas would say if they saw me now, I thought. There they'd be, so virtuously fasting, gazing at me with pity. *She's chosen the path to hell, the path of the senses,* they'd say, and then they'd sigh. But the freedom to decide things for myself felt good, even if the ice cream wasn't.

I got to Frankfurt just as it was getting dark. I looked for Vinita's apartment building, wearily lugging my bag, which seemed to weigh more than it had earlier. I was dusty and hungry, and it occurred to me for the first time that Vinita might not be there. What would I do then?

Thankfully, she was. She welcomed me in and after hearing my tale, offered her spare room for as long as I needed it. I headed for the shower, then went to bed and slept more soundly than I had for days.

The next morning, Vinita and I had a long talk.

"You should think about it carefully," she said. "In some ways, I really miss the life I had as a didi."

"I'm sure you do," I said, "but would you consider going back to it?"

Few who left ever returned. It wasn't an easy thing to do. You couldn't just come back and say you were a didi again; you had to go back to training. For someone in their forties who'd been doing sadhana for years, it would indeed be a trying experience to return to the training center; you'd be surrounded by all those overly enthusiastic nineteen- and twenty-year-olds who'd likely look upon you as someone fallen. Vinita, of course, knew all this. Tall and thin, with a plain, freckled face, she had a sweet smile. She smiled now.

"Well, no, now that I've left, I won't return," she said, "but you should still think about it before you do it."

"I've thought about it a lot. This retreat was just the last straw."

There were, however, practical considerations with the idea of leaving. The first one was money. I would need plenty, not only for a plane ticket, but to live on when I first got back to the States. As was usually the case, I had none. But raising funds shouldn't really be too difficult, I thought. I had baked cakes and made any number of sweets, had spray-painted Christmas decorations on windows, grown cilantro, sold pencils and erasers—all for the mission. Surely I could come up with some way to raise money for my own needs! But where I would stay once I got there: that was the real problem. That cold night spent at Thirtieth Street Station in Philadelphia trying to avoid the guards was still a painful memory. None of my relatives will want to have anything to do with me, I thought.

Truth be told, even before the retreat, I had thought of leaving—more than once. The dilemma of where to go once I had returned to the States had always stopped my ruminations cold. Every time I pictured myself back there, I saw myself as a bag lady with unkempt hair, wandering the streets of Philadelphia with my few possessions in plastic bags, fighting with other homeless people for a steam vent to keep warm during bitter winter nights.

I stayed with Vinita for about a week. Somehow the didis found out where I was. Ananda Preyasi called me. "Madhuchanda," she said, "just come here and rest for as long as you need to." I let her persuade me to go back to Mainz.

Months passed. Through the rest of the summer and into the fall, I stayed in the didis' room, and except for RDS meetings, I had the place mostly to myself. Any didis who came and went left me alone for the most part, giving me as much space as possible, or maybe just avoiding me. It made me wonder again if they really cared. Ananda Preyasi sent me to Russia for a month or so, hoping that a trip there would re-inspire me, but it did not.

Almost daily, I went for long walks downtown or in the park near the Mainz office. I turned the problem of where to stay once back in the States over and over in my mind, hoping to uncover a solution. None was forthcoming. I felt stuck. I didn't want to continue living the way I was. The role I was in no longer fit. Maybe I had grown out of it, or maybe I had shrunk spiritually and could no longer fill my robes. Whatever the reason, I had to face the fact that the role of acarya was no longer for me.

Still, how could I leave? I had nowhere to stay, and no hours of agonized casting about would land an address or friend to stay with. I couldn't ask either of my brothers. Barry was out of the question, and David had a small apartment and would most likely have a girlfriend coming and going. My rich aunt? No way. My uncle? He was living somewhere in California. Friends? I'd been out of the country for close to twenty years and had lost touch with all of them. The only people I still knew were Margiis, and I didn't want to stay with any of them. They would be judgmental, and I was going through enough of that on my own. (And there was no guarantee that Margiis would help me, either. At one point, I contacted Ainjali, an American didi who had left the organization, returned to the States, and was living in Cleveland. I called her and asked if I could stay with her for a week or two. She turned me down.)

So, on and on I would walk with no solution to my dilemma forthcoming. It got so bad that whenever I crossed the overpass above the autobahn, I would stop and gaze at the traffic whizzing by below and think of jumping.

Meanwhile, Christmas was fast approaching and with it a chance to make some money for my ticket. A Margii who sold jewelry every year at an outdoor bazaar a few hours from Mainz told me about an opportunity there. I could sell Christmas window stencils, he said. It didn't sound very promising, but any money at all would help, so I accepted.

I took a bus to the town and checked into the local youth hostel. It was cheap, and as it was the off-season, I had a room all to myself and could do my meditation and postures without having to explain anything to anybody.

Early every morning I would leave the hostel for the bazaar located in the town square. Lining both sides of the square were brightly decorated little wooden stalls, which the owners unlocked early every morning. Christmas music and one carol in particular blared constantly over the loud speaker. *O Tannenbaum, o Tannenbaum, wie treu sind deine Blätter* . . . It was cold. Most merchants had portable heaters in their stalls. I stayed warm by hopping up and down and blowing on my hands. Whenever people stopped at my stall, I showed them stencils of trees, bells, and Santa Clauses. I managed to get by. I had learned enough key words to deliver a bare-bones description of the stencils and knew enough numbers to handle the money.

"Ja, ja, das sind Fensterbilder," (Yes, those are window stencils) I would say, nodding my head sagely. It was only when customers would rattle off a reply and I would just smile vacantly or clear my throat that they realized I didn't really speak German. Still, despite my linguistic limitations, I managed to sell a fair number of stencils. Business wasn't exactly booming as it was at some stalls, but I had at least something to show for my efforts and frozen hands. I returned to Mainz with just enough money for a one-way ticket to New York.

Now that I had the money, a new worry began to occupy my mind: how would I break the news to the didis and say goodbye to the organization—my family for so many years? That concern, along with the as yet unresolved dilemma of where to stay, nagged at me constantly. One day, tired of thinking of it all, I impulsively threw my belongings into my suitcase and left for the Frankfurt airport, planning to get on the first flight to the States I could find. Before I could buy a ticket, though, a solicitous threesome of didis tracked me down and brought me back to Mainz. Maybe it was their show of concern that convinced me to go back with them, but one thing was clear: I was still in two minds over the issue. If I had really decided to leave, I wouldn't have listened to them.

Ananda Preyasi promptly sat me down to deliver a sermon on the dire consequences of leaving whole-timer life.

"Madhuchanda," she said, "you'll never be happy if you leave. Your mind is on such a high level, you will never adjust to that kind of materialistic life." She went on to relate some horror stories of didis who had left the organization and had fallen on hard times. Those stories did give me pause. It occurred to me later, however, that she was talking about Indian didis, who didn't have many options. An Indian didi contemplating such a step would have only one alternative: marriage. If she was too old for that, there would be no place for her in traditional Indian society. As an American with a college degree, I had other options and was thankful that I did.

Ananda Preyasi was aware of some of the issues I had with the organization and suggested I go to India and talk to the General Secretary, Dada Satyajitananda, about my concerns. "Just go and talk to GS Dada," she kept saying. "Tell him everything. I'm sure he'll listen and try to help."

I knew that Satyajitananda wasn't about to change the culture of the organization, and he certainly wasn't going to take any advice from me. So what good would talking to him do? I doubted he'd even take the time to see me. And how would talking to Satyajitananda do anything about what was at the heart of my dilemma: how to continue working in a role I no longer felt inspired to fill. It was a spiritual issue between Baba and me and not something that meeting with GS Dada would likely help resolve.

Despite the odds of anything happening to change my mind, I decided to give it a try. Maybe just being in India will help, I thought. I had nothing to lose—except my hard-earned plane fare.

I arrived in Tiljala in mid-February. The next day I went to Satyajitananda's office. Much to my surprise, he welcomed me in; advance notice of my situation had clearly gotten to him. Since I was one of the most senior Western workers, the Central dadas and didis must have thought it worth their while to try to keep me from "falling," to salvage me from the junkyard of rampant materialism found in mainstream life. I could picture them sitting around, discussing the issue. *Such a senior worker,* they would have said, shaking their turbaned and veiled heads gravely. *We have to try anything we can to save her.*

I had a number of visits with Satyajitananda. Every time I went, I would stand outside his office with other workers waiting to see him. There were neither chairs nor room for us; we waited in a narrow corridor near a stairwell, where others heading elsewhere would have to squeeze by. Sometimes the orange of waiting workers would fill the corridor and overflow down the stairs. GS Dada would come to the door to tell the next worker waiting in line to come in, see me, smile and say, "Ah, Madhuchanda. I'll meet with you shortly, *accha?*" cocking his turbaned head and fingering his curly salt-and-pepper beard. Once he had seen me, I usually got in next or after one or two others.

Our conversations touched on a wide range of issues. Speaking at length about Ananda Sudha and how abusively she had treated me and other workers, I provided details and asked how someone that harmful to her workers and to the mission as a whole was allowed to continue in such an important position. Dada listened and nodded his head. He seemed to commiserate with me but promised nothing except a vague "I'll look into it."

We discussed other issues, including the position of women in the organization. Satyajitananda always listened sympathetically to what I had to say, but he never made any promises about changing anything. "Come again at the same time," he would say after each visit. "I'm always happy to talk to you." Then he would smile. I would thank him, do namaskar and leave, the next person in line passing me on his or her way in.

But I never could bring myself to talk about the main issue. I saw him only as an organizational leader, not someone who inspired me to open up about my spiritual dilemma. He never asked and I never told.

Nothing ever did change for Ananda Sudha. After all, the story went, Satyajitananda had known her since he'd been a boy in an Ananda Marga children's home. How could anyone expect him to do anything? I don't know if that was true, but this hard fact was: Ananda Sudha always brought plenty of cash with her to every RDS, money bled from Australian Margiis and projects. As long as she brought money, nothing would happen to her, the cynics said. And they were right: nothing ever did.

In March I went to Ananda Nagar, intending to do some intense sadhana in the Kaoshikii hills nearby where, stories went, great sadhus had achieved realization over the ages. According to Baba, these were among the most ancient mountains in the world; time and erosion had greatly reduced their once lofty peaks to the broken up, jagged, and bare hills they had become. I was hoping that the subtle vibrations to be found there would help me rededicate myself to whole-timer life.

I climbed high one day and meditated, trying to absorb the vibrations of those who had been before. In that austere landscape and after days spent with Indian devotees and workers, my tumult seemed like the shallow *sturm und drang* of the little ego, as the German phrase went. After finishing my sadhana, I sat there for hours, gazing over the desert valley, watching the subtle changes of color as the day wore on towards evening, writing poetry and trying to rekindle my inspiration. I came down only as sunset colored the sky in soft orange and purple.

Late in April, I flew out of Delhi and returned to Germany. Not long after returning, I knew I had to go. The trip to India had only postponed the inevitable. Nothing GS Dada had said had changed my mind. Maybe if he had promised to do something about the issues I had raised, it would have made a difference. I doubt it, though. It was ultimately a matter of inspiration, and I had lost it. If two months of meditation at the very heart of the organization could not rekindle it, I was sure nothing else would.

The long and short of it was I no longer wanted to represent Ananda Marga. To continue doing so would be a lie. I no longer wanted to be a nun. I wanted a relationship, and although I knew it might be too late, I wanted a family. The years of looking down upon motherhood were long over. Now I wanted to have a child more than anything else in the world—and time was running out.

Meanwhile, I had somehow gotten hold of Maetreyii's most recent phone number in Philadelphia. She was different from other Margiis. Being older, she was more like a mother figure to me and I was sure she wouldn't be judgmental. Maetreyii had helped me out of many a tight situation in the past, including that time she'd called my parents for me; maybe she would help again. At first I shied away from making the phone call. I went back and forth about it, afraid she might no longer be at that number, or even worse, would not be able or want to take me in. If that happened, I told myself, it would be the end. I would be forced to stay and live the lie I'd been living since my inspiration had died; there would be no other choice.

One afternoon after another I would walk to the pay phone not far from the Mainz office, pick up the receiver, dial, and hang up before the call would go through. Sometimes I walked deliberately there; other days I wandered through the park and down into town, arriving at the phone booth after a circuitous route. I debated about the best time to call. It wouldn't do to ring Maetreyii too early in the morning, her time. On the other hand, I didn't want to call too late and risk missing her entirely. Calling Maetreyii in the evening—seven o'clock her time, for example—was out of the question because I'd have to place the call around midnight.

One afternoon, I found myself at the pay phone yet again. I picked up the receiver, took a deep breath, and dialed the number. When the phone started ringing, it took a supreme effort of will not to hang up. My heart skipped a beat when Maetreyii answered. She sounded happy to hear my voice as I told her I would be coming to the States for a while and needed a place to stay. I didn't go into any details, not yet being able to use the phrase "leave Ananda Marga" with myself, let alone others.

"Of course you can stay here, Didi," Maetreyii said. "Just let us know when you get into Philadelphia, and we'll come and pick you up." I exhaled as relief and gratitude rushed through me. I thanked her, and we said our goodbyes. Hanging up the receiver, I noticed it had become sweaty in my hand.

Now all that remained was arranging my ticket and taking my leave in the least painful way possible. Although I knew I was leaving never to return, I wasn't quite ready to acknowledge it openly. I simply asked for and received permission to go to the States for some time to sort some things out. Since I was, in the eyes of the organization, just leaving temporarily, one didi gave me some money.

"You have to have some money in your pocket while you're there," she said, leaving unspoken her expectation that I would soon be back. Another didi supplied me with documents detailing our food distributions to orphanages in Russia; I'd partly convinced myself I would try to do some fund-raising.

Except for Didi Arpana, no one tried to convince me not to go. It appeared that everyone else was going along with the story that I was leaving temporarily. Perhaps they knew I wasn't just leaving for the short term and chose to say nothing because they felt I was already a lost soul. Ananda Preyasi, of course, had tried earlier when she warned what would happen if I were to leave, but she said nothing now. Her earlier warnings about never being happy had affected me, but fear wasn't going to stop me.

Arpana, though, tried her best. "Madhuchanda," she said, her voice breaking, "I'm afraid you won't come back." Then she cried. I had known Arpana since the Denver days when we had both been young Margiis. She was an exceptionally good-natured and soft-hearted soul, but although she'd been a didi for many years, the organization had never seen fit to make her an avadhutika. For some reason, they didn't think she was suited for it. Maybe it was because she suffered from a lack of confidence.

Still, Arpana was a selfless individual who did all the tasks others thought they were too good for. She worked harder than most, driving our van, a cantankerous vehicle without power steering; and shuttling didis, most of whom had no driver's licenses, to and from RDS meetings and other events. She also did everything connected with our market stalls: packing the merchandise, driving to the markets and staffing them, returning and unloading the remaining goods, sometimes all by herself. Her appeals affected me more than those from others would have.

"Don't worry. I'll be all right," I said, blinking back tears as we hugged one last time.

Chapter 28

Re-entry

I flew from Frankfurt to New York in September. Compared to most of my past journeys, this time I was traveling light: after spending almost half of my forty-three years in Ananda Marga, all my personal possessions fit into just one modestly sized bag. True, I'd left a few boxes behind in the storage space on the third floor of the Mainz office (as if to say, *See? I'll be back.):* a uniform, my guitar, several books, some photos, and a few soft-covered Indian notebooks filled with accounts of my visits with Baba in jail and other experiences. With me I had my other uniform, a couple of Ananda Marga magazines containing some of my poems and articles, and the documents about our relief work in Russia. I also had two hundred fifty dollars, not a small amount of money to me at the time.

In New York, the first thing that struck me was how big everything looked. Sitting in a taxi on my way to get a bus to Philadelphia, I looked out at cars that looked as big as boats compared to the ones I'd grown accustomed to in Germany, and they were making their way down streets as wide as rivers. Even though it hadn't been all that long since I had last been in the States, things felt foreign and strange. It would be many months before I stopped feeling myself a foreigner in my own country. (The sense of everything being oversized would remain with me for quite some time. The first trip I took to a supermarket, I remember feeling shocked not only by its size, but by that of the shopping carts, nearly twice the size of their counterparts in Germany.)

When my bus pulled into Philadelphia, Maetreyii and her husband Herb were waiting for me. It was good to see them. Maetreyii and I hugged, and she asked me if I was hungry. I said that I was, and she suggested Chinatown, just a few blocks away from the bus station. We drove under the ornately carved Chinese gate, found a parking space, and went into one of the restaurants lining both sides of the street. Determined not only to remain a vegetarian but to persist in avoiding onions, garlic, and mushrooms, I ordered a rather bland tofu and vegetable stir-fry. But this, my first meal as an ex-acarya, felt liberating because whole-timers weren't supposed to eat in restaurants. *Even sattvic food taken in a restaurant will be regarded as tamasic,* went the conduct rule. Like most workers, I had broken this rule occasionally when necessary but hadn't felt good about it. Now I could eat in restaurants without feeling guilty.

Maetreyii and Herb had an extra bedroom, but I was going to stay in their living room because Marci, one of their daughters, would be coming from Denver in a few days. I was going to sleep on the floor, just like always. I would have done so even if I'd had a bedroom as I wasn't yet ready to sleep on a bed. I wasn't about to throw all my conduct rules out the window, I told myself. So every evening, I would roll out my sleeping bag; in the morning, I would roll it up and put it away. My sleeping arrangements, at least, would differ little from the life I had left behind. I also continued with my practices, although my meditations were shorter and my asanas sessions were reduced to once a day. Everything else about my life, though, would bear little resemblance to the one I had led for so many years.

The morning after my arrival, I left the apartment, walked up the street, and encountered Roosevelt Boulevard. It was a twelve-lane highway, with six lanes going in each direction. I remember standing there dumbstruck at its size, gaping as cars whizzed by at top speeds. Finally I roused myself and ventured across. The light turned red before I got to the other side, so I had to break into a run. Once across, I walked over to the little strip mall I had noticed and found a small bookstore. I spent a few hours browsing, eventually buying a paperback about self-acceptance. It was my first purchase as a private citizen, not connected with my role as an acarya, in more than eighteen years, and I felt kind of guilty about it. Would I become the kind of materialistic person I had scorned for so long? What would my life bring, now that I was just an ordinary person and not someone exalted with a great mission to fulfill? The whole day stretched in front of me empty and unscheduled with no train or bus to catch, no RDS to attend, and no one to tell me what to do or where to go. There was nothing to do but what I decided. It felt unfamiliar, exciting—and more than a little scary.

Some days later, I went for my first walk in the large park across the street from Maetreyii's apartment building. There, I took to taking long walks, shuffling in red and yellow leaves during the still-warm days of early October. There was a creek in the park, and I would sit by it for hours, watching sunlight move across the water and sometimes writing poetry as, one by one, leaves clinging to branches that hung over the creek would fall, twirling gracefully until they were caught in the water's flow and carried downstream.

I knew that difficult days lay ahead. Soon I would have to contact my brothers, my aunt and uncle—and face anger and possible rejection. I'd have to get my old name back; my passport identified me as Hanna Hartt, a name I couldn't possibly try to use now. I would have to find a job somehow. Even before doing that, I would have to figure out how to put a résumé together and account for all the years spent away. I knew it would take me a long time to sort out the feelings I had about Ananda Marga: guilt about leaving and breaking my vows, confusion about the

Guru and my relationship to him, and anger at how I'd been treated and at the loss of all those years, the best ones of my life. It would also take time before I would be able to confront the truth about the lies I had told my parents and what those lies had done to them.

But that was all in the future. For now, it felt good just to sit by the creek and listen to the chuckling of the water as it passed me by.

Chapter 29

Twelve Years On: The Letters

One day not long after I had returned to the States, my brother Barry handed me some papers in a plastic bag.

"Mom and Dad saved all of your letters," he said.

"Thanks," was all I managed to say. I took the bag home and put it in the bottom drawer of my desk.

Every time I sat down at the desk and opened that drawer, I felt the letters waiting for me and knew that one day I would have to read them. I was afraid of what I would find there: the old me, the one who had told her parents so many lies. I didn't want to read the details and feel the pain and guilt. If it weren't for my writing this book, I might have put it off forever.

It had been almost twelve years since I had returned. I had married, and my husband David and I had moved twice; as we did, the letters, still in the same plastic bag, were transferred to another desk, then another, still unread. I knew the day was approaching when I would have to read them. During this time, I tried to remove myself emotionally and prepare for that day by thinking of the letters as documents—archeological artifacts, almost.

One afternoon, I took a deep breath and opened the bottom drawer of my desk. I pulled out the bag, carried it downstairs to our office, and plopped it down on the desk in front of my husband. He was working on the desktop computer.

"What's this?" he asked.

"The letters," I said. David knew about the letters.

I drew up a chair and opened the bag. There they were, all in their original envelopes. I had expected all the letters I had sent my parents to be there, but a quick look at the stamps revealed that they were all from Australia, with a few from American Samoa mixed in.

"There's nothing here from Israel or Fiji," I said, puzzled.

My plan had been to open them all and read them in order. Instead, I picked up one at random. Dated January 28, 1983, it was written on the kind of thin rice paper I had used to save money.

Dear Mom and Dad,

I just received your letter about a week ago. I have to say I'm very upset by the type of letters you've been sending me and don't even like to answer. What do you think I did with the money? Why are you asking for a copy of the deed and photos? I think you don't believe I bought land with the money.

The land. It was all about that, how I had gotten my parents to give me money to buy land for Ananda Marga.

. . . I thought you would understand from my answer about having my personal life that I don't have the same connection with Ananda Marga as in the past. I remember in Philadelphia when I saw you, you expressed your feeling that you had no objection to my being a member—only that it should <u>not</u> be my whole life. So I am taking your advice—I am still a member, but have my <u>own personal life</u>. When I

spoke to you asking for the money for the land, I told you that I was no longer in the same capacity in the organization (wearing uniform and whole life) but was still a member. Why all this fuss?

There couldn't possibly be a worse letter to start out with. I handed it to David. "This is terrible," I said.

I picked up and read another letter, then another, devastated by the attitude it revealed and the details of my duplicity. Before rereading the letters, I had remembered getting my parents to give me money by telling them I was buying land for myself, but I hadn't remembered the specifics. Now, I was coming face to face with the elaborate web of supporting lies I'd spun to support the big one.

I read one letter after another until I'd absorbed them all, swallowing one foul-tasting dose of medicine after another, struck by the way I had taken half truths—about the land, my teaching job, my marriage—and twisted them.

The purchase of the land, of course, was not a total lie. Land was being bought. *The total price of the land is $16,000,* I had written. *We are getting an amazing deal due to the reasons which I wrote earlier. My share is $8,000.* But the "we" was not me and a friend named Karen *(she is originally from Britain and has now settled in Australia. She is also a teacher)*—it was Ananda Marga.

Once they sent me the money, I had the audacity to ask for more. *I spend weekends on my farm. Presently, I am trying to construct a house, but it is difficult due to lack of money. I've begun, but I need about $6,000 to get it fairly together. Please let me know if you can help me in any way with this.*

In an effort to make it seem like I was no longer working for Ananda Marga, I wrote that I would be applying to teach in Australia. I asked my parents to inquire about getting my college transcript. One letter detailed how I'd heard from Penn, how they wouldn't issue the transcript because I hadn't paid off my college loans. I hinted to my parents that they should pay off the loan so I could get the transcript. *I received this letter from the university concerning a debt I owe. I thought that it had been paid off. Please inquire and let me know how much it is for. I really need the transcript soon to get my post by January.*

They paid the debt and I got my transcript. I eventually did get a teaching job, but it was in American Samoa, not in Australia like I'd told them.

In 1984, I wrote my parents that I had been married. That was true. But the marriage was a bogus one in order to stay in Australia. *I've been married—on July 16, and am very happy. My husband's name is Andrew. He is a bit younger than me—by six years. He teaches and also is a licensed pilot! So that is some good news. I'll try to send some photos. (We didn't take any at the wedding—it was very simple.)*

The biggest detail and most calculating of all that I had forgotten was this: From 1981 to 1983, when I had written most of the letters, I hadn't been in Australia at all, but in Fiji and American Samoa. I must have enclosed each letter (except for one sent directly from American Samoa in which I wrote that I had gone there for my term break and was getting some "almost free" dental work done, supported as it was by U.S. grants—a total fabrication, of course) with the envelope containing the letter addressed to my parents in another envelope and sent it off to the didis' office in Melbourne. I must have added a week or two to the actual date to give time for the letter to arrive in Australia, where it would have been opened, a stamp put on the second envelope and then mailed once again. Several letters referred to the mail and how slow it was: *Mail takes a long time to reach here from the U.S. I don't know why. . . . Mail from the U.S. comes late sometimes. . . . I've arrived back in Melbourne and finally received your last letter, which took a very long time to reach me due to the postal strike. . . .* I had no clear memory of doing this, but the evidence was sitting there right in front of me.

And I realized something else. I had actually slipped up and let the truth out in one of the letters by mentioning Fiji.

Dear Mom and Dad, Much love. I hope this finds both of you well. I just returned here a few days ago. Some of your letters were forwarded to me in Fiji, so I received them late. (Fiji? Why has she been in Fiji? they must have asked each other. Could it be that she's lying to us?)

The enormity of it all passed over me like a wave, and I felt nauseated. "Just imagine how my parents felt when they realized their suspicions were correct and that it was all a lie," I said to David.

He gave me a hug. "Honey, all this happened over twenty years ago. You're not the same person you were then. You have to forgive yourself."

But I was staring at the wall, lost in thought. I remembered the time I had visited Barry and Diane all those years ago. No wonder they hadn't wanted me to stay with them. After doing that to Mom and Dad . . .

"This is horrible. I'm a terrible person. How could I have done this?"

I left the letters in a chaotic pile on one side of the desk for a week or so. When the initial shock of reading them had abated somewhat, I took the pile upstairs to read again. This time, I read them in order and ended up focusing on the last two letters I had written, one to my mother and the other to Barry.

The letter to my mother had been written in August of 1986 after my father had passed away and a few days after I had called her from Lismore.

> *Dear Mom,*
> *Much love. I hope this finds you feeling better. It was good to talk with you on the phone the other day and hear your voice.*
> *I want you to know that you are often in my thoughts. I'm not a very demonstrative person and am pretty quiet in*

nature. So even though I'm not very good at writing letters and I don't write often, I love you. Please understand that.

I often feel fortunate I had such good parents as you and Dad. Here in Australia, many people I know had terrible childhoods—with alcoholic fathers, beatings, divorce, etc. When I hear their stories, I often think back on my happy and secure childhood with you and my brothers.

Even though we are separated physically, on a deeper level, we are together. Communication of the heart doesn't require physical closeness. Even when we leave this world, our deeper self lives on and we live on in each other's hearts. I hope you feel the same way about this and know what I mean.

With deepest love and affection,

Marsha

Ever since my mother's death, I had comforted myself with the thought that I had at least written this letter and that she must have read it. But now I doubted that she had. My mother died on August 16 of that year, so there was a good chance that the letter hadn't gotten there in time.

Over the years, I'd forgotten that I had written the letter only to her and had come to believe that I had written and sent it to both my parents, months before either had passed away. It was a shock to realize that even for my mother, it must have arrived too late. Someone had opened the letter, but I'll never know if she ever read it.

The last letter I wrote home was dated September 20 of the same year and was to Barry.

Dear Barry,

I received your telegram about Mom about a week ago after arriving back from Sydney. I was very sad to read about Mom's passing. She must have been very sick and in a lot of pain at the end, so it was a release for her. Did she receive my letter in time? I do hope so.

I am still up in the air about my citizenship, which is one reason it would have been difficult to come for a visit. I hope you receive this letter as I do not know your home address. What will be happening with the house now? Please let me know if there has been any inheritance left to me by Mom and Dad and any particulars.

Much love to Diane and Sascha and David. What is David doing now? Is he still living in Philadelphia? Australia is a beautiful and unique place—very different from the U.S.—not so built up as over there. I like it here very much.

What are you doing? Are you still teaching? I hope you are all happy in your life.

With much love,
Marsha

Barry never wrote back—and who can blame him?

Chapter 30

Hot Tub in the Snow

"How's the book going?" my sister-in-law Kathy asked. We were taking a relaxing soak in the hot tub after a day of skiing at Lake Tahoe. My in-laws had rented two houses over the Christmas holidays, and we were in the midst of a big family reunion. Besides my husband David's three brothers and their families, there were various cousins of his I was meeting for the first time.

I sat up on the edge of the hot tub to cool down for a moment and looked up at the stars. "Okay," I said. "I'm almost finished the second draft."

"That's great! Send me some chapters when you get home, okay?"

"Sure," I said. Kathy had been supportive of my project all along. A psychology professor at a college in Maine, she'd even mentioned the possibility of using some of the material in her women's studies classes.

I settled back into the water. "You know, it's interesting about memory," I said. "I clearly remember my father talking about his life as a child in Ukraine. My brother Barry remembers, too, but his memories are different from mine."

"How so?" Kathy asked.

"Well, I remember my father talking about the pogroms. He said that Cossacks would thunder into his village on horseback looking for Jews, and they all would hide in his grandfather's cellar. That's because his grandfather had been conscripted into the tsar's army at a young age and had served for a long time. The villagers knew the Cossacks wouldn't target him, even though he was Jewish."

"Wow."

"But when I asked Barry if he remembered this, he said that Dad wasn't talking about pogroms but about the tsar's men coming into the village to grab new recruits for the Russian Army."

Kathy was silent for a moment.

"Well," she said finally, "whichever it was, can you imagine how traumatic that must have been for the small boy your father was at the time?"

It had never occurred to me. My father, whether he had been talking about pogroms or conscription raids, had related the stories over Sunday dinners and a few beers in a folksy, almost joking manner far different from the silent and angry way he had about him during the week.

"And even the fact that your father's grandfather had been forced into the army at a young age must have had a terrible impact on the family as a whole. Those kinds of trauma can impact generations, you know," Kathy said.

She was right about the young age. My great-grandfather had been taken from his home by force when he was barely a teenager. She was probably right about the trauma, too. And it had never occurred to me.

The full impact of it hit me. My great-grandfather's pain had been passed down to his son and, in turn, to my father. Then it had been compounded by my father's terror as he had hid, trembling in his family's cellar, hearing the thunder of horses' hooves approaching and the muffled cries and whispered prayers of the villagers hiding alongside him. Later on, dreaming of a better life, he had left for America, embarking on the perilous journey with his mother and sister, crowded in with scores of other immigrants in steerage with no facilities, no way to wash, no privacy, and skirting near disaster when fire broke out after someone had tried to light a stove.

But that young boy's dreams of America hadn't really been fulfilled. My father struggled for most of his life just to make a living. His children, growing up in the fifties and sixties, hadn't had any idea what he had been through, save for those Sunday stories when he'd had a few beers.

Secrets. My father had kept his true feelings about years of pain and struggle to himself, perhaps thinking them unworthy of a grown man. He had kept the existence of his other son and grandchildren from us, too. And the secrecy and silence had settled into the house and into our very bones. Early on, we learned to keep our feelings to ourselves, just like he had.

As I gazed at the snow glistening on the trees, the stars like bright chunks of ice in the nighttime sky, I felt swept through and filled up with the history of generations. Despite the warm waters of the tub surrounding me, I shivered.

Words from a Bob Dylan song ran through my mind unbidden:

I pity the poor immigrant who wishes he would've stayed home . . .
But in the end is always left so alone
Whose visions in the final end must shatter like the glass
I pity the poor immigrant when his gladness comes to pass

"Time to get out and get ready for dinner," Kathy said.

Together we got out and covered up the tub, wrapped our towels around us, and went inside.

Epilogue

It has been more than eighteen years since I left Ananda Marga. Despite working a lot of things out about my experience, there are still times when I feel confused about it, more than I would have expected to after all this time. In many of the dreams I have had about the organization, I find myself a didi again and ask myself, *How did I get back here? I thought I was finished with this once and for all!*

In some dreams, I experience a kind of mixture of lives, didi and post-didi. I find myself in orange, but at the same time, I know I have a husband. *I'm married,* I think in dreams like these. *It's not possible to be married and a didi at the same time.*

I still also have occasional inspirational dreams about Baba. When I wake up on these occasions, I find myself thrust back into a way of thinking I'd thought long left behind. My writing of this book comes to mind, and I feel conflicted, almost guilty, about having written it.

Dream Entry: April 28, 2004

I am attending spiritual classes run by a woman. She is strict and expects the students to stick to the rigid routine, but I resist doing what she wants.

In the evening, we gather for another class. Baba appears and takes a young girl with him into a room. We students look at one another, silently asking if he's going to do something improper. Then we shake our heads. We know he wouldn't do something like that.

The next thing I know, I am driving, coming out from underground, as if from a tunnel. It is dusk and snowing. I'm happy when I see the snow. Then I catch sight of a large, clunky car from the seventies coming straight towards me. I have no time to swerve and am certain I am going to die. The cars collide with a huge bang and I feel myself flying through the air.

I land and find myself clutching at something white: snow. I realize I have landed on a street in Germantown, a section of Philadelphia where I lived shortly after returning from Ananda Marga. And I realize this: I have been saved from death.

All around me, people are playing in the snow. I get up and join them. I laugh and run and jump. I feel ecstatic, as if reborn.

Then I find myself back in class. I go up to the teacher and ask to speak to her. We go to one side of the classroom, and I tell her about the collision. The last thing I say is, "Baba saved me!" The teacher does not reply.

Whatever such dreams mean, I keep coming back to certain questions regarding Ananda Marga and my experience of it. Were my experiences with the Guru real? Was he a true master? Were all those years I spent in the organization a waste?

The depth of feeling involved and how vividly I still recall them convinces me that my experiences with the Guru were genuine. However, I now have serious reservations about attributing perfection and divinity to any person, no matter how highly evolved one may believe him or her to be. Despite Baba's spiritual attainment, it seems to me that he allowed corruption and questionable practices to creep into his organization. To my mind, he permitted himself to be influenced by his own culture, and that was why, in spite of his words about women being the equals of men, he allowed them to be mistreated within his organization.

When I first returned to the United States, I felt that Ananda Marga had stolen the best years of my life. While I did marry a few years later, it was too late to have children, although we tried. After a year or two, we decided to adopt. But even that effort was affected by Ananda Marga and the bogus marriage I'd had in Australia. David and I assumed that the Australian marriage was not legally binding because it hadn't been consummated. Before adopting, though, we decided to get some legal advice just to be sure. To our dismay, we learned that the marriage was valid. We then embarked on a frustratingly long divorce process that involved contacting authorities in Australia and the man involved. It ended up taking two full years for the paperwork to go through. Once that was completed, we had to petition the Philadelphia authorities to have our own marriage recognized as legal. By then, we both felt a bit too old to raise a child. (Not being able to have my own child had been a huge blow to me. Now, though, I've mostly come to terms with it. I tell myself that it is better not to have brought a child into a world that will prove ever more difficult to grow up in, with global warming and all its effects. Not to mention the fact that there are far too many children on this over-populated planet already.)

Things didn't go smoothly in my professional life either. Even the master's degree I went back to school for didn't help me secure the kind of positions I felt I had earned with my varied experiences and educational qualifications. I had to remind myself that for the professional world, those years abroad listed on my résumé, while interesting, hardly counted as an employment history. As a result, I often found myself supervised by people with less education and experience, making significantly less than they, a situation that often left me feeling frustrated and exploited. For the past several years, I have been teaching English as a Second Language, which I enjoy, understanding as I do how difficult it can be to live in another culture. But I find I'm not committed to it as much as I would like to be. It may be because I'm older and getting closer to retirement; more likely, I suspect, it has something to do with not wanting to commit myself totally ever again to any one thing.

Another major struggle since returning has been figuring out what my values truly are. When I joined Ananda Marga, I'd had a set handed to me. For the confused young person I'd been at the time, that was one of the great things about it: I didn't have to grow up any more on my own. So when I left the group, I felt almost like an adolescent leaving home for the first time. Although some things from Ananda Marga (like considering the consumption of onions, garlic, and mushrooms as close to a sin, for example) have long been left behind, others have remained.

One that has is the sense of inner-connectedness and sacredness of all things, living and non-living—a value at the heart of all yogic teachings. I am a lover of animals and have an active concern for the environment. This led me to help start an environmentally based charter school in Philadelphia; I've also worked on committees and boards of local environmental organizations for several years now. In my personal life, I try to live as consciously as possible, residing in a modest home and driving a hybrid car. Another thing that drives my environmental ethic is a leftover distaste for all things overly materialistic. I am still uncomfortable with having things that most Americans wouldn't consider excessive and don't let myself forget that most of the world doesn't live like we Americans do. (It seems I've replaced suffering for the mission with suffering for the environment. Even though summers in the Philadelphia area can be excessively hot and humid and our home has central air conditioning, we use it only on the hottest of days. Instead, we rely on fans. At least I'm wearing shorts and a T-shirt and not robes!) And whenever I cut off the ends of carrots or am about to leave a room without turning off the lights, I think of those girls from the children's home in Madras and resolve not to be the kind of American I was so ashamed of all those years ago.

Predating Ananda Marga, of course, are issues with my family that I am finally no longer running away from—issues that had their origins years ago, well before I was born—brought about by the Great Depression and, going still further back, by the pogroms and anti-Semitism that my father and his family and my mother's parents and their families had to face in Eastern

Europe. There are still some big issues in my family (the main one being that, for a variety of reasons, my brothers don't talk to each other), but I do get the sense that they have forgiven me for what I did and have come to understand what led me to do it.

I see each of my brothers occasionally. Some time ago, I was visiting David when he told me what it had been like for my parents while I had been away. "Whenever anyone said your name, Mom and Dad would be close to tears," he said. "Mom didn't talk about how she felt. Dad would sit around and cry sometimes. He seemed depressed, especially after he retired. One time he said, 'I feel like I've lost my daughter. I wish I could see her once before I die.'" When David said these words, I sat there in silence, staring down at the table. There was nothing I could say that could change the past and all the pain I had caused. Still, the words stabbed at my heart. David also told me that my uncle Danny, my mother's younger brother, had suggested hiring someone to capture and deprogram me. "Danny told me that Mom and Dad didn't want to do that," David said. "They felt that it was your life to live. They didn't want to force you out of Ananda Marga."

One time, Barry and I got to talking about the time he wouldn't let me stay in his house. "You told me you were going to stay with a friend," he said. "If you had told me you didn't have any place to stay, we would have made some arrangements—put you up in a hotel or something." That was news to me. Although I have no memory of having said that, it's entirely possible I did in order to save face. None of that matters anymore, though.

As far as my other relatives go, the person I ended up feeling the closest to after returning was my uncle Danny, who passed away in 2008 at the age of ninety-three. From time to time, I would call him and we would have long conversations about the family. Danny had a fantastic memory and could recall events that happened long ago in great detail. He also possessed a sharp intellect and a great deal of wisdom and compassion. Sometimes we talked about the impact my leaving had on my parents.

"They couldn't understand what you were doing," he told me once. "They concentrated on the effect it had upon them. One day your mother showed me a letter you had written in which you said how you only happened to be their child by an accident of nature. She felt that the organization had replaced her, and she was devastated. It made her life a life of tragedy. She mourned for many years. I saw in her eyes a sadness that never went away."

Still, I felt from Danny a sense of acceptance and forgiveness. He knew I was writing a book. From time to time, he would ask me how it was going and say, "You are redeeming yourself. To persist in the mistake is worse than the error itself." A few years before his death, my husband and I visited him in California and brought him a copy of the draft I had been working on at the time.

Some of the guilt I've been carrying around for so long regarding my parents is still there. For years, I couldn't bring myself to feel what it must have been like for them, but bit by bit, I have allowed myself to imagine their pain during those years I was away, the last twelve years of their lives. They said goodbye at Reading Terminal Station fully expecting to see me again a few months later, only to have me disappear from their lives almost completely. For years, they received only a letter or two and the odd phone call. Then came the news that I was no longer working for Ananda Marga and wanted to buy some land in Australia. The flurry of letters and phone calls that followed must have given them hope that I would soon be part of the family again. But then came the slow realization that I had been lying. Perhaps the first sign was when I let it slip that I had been in Fiji. Or maybe it was when I told them that I was teaching in a school near Melbourne during the week and was spending my weekends at "the farm" as I put it. Maybe they looked at a map of Australia and saw how far it was from Melbourne to the location of the land north of Brisbane, and put two and two together.

It makes me incredibly sad to think about how they must have felt when they realized I had deceived them, and I find myself wondering if I'll ever manage to overcome the guilt I still feel. Sorrow still wells up in me at odd moments. Sometimes it comes when listening to a melancholy song on the radio while driving somewhere. My eyes fill with tears, and I find myself overwhelmed by sadness. (Perhaps ironically—or fittingly—songs from *Fiddler on the Roof* particularly affect me this way, and I wonder about my father's tears on those Sundays when he would listen to those same songs and cry. Were his tears for memories of the boy he'd been in a shtetl so like the fictional Anatevka? Or could they have been for the relatives left behind and lost in the pogroms and death camps that followed his departure?) Still, I do gain some comfort from knowing that the person I am today would never do something to hurt my parents the way I did back then.

Although I'm not proud of some of the choices I made, I do realize that they didn't happen in a vacuum. I know my parents did the best they could for my brothers and me (considering the people they were and the pain they carried around with them every day), and I remind myself that my childhood was free from the trauma of physical abuse that others have had to face. That doesn't mean I haven't wrestled with feelings of anger at my parents. While our physical needs were provided for at the cost of a great deal of struggle and hard work on their part, our emotional needs were not. I know that those early years spent in the emotionally cold place that was my home have left their indelible mark on who I am today. I know I can't continue to live in the past or blame my parents for the issues I still have, so I have worked hard on forgiving them—and myself. As time passes and I gain more perspective, I find the feelings of anger have dissipated and have been replaced by those of regret for the way things turned out, for the things that my parents had hoped for in their lives that never came to pass and the losses they had to cope with. Besides the loss of their daughter, they also had to come to terms with the lack of grandchildren. They likely thought that they would have many. Instead, they were left with only one, Barry's daughter Sascha. (My father also had two grandchildren by way of Howard, the eldest son we hadn't known about, but he rarely saw them. That state of affairs must have only served to increase his sadness.)

One spring day, not long after reading the letters I had sent home, my husband and I paid a visit to my parents' gravesite, the first since that cold day of spare winter sunlight when I had visited with my brothers so long ago. Along with being pleasantly surprised at how green the cemetery was (in stark contrast to my memories of it), I noted the row of small stones placed by someone upon the tombstone. "A Jewish tradition," I said to David. We weeded around the tombstone for a bit, and then I settled down to express myself to my parents as best I could, as I had never been able when they were alive.

"I know you loved me in your own way," I began, "but as a child I never felt loved. I don't remember being held or cuddled much or any bedtime stories. I don't know if you ever came to understand why I left. I never had much self-confidence growing up or any real sense of belonging, so I felt compelled to go out and look for a place where I could get those things. Ananda Marga was like a family to me. It's tragic that they wanted me to leave my real one behind, and that I listened to them and caused you so much pain.

"Mom, I never knew what your feelings were about things because you never showed any. I imagine you didn't get much attention growing up, being the third of six children and having two younger sisters who you must have felt were more attractive. Maybe you never felt loved or appreciated. At any rate, you sure didn't seem very happy, and there were so few happy occasions in our house. Everything was always so cold. We never knew exactly when either of your birthdays was, and you and Dad never gave us any parties. I can remember only two: one for David's bar mitzvah and one for my sweet sixteen. Maybe you and Dad never celebrated birthdays growing up, so that's why you never celebrated ours.

"Was it your family who made you feel it necessary to keep the existence of our half brother a secret? They must have made you feel bad for marrying a divorced man. And probably you never wanted to move to Elkins Park, given that you didn't drive and suddenly had no neighbors to talk to. All you had was us. Maybe that's why you ended up cleaning all the time. Or maybe you felt that you'd only be loved if the house was perfect. Did you ever really express yourself to Dad? Were you scared of him, too? I wish you were here, so we could really talk."

Then I said to my father, "Dad, as a child, I was scared of you all the time. But now I can imagine how frightened you must have been, hiding in the cellar when you heard the Cossacks' horses. What was it like coming over to this country on a boat overcrowded with other immigrants? What were your dreams for America? I wish I knew if any of them came true. You must have been angry and frustrated when your own father died and you had to take care of the whole family—even to the point of putting Bernie through medical school. You worked so hard in your hardware store, lifting those heavy bales of peat moss well into your sixties, and no one thanked you for it or showed you any appreciation. And it was so sad that we never had our half brother and his children as part of the family. I'm sure we would have been a much happier family with them in it. I'm sorry I couldn't understand your struggles or your disappointments, but I was only a child."

Then I went on to tell him that I'd met my half brother Howard, along with his children and grandchildren. "Your grandson Myron is a dentist, and David and I both go to him. Whenever I go to his office and there is someone he wants me to meet, he introduces me as his aunt. They look at him and then at me with puzzled looks, and then I say, 'Yes, I'm his aunt, but he's older than I am!' and we have a good laugh."

David, too, spoke to my parents, relating his own feelings to people he had never known.

*   *   *

This book, which began as a collection of little tales, has grown and changed over the years to incorporate my parents' story as well. It's the story of an immigrant, the daughter of immigrants, and of their daughter, all of whom struggled with issues of identity. The father left his country of birth and spent his life trying to establish a new identity within the melting pot of America. The mother was an insecure woman from an orthodox Jewish family who was never quite comfortable with herself. Their daughter, rejecting everything she was born to and had given to her, left the country of her birth and strove for a new sense of self in a spiritual group.

I was once a seeker who thought that no one truly belongs to a family or another person. I identified with spirit only. Although still on my own journey, I now recognize my own history and heritage; I've begun to search for details of my family's Eastern European and immigrant experiences and to delve into my Jewish identity—the very identity I rejected outright in my younger years. I have come to believe that true spiritual understanding comes only through accepting oneself on all levels, so I choose to embrace my history and with it, my humanity.

That history, of course, includes Ananda Marga. When I first returned, I could see very little good in it. Now, I think I have succeeded in coming to a more balanced view of the group. There were positive things about Ananda Marga, including its ideals, philosophy, and spiritual practices. However, there was something profoundly warped about how some of its members tried to live up to those lofty ideals, a great disconnect between the ideals and what people did to implement them, a kind of hardness and a judgmental attitude antithetical to what I think it means to be a truly spiritual person. Many of us had little or no compassion for ourselves or, consequently, for others. Now, I'm learning to treat myself and others with compassion; the Buddhist practices I've taken up over the past few years have really helped me do that.

Recently, I have been able to feel compassion even for Ananda Sudha and let go of the feelings of hurt and anger I've carried around for so long by imagining the difficult situation she would have found herself in, being pregnant as a young didi. Even if she had wanted to leave acarya life and have the baby, she would have found it close to impossible because at that time it was practically unheard of for an unmarried Indian woman to raise a child on her own. On the other hand, returning to whole-timer life must not have been easy, with all the stigma she had to face. To me, Ananda Sudha was a victim of Indian society in general and of Ananda Marga in particular. And as is common in such cases, the victim victimized others and passed her pain on to them.

I would be dishonest if I were to say I don't occasionally still feel like a victim of Ananda Marga and its way of thinking. Even today, there are times when I find myself wondering if I have become too materialistic or if I've "fallen" from the high spiritual life I was living as a didi—evidence that my spiritual superego is still alive and well. *You were warned about that before you left,* it occasionally reminds me. *Now you're just an average person, no longer an exalted personality with a great mission to fulfill.* I know that how I saw myself back then was based on a good deal of illusion, but that old conditioning is hard to overcome, and I fall into those old patterns more than I would care to admit. Feeling important and more spiritually evolved than others was a drug that masked my profound lack of self-esteem, but it is a drug that I sometimes find myself craving, even after all this time.

That said, I no longer blame the organization for all those years I spent with it—no one forced me to join, and no one compelled me to remain. In spite of the many struggles I've had since leaving, I'm thankful for the life I have now. I especially feel fortunate in having such a loving husband, who has been a tremendous source of support throughout my journey, and a wonderful family of in-laws.

It is futile, of course, to think about the person I might have become or what I might have achieved if I hadn't devoted nearly twenty years of my life to Ananda Marga. Still, I do think about it sometimes. Maybe I would have become a professor of linguistics or of French, Russian, or English. Maybe I would have married earlier and had children. On the other hand, with my hippie-related doings at Penn, maybe I'd have ended up a drug addict or even dead. When I came across Ananda Marga all those years ago, I had been making steady progress in that direction.

I sometimes think of the dream I had of being hit by a car from the seventies and of being saved from certain death by Baba. Who knows? Maybe he really did save me. In any case, Ananda Marga will always be a part of who I am, just as I am the daughter and granddaughter of immigrants who came to this country seeking a better life for themselves and for those they loved.

I thought I'd end with a final dream.

Dream Entry: December 9, 2007

I am in another country, perhaps China or India, with my husband. At one point, I leave my glasses on the floor and someone steps on them. I pick them up and see that one lens is cracked. Since I have no spare, I decide to go get a new pair. I put the cracked glasses on, and they suddenly become sunglasses.

I get into a small car and drive until I come to an intersection. It is blocked by a huge truck with a platform on top. Standing on it and facing me are five dadas in their orange uniforms. One of them is Yogeshananda, the dada who sent me to training. All of them, Yogeshananda included, are young. They are looking down at me, and I am terrified that they will recognize me. But they don't. I think it is because of the sunglasses I am wearing. I want to get out of there, but how can I, with the intersection blocked?

Then I notice a narrow dirt alley to the left of the truck. I want to escape down it but am afraid someone will stop me. Maybe it's against the law to drive there, I think. But I can't worry about that now. Deciding to take the risk of doing something illegal, I drive down the alley and get away.

Acknowledgments

From its beginnings as a collection of humorous tales to its present incarnation, *The Orange Robe* took an exceedingly long time to write. There are many people I wish to thank who, along the way, helped me in different ways. First and foremost is my husband, David. Not only did he offer emotional and practical support while I was writing the book by helping me find the space and time to do it, but he also put in countless hours as an editor and as someone to bounce ideas off of. Next is Robert Dennis, who designed the cover and interior photo spread. He generously gave of his time for what we called our "over-the-shoulder" sessions; I watched and gave feedback while he performed magic on his Mac. In addition, I'd like to thank friends and relatives who read drafts and offered valuable feedback, including Jacqui Good, Marci and Terry Stern, and my sister-in-law Kathryn Low. Ellen Watson, who also read a draft, helped me unpack my experiences and develop a less judgmental and more compassionate attitude towards myself. Barbara Kotzin, who often calls me her "oldest-living friend" because we've known each other since we were four, shared her memories of our early years, which helped inform the book. I'd also like to thank members of my family who answered questions that came up for me as I wrote: my brothers David and Barry; my niece, Sascha; my half brother Howard and his son, Myron—and my mother's brother Danny, now deceased, who, along with his amazing memory for events and places, offered me his compassionate wisdom. Another elder, now deceased, to whom I owe a lot is Harriet Jenkins (Maetreyii), the woman who treated me as a member of her family and often referred to me as her "honorary daughter," who offered me both a place to stay when I first returned and her unique spiritual vision. Lastly, I'd like to thank my mother-in-law, Franna Low, now deceased, and all my in-laws, who welcomed me into their family as one of their own.